WATCHING QUEBEC

CARLETON LIBRARY SERIES

The Carleton Library Series, funded by Carleton University under the general editorship of the dean of the School of Graduate Studies and Research, publishes books about Canadian economics, geography, history, politics, society, and related subjects. It includes important new works as well as reprints of classics in the fields. The editorial committee welcomes manuscripts and suggestions, which should be sent to the dean of the School of Graduate Studies and Research, Carleton University.

Watching Quebec

Selected Essays

RAMSAY COOK

Carleton Library Series 201

McGill-Queen's University Press
Montreal & Kingston • London • Ithaca

© McGill-Queen's University Press 2005
ISBN 0-7735-2918-7 (cloth)
ISBN 0-7735-2919-5 (paper)

Legal deposit third quarter 2005
Bibliothèque nationale du Québec

Printed in Canada on acid-free paper that is 100% ancient forest free
(100% post-consumer recycled), processed chlorine free.

McGill-Queen's University Press acknowledges the support of the
Canada Council for the Arts for our publishing program. We also
acknowledge the financial support of the Government of Canada
through the Book Publishing Industry Development Program (BPIDP)
for our publishing activities.

Chapters in this book appeared first in the following publications:
Chapters 1, 3, 7, 8, 12, 13, 14   *Canada and the French-Canadian
    Question*. Toronto: Macmillan, 1966
Chapters 2, 4, 5, 15   *Canada, Quebec and the Uses of Nationalism*.
    Toronto: McClelland and Stewart 1986
Chapter 6   *Maple Leaf Forever*. Toronto: Macmillan, 1966
Chapter 10   *Literary Review of Canada*, 1995
Chapter 11   *Mens* 1, no. 2 (spring 2001): 97–114

Library and Archives Canada Cataloguing in Publication

Cook, Ramsay, 1931–
    Watching Quebec : selected essays / Ramsay Cook.

(Carleton library ; 201)
ISBN 0-7735-2918-7 (bound). – ISBN 0-7735-2919-5 (pbk.)

    1. Québec (Province) – History.   2. Québec (Province) – Politics and
government.   I. Title.   II. Series.

FC2911.7.C57 2005   971.4   C2005-901346-X

Typeset in 10/12 Sabon by True to Type

Contents

Introduction

*Donner au public des détails sur soi-même est une tentation de bourgeois
à laquelle j'ai toujours résisté.*

Gustave Flaubert, 1879

Most of the essays collected in *Watching Quebec* were written over a
period of thirty years between the beginning of the Quiet Revolution
and the failure of the Meech Lake Accord. During those years, much
of my teaching, research, and writing focused on Quebec and the challenge that French-Canadian/Quebec nationalism presented to other
Canadians. These were extraordinarily exciting years, a time of profound crisis for Canada. The country came out of that crisis – if indeed
it has emerged – looking constitutionally much more like pre-1960
Canada than like most of the radical options proposed by many par-
ticipants in the debate over "the Quebec and Canadian question." But
that should not disguise the truth that it could have been otherwise.
Canada could have ruptured and ceased to exist, at least as the nation
was understood during its first century. I hope to explore the reasons
for the failure of the radical, and even moderately radical, options at
another time. Re-reading these essays has provided me with some
clues, but much more systematic thought and reading is required
before a documented interpretation can be advanced.

The excitement of these years drew me into the discussion both as a
scholar and as a citizen. I wrote quite a lot of journalism for *Le Devoir*,
the Montreal *Star*, the *Globe and Mail*, and especially the *Canadian
Forum*, where I also frequently translated articles from *Le Devoir* and
Cité libre. As well, CBC Radio and Television often asked me to comment on events involving Quebec, including, for example, most of the
constitutional conferences between 1968 and 1990 and the provincial
election of 15 November 1976, which brought the separatist Parti
Québécois to office for the first time. I also wrote scholarly articles.
Sometimes the line between scholar, journalist, and citizen was
breeched, for I had strong opinions about such matters as federalism
and nationalism, opinions that were developed during my training as a

professional historian. In my teaching I tried to provoke my students
to think for themselves, but they were always eager to ferret out my
views. On the day of the assassination of John F. Kennedy, forty years
ago, I was one of two professors who participated in a demonstration
at Queen's Park, organized by the Students Administrative Council at
the University of Toronto, calling on Premier John Robarts to listen
sympathetically to Quebec's demands during the federal-provincial dispute over the proposed Canada Pension Plan. Our march, intended to
win widespread newspaper and television coverage, was totally
upstaged by the events in Texas that day – events I learned of only after
the demonstration. But public protesting was never much to my taste,
believing, as I always have, that the essay is mightier than the slogan.

Naturally I have often wondered how I became – and remain – so
involved intellectually with French Canada and Quebec. Here (with
apologies to my favourite French novelist) is what is certainly only a
partial answer.

Growing up in western Canada prepared me thoroughly for what
became known as multiculturalism, the normal state of things in small
towns and even large cities on the prairies, and hardly at all for French-
speaking Canadians, who were isolated, ignored, or suppressed in
most of the west. I was nearly twenty years old before I ventured east
of the Lakehead for brief visits to Ottawa and even briefer ones to
Montreal, where the Café Martin and Ruby Foo's served as my introduction to Quebec culture. In my late teens, the presence of Franco-
Manitobans touched me infrequently, most often on the rinks or the
baseball diamonds of places like Letellier and Saint Norbert, where
sports were played even on Sunday after morning Mass, though never
on Sunday in Protestant Morden, my hometown. Those were positive,
if sometimes bruising, meetings. In 1950 a more dramatic and personal
encounter took place. When the Red River overflowed its banks that
spring, most of the small French-speaking settlements along the river
south of Winnipeg were forced to move to higher ground. Morden
adopted the people of Saint Jean, several hundred of whom came to
share "allophone" (mostly English and Low German with a smattering
of Icelandic, Polish, and Czech) homes and hospitality. My father was
a United Church minister, and his church became a community dining
room for many refugees, with some even camping there. He observed,
with the slight resentment that he could rarely summon up, that none
of the Roman Catholic visitors was seen in the his church's pews on
Sunday. Their priest protectively took them off to the local Catholic
Church, which normally held services only irregularly, there being virtually no "papists" among Morden's otherwise extremely diverse religious population. (I recall eighteen churches, mostly with Mennonite

congregations, and literally dozens of "reverends" who collected their mail at the local post office.) The people of the Saint Jean diaspora needed temporary shelter; Mordenites cheerfully offered it to their neighbours who accepted with warm gratitude. English was the language of communication, except among francophones, and certainly my generation, some of whom were already familiar with our athletic Saint Jean counterparts, welcomed the infusion of strangers – especially those of the opposite sex – with both curiosity and a sense of adventure. Friendships were easily established, though few survived the recession of the Red.

The French-speaking refugees' stay lasted only a month or so; when it ended it was remembered as an example of the neighbourly spirit of the prairies, which it was, but with no thoughts at all about bilingualism, biculturalism, or "founding nations." (Possibly I missed some heated discussions of "asymmetric federalism" at the local beer parlour on Saturday night.) Back at high school, those few of us who hoped to attend university continued to struggle with poorly taught French (except by Marcel Phillippe, a Franco-Manitoban, who abandoned Morden in disillusion after only one year) and insufferably boring Canadian history, which mostly ignored the French dimension (except for explorers) as presented in *Building the Canadian Nation*, George Brown's textbook. I kept up the French out of necessity, and would later do another required year at university. In my last high school year, I dropped history in favour of chemistry, only to find that at United College in Winnipeg it was much more convenient to study history than chemistry, since science subjects required thrice-weekly bus trips to the Fort Garry campus of the University of Manitoba. On such weighty considerations my career choice was made, though I did not suspect it at the time.

History, as an intellectual discipline, led by a crooked path to the study of French-Canadian and Quebec nationalism. Abandoning a plan to become a lawyer, a plan adopted on the insistence of my father who strongly objected to my ambition to work in a sporting-goods store, I decided to major in modern history with the vague intention of joining the Department of External Affairs. By my final year, encouraged by several remarkable teachers, J.H.S. Reid, Kenneth McNaught, and Harry Crowe (the whole regular Department of History), I began to think of postponing final decisions by applying to graduate school. My interests now focused on the history of Canada, a field that McNaught's left-wing perspective finally brought alive for me, and nationalism, a subject introduced to me by a distinguished, retired scholar of Eastern Europe, W.J. Rose, during a visiting professorship at United College. Given his subject (Eastern Europe and the collapse of the Hapsburg Empire), and his Edwardian education, Rose's positive attitude to nationalism and Wilsonian ideals of national self-determination were unsurprising. Nevertheless, he accepted, even encouraged, my more critical attitude towards a phenomenon that I already believed had contributed to international anarchy, the Second World War and the destruction of most of Europe's Jews. I read Johann Gottfried Herder, the intellectual father of nationalism, and disliked him. I came to admire Thomas Masaryk, the Czech intellectual and politician, who preferred a reformed to a dissolved, Hapsburg Empire. I worked hard, but not altogether successfully, to pronounce Eastern European names and to distinguish between Pan Slavs and Slavophils. Nationalism, as a subject worthy of careful study, excited me, perhaps because it represented such a potentially destructive ideology in the Cold War world of the 1950s. The contemporary world seemed to confirm the conclusion that internationalism belonged to the left, nationalism to the reactionary right.

All of this may seem a long way from French Canada and Quebec, but, as things turned out, it was not. Still uncertain about my future, I was attracted to Queen's University by a generous scholarship ($1,500, in those days, was generous, especially compared to Toronto's offer of $500) and the prospect of working with Professor A.R.M. Lower. No specific research topic interested me other than the possibility of examining some aspect of the history of civil liberties in Canada. I had been involved in a controversy over McCarthyism as a student in Winnipeg, and Lower was a staunch civil libertarian. My thesis topic was civil liberties in wartime Canada (1939–45). In my preparatory reading, which Lower insisted should be very wide, I discovered for the first time Lord Acton's *Essays on Freedom and Power*, where I found his incisive dissection of John Stuart Mill's conventional view of "nationalism" (ethnic self-determination) and his advocacy of federalism as a counterweight to nationalist threats to liberty. Acton seemed to advance a perfect formula for a bicultural, even a multicultural Canada: "The coexistence of several nations under the same State is a test, as well as the best security of its freedom ... and indicates a state of greater advancement than the national unity which is the ideal of modern liberalism."[1] I quickly became a convert.

At Queen's, I gradually discovered that my real interest was the seminar on French Canada, taught by Arthur Lower and Fred Gibson. It opened a whole new world to me. The sympathy that both Lower, who focused on French-Canadian culture, and Fred Gibson, whose specialty was politics, demonstrated towards the francophone minority infected me almost at once. As a westerner, I had viewed French Canadians as one minority among many; as Lower's student, I came to realize that such a view lacked historical understanding. Immigrants chose to become Canadians; French Canadians, the original European settlers, I realized, became Canadians not by individual choice but as a consequence of a military defeat, the British Conquest. That explained why their nationalism expressed aspirations – the survival of French-Canadian distinctiveness – that sometimes conflicted with (English) Canadian nationalist aspirations identified with English-Canadian culture. In every generation, the Conquest, knowingly or otherwise, had to be renegotiated in a search for an acceptable equilibrium between the two cultures, one a majority, the other a minority. Lower's cultural emphasis explained the two ways of life and the French Canadians' persistent will to survive the English Canadians' will to create a homogeneous nation. Gibson's political emphasis examined the battlefield where the struggle was most visibly played out. Lower introduced me to Canon Lionel Groulx, the nationalist priest and historian, obsessed with *la survivance*; Gibson set me to work on Henri Bourassa and his formula for what F.R. Scott once called the two miracles of Canadian history: *la survivance du Canada français* and the survival of Canada. Like Bourassa, I concluded that the two miracles were really only one. During the following two summers, working as a research assistant for Fred Gibson, I came across material that allowed me to publish my first piece of serious scholarship. "Church, Schools and Politics in Manitoba, 1903–12"[2] (1958) examined the fate of French and Catholic schools during the negotiations over the annexation of Keewatin to Manitoba through an Actonian microscope: in Canada, national unity was often maintained at the expense of minority rights. Queen's, and especially Arthur Lower, fortified my liberalism (without weakening my support for the Co-operative Commonwealth Federation, or CCF, forunner of the New Democratic Party), by awakening a deep admiration for the French-speaking minority's way of life.

While my year at Queen's opened up the history of French Canada to me for the first time, and encouraged a sympathetic understanding of the minority culture, it did not alter my conviction that nationalism was a reactionary ideology. Maurice Duplessis's repressive, corrupt, apparently permanent, anti-federal regime seemed to confirm that conclusion. So did many of the authors whose books and articles we read in the Lower-Gibson seminar. Lower, for example, urged us to become regular readers of *Le Devoir*, a nationalist newspaper founded by Henri Bourassa. By the mid-1950s it was engaged in both fighting Duplessis and attempting to reformulate French-Canadian nationalism in terms better fitted to the modern urban-industrial society that Quebec had become. André Laurendeau, then the paper's ascetic-looking young editor, quickly captured my admiration, sometimes even tempting me to accept his version of nationalism. When I later became acquainted with him, I realized how subtle a balance between nationalism and federalism he had devised, combining Bourassa and Groulx. That subtlety both gave intellectual excitement to his writing, and, I think, prevented him, in the last years before his premature death, from realizing that the forces set loose by the Quiet Revolution had radically undermined the delicate balance that he had fashioned. That is the meaning of the famous "Blue Pages" of the only volume of the *Royal Commission on Bilingualism and Biculturalism* that bears his stamp. It is, in fact, his last intellectual will and testament.

If reading Laurendeau and *Le Devoir* reaffirmed my belief in the reactionary nature of traditional nationalism in French Canada, it at least made me consider that a reformed nationalism, a liberal nationalism, might be possible. (My memory of Lewis Namier's incisive little study of the *Revolution of 1848* should have left me sceptical.) But in 1956 I read in *Le Devoir* about a brilliant, controversial set of essays on the asbestos strike of 1949, *La grève de l'amiante*, edited by Pierre Elliott Trudeau, a name then unknown to me.[3] An Ottawa bookstore obtained a copy for me and I read it voraciously, especially Trudeau's opening essay. Here was a passionate tour de force, one that analysed the nationalist ideology that had dominated social thought in Quebec for half a century, and established its failure to connect with the developing social realities of urban-industrial Quebec. The other essays in the book, overshadowed by the power of Trudeau's analysis and prose, demonstrated the accuracy of his analysis as applied to the bitter clash involving workers, industry, government, and the leaders of the Catholic Church in the Quebec asbestos industry. I concluded then, and continue to believe, that Trudeau's essay is the finest piece of political thought and ideological analysis written by a Canadian, an essay on which his entire future career as a thinker and politician was founded. It taught me a great deal about Quebec, nationalism, and political ideas. It also confirmed views about those subjects that I had arrived at over a longer period.

Perhaps I had been prepared for Trudeau by George Orwell, whose volume of essays *England Your England* I had read the previous summer. In that collection his "Notes on Nationalism" had especially struck me. Orwell's precise prose set out the essential distinction between "nationalism" and "patriotism": "Patriotism is of its nature defensive. Nationalism, on the other hand, is inseparable from the desire for power."[4] This sentence remains a more valuable insight into nationalist ideology than all of the learned arguments of contemporary political philosophers about the morality and justice of nationalism and national self-determinism.[5] Orwell, I think, encouraged me to suspect what he once called "all the smelly little orthodoxies which are now contending for our souls,"[6] and demonstrated that the essay form could still be as powerful as it had been in the nineteenth century.

Moving from Queen's to the University of Toronto, in the autumn of 1955, to continue my graduate education, I shifted my research interests back to western Canada, proposing to write a doctoral thesis on the political ideas of the great Winnipeg editor, John W. Dafoe of the *Free Press*. In a backhanded way, Dafoe's attitude to French Canada, an attitude I had once shared, confirmed my revised opinions. For him, French Canada was more a problem than a positive feature of Canada; his nationalism was very English-Canadian even though he welcomed French-Canadian support for his campaign for Canadian autonomy within the Commonwealth-Empire. French and Catholic schools outside Quebec, and French Canadians' opposition to collective security and to conscription during two world wars, frustrated and angered him. His French Canada/Quebec was a caricature, one shared by most of his readers and doubtless many others. His nationalism and French-Canadian nationalism were mirror images, convincing me that Canada's difficulties came from too much, not too little, nationalism. More Lord Acton and less John Stuart Mill seemed an obvious prescription.

Without the Quiet Revolution I would probably have set off on my academic career at the University of Toronto as a Canadian political and intellectual historian. But as the noise from Quebec grew in intensity, so too did my conviction that my department did far too little to inform its students about what was called "French Canada." I proposed the appointment of an expert in that field. Such a proposal, coming from a junior member of the staff at a time when hiring new professors was still infrequent, met with little encouragement. So I volunteered to become that expert. In 1962 I began teaching a senior seminar entitled "French Canadian Nationalism." The students were required to have a reading knowledge of French – the professor was required to keep ahead of them.[7] The language requirement, in those years before the Ontario educational system was "reformed," caused no problem, though by the end of the 1960s it would. As for the professor, well, the harder I worked the greater my enthusiasm grew. French Canada/Quebec, so distinct a society, ensured that I would remain a historian of Canada, while, for the most part, leaving my own culture and past in the hands of my colleagues.

At the University of Toronto, and then at York University, where I moved in 1968, I regularly taught students who were eager to learn about both nationalism and French Canada/Quebec. Susan Mann, who published two fine books about Quebec, and Graham Fraser, who first introduced me to René Lévesque and who wrote a valuable book about the Parti Québécois and reported on Quebec for several Canadian newspapers, were among my earliest and most challenging undergraduates. (My teaching about francophone Canada at Harvard in 1968–69, and at Yale in 1978–79 and 1995 also attracted many stimulating students.) As the years passed, even those whose French was inadequate could manage to follow their subject from a growing number of translated works or studies written by anglophone scholars. Some of the latter were my own graduate students. At Toronto, Joe Levitt explored Henri Bourassa's social thought, Paul Crunican documented the role played by the Catholic hierarchy in the Manitoba schools dispute, Arthur Silver re-examined the role of French-Canadian politicians and journalists in the evolution of Confederation, and Pat Dirks analysed the Action libérale nationale. Among my York students, Phyllis Sherrin elucidated the ideas of Abbé Lionel Groulx, Gail Brant minutely described the movement of francophones into the Sudbury region, Ralph Heintzman detailed French-Canadian attitudes to economic development, Michael Behiels revealed the intellectual roots of the Quiet Revolution, Patrice Dutil wrote a biography of the reformist-liberal Godfroy Langlois, Sylvie Beaudreau tackled the question of massive French-Canadian emigration to the United States, Marcel Martel unravelled the complex relations between Quebec and the Franco-Ontarians, Xavier Gélinas probed the ideas of the intellectual right in Quebec during the Quiet Revolution, and Molly Ungar reconstructed a remarkable Montreal salon in the 1930s.[8] Each of these apprentice historians opened up new territory and explored it for the benefit of students of Quebec history in both anglophone and francophone Canada. And nothing pleased me more than the growing number of francophone students (and the number continues to grow), who discovered that universities in anglophone Canada welcomed their presence and willingly nurtured their intellectual development.

So, too, in these years I developed friendly relations with many of the leading historians and intellectuals in Quebec: Michel Brunet, Jean Hamelin, Pierre Savard, Jacques Monet, Jean-Pierre Wallot, Paul André Linteau, Jean-Claude Robert, Gérard Bouchard, and many others. Moreover, I helped to convince York University to appoint three successive French-speaking historians: René Durocher, Jacques Rouillard, and Fernand Ouellet. Claude Ryan (who invited me to write for *Le Devoir*), Pierre Trudeau, (who published my views in *cité libre* and became a lifelong friend), Marc Lalonde, Léon Dion, and Abbé Gérard Dion were francophone intellectuals who encouraged my interest in Quebec and contributed to my education. In my late-career role as general editor of the *Dictionary of Canadian Biogra-*

phy, I have had the good fortune to share the trials and achievements of that bilingual national treasure with two of Quebec's most distinguished historians, first Jean Hamelin and subsequently Réal Bélanger, both of Laval University. This has been a rich experience in which I once again recognized the intellectual clarity and the warm humanity that is characteristic of francophone scholars. Having retired from teaching, I now take the greatest pleasure in admiring (and doing what I can to support) members of the rising generation of Quebec scholars, those who have founded the important scholarly journal *Mens:* Damien-Claude Bélanger, Sophie Coupal, Yves Bégin, Michel Ducharme, and Mathieu Lapointe, among others. To have my work published – and translated-by these energetic young historians and to be invited to join *Mens'* advisory board is a generous reward for half a century of studying French-Canadian history and commenting on – even occasionally intervening in – Quebec's heated debates.

Canada and the French Canadian Question (1966), *The Maple Leaf Forever* (1971), and *Canada, Quebec, and the Uses of Nationalism* (1986 and 1995), from which these essays are mainly drawn, were the products of my enthusiasm as a teacher, a writer, and a citizen. For the most part, the presentation is thematic and only occasionally chronological. Each essay has been dated. I have chosen these essays, leaving many others unselected, because they seem to have some continuing significance as historical studies or they reveal something about the times in which they were composed that is worth recalling. If these essays have some staying power, and I hope they have, it is because some of my engagement with Quebec still pervades them. I have not modified them[9] or attempted to make them more relevant to the present. To have done so would have been to play tricks with the past, something no historian should ever do. It might also be taken to mean that I have revised my essential views about nationalism in general and about Quebec in particular. I have not. The intellectual lenses that, I believe, clarified my vision in the past remain in focus as I continue, a fascinated outsider, watching Quebec.

Ramsay Cook,
10 June 2004

NOTES

1 Lord Acton, *Essays on Freedom and Power*, (Cleveland and New York: World Publishing 1962), 160.
2 *Canadian Historical Review*, 39, no. 1, (March 1958): 1–23.

3 Pierre Elliott Trudeau, *La grève de l'amiante* (Montréal: Les éditions Cité libre 1956), especially 88–9.

4 George Orwell, *England Your England and Other Essays* (London: Secker and Warburg 1953), 42.

5 For example, see Joseph Carens, ed., *Is Quebec Nationalism Just? Perspectives from Anglophone Canada* (Montreal: McGill Queen's University Press 1995), 137–59, and Margaret Moore, *The Ethics of Nationalism* (Oxford: Oxford University Press 2001).

6 George Orwell, "Charles Dickens," in Sonia Orwell and Ian Angus, ed., *The Collected Essays, Journalism and Letters of George Orwell*, 1 (1920–40), (New York: Harcourt, Brace and World 1968), 460.

7 Ramsay Cook, ed., *French Canadian Nationalism: An Anthology* (Toronto: Macmillan 1969), contains much of the documentation that I used for my seminar from 1962 until my retirement from teaching in 1995.

8 A list of my students and their research topics is found in Michael D. Beheils and Marcel Martel, ed., *Nation, Ideas, Identities: Essays in Honour of Ramsay Cook* (Don Mills, Ont.: Oxford University Press 2000), 238–9.

9 The Introduction and chapters 9, 10, and 11 consist of either new material or material that has not been edited before, and so these parts of the book have been edited for publication here. The other chapters, however, are republished as they originally appeared, with the inevitable editorial inconsistencies that this entails.

WATCHING QUEBEC

ONE

Canada and the French-Canadian Question

Since 1962 Canada has been passing through a period of critical national and political instability. In the federal general election of that year the Progressive Conservative government, which four years earlier had won the most resounding victory in Canadian electoral history, was barely returned as a minority government. The next year was marked by fumbling indecisiveness, economic uncertainty, almost unbelievable confusion in defence and foreign policy, a palace revolt within the cabinet, and finally a new election. Confronted by these events it is not surprising that one French-Canadian editor wrote, 'Y a-t-il une politique militaire canadienne? Y a-t-il une politique étrangère canadienne? Y a-t-il un gouvernement canadien?'[1] In the circumstances, none of the questions was entirely fanciful.

The election which look place in the spring of 1963 was only slightly more decisive than its predecessor: the Conservatives lost a few more seats, giving Lester Pearson's Liberal Party an opportunity to form a minority government. While order has largely been restored to the country's economic affairs, and some of the confusion in foreign and defence matters swept away, the general sense of uneasiness about the country's direction and future remains widespread. Bruce Hutchison, a veteran journalist and staunch Canadian nationalist, observed recently that Lester Pearson is the first prime minister 'who can no longer be sure' that Canadians are willing to continue to pay the price of nationhood.[2] While there is continuing concern about Canada's unequal partnership with the United States, the major source of the country's present difficulties is domestic, not foreign. That source is the most sensitive area of the Canadian polity: the relations between French- and English-speaking Canadians and, more particularly, the relations between the federal government at Ottawa and the government of the province of Quebec. Never have federal-provincial relations been so unsettled, so complicated, and even so strained as they have been in the past two years. There is an obvious irony (though it is probably also a fortunate coincidence) in the fact that the governments of both Canada and Quebec are Liberal and that the Prime Minister of Canada, Lester Pearson, and the Premier of Quebec, Jean Lesage, were colleagues in the St. Laurent government before the Conservative victory in 1957.

The tensions between Quebec and Ottawa must be seen in a wide perspective. In the first place there is a kind of rhythm in the Canadian federal system in which periods of centralization are followed by provincial revolt and decentralization. The years between 1939 and 1957 were characterized by vigorous federal leadership and the dominance of Ottawa. Quebec never accepted this centralization fully, though its attitude was ambiguous: it consistently elected a firmly provincial autonomist Union Nationale government in Quebec, but just as regularly re-elected the supporters of the centralizing Liberals at Ottawa. By the mid fifties provinces other than Quebec were growing restive under federal tutelage and the number of provincial Conservative régimes increased. John Diefenbaker successfully took advantage of this provincial unrest in his campaign to dislodge the twenty-two-year-old Liberal régime in 1957.

The Diefenbaker victory had a peculiar effect on French Canada. The slim 1957 success was won despite Quebec, which clung to its traditional Liberal allegiance. But that election frightened French Canadians, for it proved that a federal election could be won virtually without the support of Quebec. It was a long time since the minority position of the French Canadian had been so graphically illustrated. In 1958, however, the situation was rectified when the Diefenbaker landslide included a Conservative majority in Quebec for the first time since 1887. But the apparent strength of the Conservative Party in Quebec was misleading. In the first place the Quebec wing of the federal party included almost no one of experience who could both state Quebec's case in the federal cabinet and fulfil his ministerial duties effectively. The one man who might have played that role, Léon Balcer, had opposed John Diefenbaker's candidacy for the party leadership and was therefore somewhat under a cloud. The result was that the Diefenbaker government was never *en rapport* with the aspirations of French Canada.

The lack of French-Canadian leadership in the Conservative government reflected something that proved an even more serious weakness: Conservative electoral strength in Quebec was built on the shakiest of foundations. In Quebec there had been no provincial Conservative party since it merged with a group of dissident Liberals in 1935 to form the Union Nationale led by the one-time Conservative, Maurice Duplessis. In 1957, and especially in 1958, the federal Conservative Party succeeded where it previously had failed in obtaining the support of the Union Nationale machine. The alliance was an unnatural one based only on a common hostility to the Liberal Party. The result was that the Union Nationale, an ardently French-Canadian nationalist party, helped send to Ottawa French-speaking Conservatives whose intense autonomism was bound to make them unhappy in a party dominated by Diefenbaker's 'one Canada' philosophy. It is not surprising that one French-Canadian Conservative backbencher was, in 1961, openly describing Confederation as a 'fool's paradise' for Quebec.[3]

The Diefenbaker landslide in Quebec in 1958 bore within itself the seeds of its own destruction. The Union Nationale, which had held power in Quebec since 1944, had become a corrupt, autocratic, and intensely conservative régime, which stayed in office by skilfully playing on traditional French-Canadian fears of an Ottawa dominated by the English-speaking majority. Since the federal government was Liberal, Duplessis convinced Quebec voters that provincial autonomy could only be defended by keeping the provincial Liberals out of power. But once Diefenbaker had removed the Liberal menace from Ottawa the old game could no longer be successfully played. This gave the provincial Liberals a new lease on life, which they grasped impatiently. For several years, under the guidance of the impressively intellectual but cold George Lapalme, the party had been building up an organization and defining a progressive program. At the same time it was losing elections. In 1958 the crushing defeat of the federal Liberals made an extremely dynamic young politician available to the provincial party. He was Jean Lesage, a capable, attractive former cabinet minister, well known as a persistent spokesman for Quebec's interests in Ottawa. Doubtless when Jean Lesage took over the leadership of the provincial Liberal party, one of his main concerns was to rebuild the fortunes of his party at Ottawa. But a series of unpredictable events thrust him into power in Quebec in less than two years.

In 1959 the Union Nationale experienced almost unbelievable bad fortune. First its founder and leader, a man who had been a true 'chef' in the French-Canadian tradition – Maurice Duplessis – died. His successor was a man more in tune with the times than the ageing Duplessis had been. But Paul Sauvé, the new leader, had very little time in which to implement the progressive social ideas he subscribed to; before his first year of office was ended he suffered a fatal heart attack. This left the party in a state of internal strife, totally unprepared for the election of June 1960. That election brought Lesage to office in Quebec and marked the beginning of the end for the Quebec federal Conservatives, who could no longer rely on the formerly powerful Union Nationale machine for support.

Since Quebec's voice was so ineffectively expressed in the Conservative cabinet at Ottawa, many French Canadians, after 1960, turned their eyes to Quebec City for leadership. They were not disappointed. While Diefenbaker's government seemed bewildered in the face of the country' s numerous problems, Lesage's Liberal *équipe* at Quebec was in the process of unwrapping a program of modernization designed to bring public policies into line with the economic and social developments of the previous twenty-five years. Before 1960 bright young French Canadians looked to Ottawa or to such federal institutions as the Canadian Broadcasting Corporation and the National Film Board as havens where they could express their ideas without fear of the penalties which the Duplessis administration used freely against its critics. Now these people found their province, and especially the provincial government, anxious to make full use of their talents. A new atmosphere of freedom seemed to prevail in Quebec and at last it was possible to question every traditional institution, including Confederation itself. Some of the noise in today's Quebec is the sound of exploding myths, some the noise of a society working furiously to modernize itself, and some an old noise rejuvenated: nationalism.

The death of Duplessis removed a cap that had kept the seething discontents of French Canada sealed up for more than a decade. It is doubtful if even Duplessis could have kept the cap on much longer, for the social and economic forces at work were much too potent. Quebec, like so much of North America since 1940, has experienced a period of accelerated industrial and urban growth. While this was not the sudden process that is sometimes suggested – the stereotyped Maria Chapdelaine view of Quebec's Arcadian culture has been outdated since the twenties – there can be no doubt that the war and post-war economic boom transformed Quebec into a society very much like Ontario or the eastern United States in its social organization. This economic development was carried out very largely through the investment of non French-Canadian capital. The result was that class lines and 'national' lines tended to coincide. Moreover, Quebec remained remarkably backward in adopting the kind of social welfare policies that make a modern industrial society acceptable to the great mass of the people who live in it without owning much of it.

The fact was that the Union Nationale government's public philosophy was a nineteenth-century capitalist's dream: foreign capital was invited to a province with enormous natural resources, stable government, low taxes, cheap and largely unorganized labour. Premier Duplessis consistently fought federal welfare policies as infringements on provincial rights, but rarely did he offer any alternative policies of his own. The bitterly fought strikes in Quebec in the forties and fifties were reminiscent of the 1890s in other parts of North America. In these labour disputes the Duplessis government openly identified itself with 'foreign' capital against French-Canadian labour. The enormous under-representation of urban areas in the provincial legislature meant that the Union Nationale had little to fear from the votes of angry trade unionists. Despite his reactionary policies Duplessis never failed to win re-election through a combination of electoral corruption, personal charisma, and an ear finely tuned to the frustrations of French Canada's minority complex. He skilfully used nationalism as a shield to protect his conservative policies in the sham battles he fought against Ottawa, while at the same time allowing the alienation of the province's economy. It is no wonder that in progressive circles, both inside and outside Quebec, French-Canadian nationalism became highly suspect. An intellectual (who today [1965] is a separatist of the socialist variety) wrote in 1958 that 'those who like me have experienced the bankruptcy of what is called our "national doctrine" must seek a new direction. They do not believe that the Nationalist orientation can ever produce a living culture, a living politics, living men.'4

In these years of Duplessis's ascendancy a new French Canadian middle class was spawned. This class was composed of people who in growing numbers were turning away from the traditional professions of French Canada: law, medicine, journalism, and the Church. Instead, though only slowly because of the continued domination of clerically-directed classical education in Quebec, the most ambitious young people turned to business, engineering, and the social sciences. These people, as well as many members of the traditional professions, began to look at society in a new fashion. Many of them discovered that to advance in their professions they had to adopt much of the culture of the dominant, English-speaking minority: they had to hang up their language with their coats at the office. The new nationalism of Quebec is partly a reflection of the tension created in the minds of young people who want both to succeed in their professions and also to maintain their culture.

It was these same people, the urban middle class, as well as the urban working class, who became increasingly critical of the out-dated social philosophy of the provincial government. They wanted the kind of positive state that would help them solve their problems by providing better educational opportunities, higher welfare benefits, better housing facilities, and equitable labour laws. If Quebec was to be modernized and if French Canadians were going to exercise any control over that society there was only one institution which could be used: the State. In the provincial government French Canadians unquestionably had an institution that belonged to them if they chose to use it. In the past the Church had been the major institution of *la survivance*; today it is the State. That is the real, indeed only, revolution that has taken place in Quebec. It is also at the root of the friction between the federal and provincial governments.

In the past French Canadians looked upon the State with a deep suspicion. For one thing the State had been for nearly a century after the Conquest an instrument of English domination. Then, too, the French Canadian, faithful to his church, believed that an active State could threaten the prerogatives of the Church. The Church rather than the State played the predominant role in the educational, medical, and social welfare fields. But the practical limitations of the Church grew increasingly obvious as the traditional parish organization disintegrated under the impact of industrialization and urbanization. By the end of the fifties the demand for State action was becoming irresistible. Today it is no longer resisted. René Lévesque described the new role of the State in his usual colourful way when he said: 'It must be more than a participant in the economic development and emancipation of Quebec; it must be a creative agent. Otherwise we can do no more than we have been doing so far, i.e., wait meekly for the capital and the initiative of others. The others, of course, will come for their own sake, not for ours. It is we alone, through our State, who can become masters in our own house.'[5]

Traditionally, French Canadians believed that if they exercised control over their language, their laws, and their religion, their survival as a distinctive community would be guaranteed. Each of these categories was placed in the hands of the provincial government at Confederation. But in recent years it became patently obvious that survival was endangered by economic and social changes. Economically and socially Quebec was becoming indistinguishable from English-speaking North America. Was cultural assimilation an inevitable consequence? If the answer was to be no, French Canadians realized that new instruments of survival were necessary.

The Liberal Party, elected in 1960, reflected this new attitude and indicated a willingness to translate it into policy. It reflected more than it created the attitude, and there can be no doubt that many, though not all, of Premier Lesage's ministers have seen the State move into areas that they would not have anticipated five years ago. Like any other democratic government, the Lesage cabinet is a coalition of different shades of opinion stretching over a fairly broad spectrum from moderate left to moderate right. There can, however, be no doubt that the left has asserted its ascendancy within the cabinet. And it is no accident that as it has shifted leftward it has also grown more nationalist. In both respects it reflects the changing temper of the province.

The first two years of the Lesage government saw a general cleaning up of corruption, the enactment of several social welfare measures and labour laws, and increased concern with education. But in 1962 a new departure was taken with the decision to nationalize eleven private hydro-electric companies, thus completing a step begun in 1944 with the creation of Quebec Hydro. It was the radical intellectual, René Lévesque, Minister of Natural Resources, who was the author of this policy. Its main intention was to give the government control of an industry that was fundamental to the economic development of the province. But while the decision was economic, it was also nationalist. In the 1962 election, called as a referendum on power nationalization, the Liberals campaigned on the slogan 'Maîtres chez nous'. The success of this appeal clearly showed that although nationalism under Duplessis may have been somewhat discredited among intellectuals it was far from dead among the populace. Indeed, under Lesage, and particularly under Lévesque, nationalism has been divested of its reactionary image and given a progressive façade and content. But the fact is that the Liberals appeal to the same sentiment of nationalism that Duplessis exploited so successfully. The difference is in the means proposed to guarantee *la survivance*; no public man in Quebec ever questions the end.

The positive nationalism of the Lesage government is expensive. To extend welfare benefits, nationalize hydro, improve and increase the civil service, enter directly into economic expansion, extend and reform education – all require the expenditure of huge sums of money. In its search for revenue Quebec found that nearly every source was already being tapped by Ottawa. Since the Second World War Ottawa had grown accustomed to initiating the country's major welfare and developmental policies. While the Quebec government had often objected, Ottawa usually proceeded in one fashion or another. Moreover, ever since the wartime and 'cold war' emergencies, Ottawa has kept a tight-fisted control on all the major sources of revenue. The Lesage government, autonomist from the start and nationalist to an increasing degree, quickly made plain its unwillingness to accept passively either Ottawa's exclusive initiative in developmental policies or its primacy in the fields of direct taxation. While the Diefenbaker government moved slightly in the direction of decentralization, this was meagre in comparison with the galloping pace of the Quebec government's reforms and expenditures.

While the friction between the Lesage and the Diefenbaker governments at first had the appearance of a traditional quarrel between Liberals and Conservatives, Premier Lesage completely dispelled that notion in his budget speech delivered on April 5, 1963. He made it clear that his government was so committed to autonomy and to costly reform measures that it would expect whichever party was in power in Ottawa to meet Quebec's fiscal demands in twelve months. This statement, widely described as an 'ultimatum', was delivered three days before the voting in the federal general election.[6] Since it was widely expected that the Liberals would be called upon to form a government in Ottawa after the election, the 'ultimatum' came as a shock to many federal politicians. In fact, it was a shrewd declaration of independence. If the Liberals were elected, Lesage wanted it to be perfectly clear, especially to the voters of Quebec, that his government would not be a mere handmaiden of federal policies. That declaration of independence has since been made formal by an almost complete separation of the federal and provincial party organizations in Quebec. Though this move shocked many English Canadians, its real purpose was nothing more than to destroy the bogey of federal domination that the Union Nationale had used so effectively against the provincial Liberals in the past.

Premier Lesage's insistence on the independence of his party was an accurate reflection of the new mood of the province. This new mood manifested itself in a profound suspicion of the federal government. Ottawa's reputation reached an all-time low during the last year of the Diefenbaker régime, and nowhere was its reputation worse than in Quebec. But while the federal government could be restored to a place of honour in English Canada, the malaise was deeper in Quebec. After the death of Duplessis a new generation of Quebeckers began to make their voices heard. Though the majority of these people found their views well represented by the Lesage government, and especially by the voluble René Lévesque, there were others who were discovering new forms of radicalism that could be fitted into the old nationalist moulds. Everywhere in Quebec after 1960 there was a questioning of traditional values. The traditional role of the State was rejected, the place of the Church in society and the layman in the Church questioned, the purposes of education endlessly debated, and, naturally, French Canada's position in Confederation was examined. There seemed so many necessary tasks to be undertaken in Quebec itself that many French Canadians lost interest in the rest of Canada. Then, too, there were those who concluded that the source of Quebec's problems was Confederation itself.

There have always been people in Quebec who have believed that French Canada's ultimate salvation could only be achieved if the full status of independent nationhood was acquired. But these groups, in the past, have never been strong. Today [1965] they represent, according to the only serious analysis that has been made, something like thirteen per cent of the population of Quebec. Of these separatists the vast majority are well educated, below thirty, with a prosperous family background. They are, in fact, typical middle-class students and young professional people.[7] Like the ideologically-minded everywhere, these young radicals reject the compromises and scorn the pragmatism of their elders in the Lesage government. Where Lesage cautiously develops the interventionist state, the radicals call for full-scale socialism and *planification*; where Lesage carefully increases State control over the previously Church-controlled educational system, the radicals advocate complete secularization or *laïcisme*; where Lesage defends his province's autonomy, the impatient youth demand national independence, or *séparatisme*. The separatist movement, which has never yet entered politics actively, is divided within itself, expressing views stretching all the way from a tiny fringe of terrorists, through Marxist anticlericals, to clerical corporatists on the far right. All, despite effusive democratic professions, verge on a totalitarianism enforced on them by their commitment to nationalist absolutes.[8] It sometimes appears that this young generation of anti-clericals has rejected the absolutes of the Roman Catholic faith only to accept the absolutes of a nationalist faith. Nearly all of their writings show an intense interest in the newly independent nations of Asia and Africa, a profound ignorance of economics, and a pride in the achievements of contemporary France.

Despite the widespread publicity the separatists have gained, partly as a result of tight organization and youthful enthusiasm and partly as a result of scattered acts of violence, the movement does not command broadly based support in Quebec. Its strength could grow rapidly, however, if the Lesage government lost its reform impulse, or if English Canadians refused to respond to the moderate demands for change being made by the provincial Liberal government. At the moment, both of these dangers are present, but not threateningly so. If the movement was to grow it would have to spread into the working-class population of the province. So far the working people have remained largely immune to separatism, suspecting that they would have to pay the undoubted price that separatism would entail. The leaders of the two major trade union organizations have made their opposition to separatism unmistakably clear. Jean Marchand, leader of an exclusively Quebec union, stated just over a year ago that in his view Quebec's problems had very little to do with the constitution.[9] It goes without saying that the business community and those responsible for the province's economic growth are opposed to separatism, which they fear may discourage investment in Quebec.

Separatism, with its several faces, is only one political manifestation

of Quebec's contemporary social turmoil. A no less striking phenomenon, and one based on much wider electoral support, is *créditisme*, the
Quebec version of the economic heresies of Major Douglas. Where
separatism is the panacea offered by the ambitious middle-class intellectual as a solution for all Quebec's problems, *créditisme* has found its
main support among the lower middle class and the urban and rural
lower classes. But, like separatism, *créditisme* is a symptom of the
revolt against the old order. Until 1962 no federal party other than the
Liberals and Conservatives had ever made any appreciable impact on
the French-Canadian voter. Yet in the 1962 federal election twenty-six
Quebec constituencies returned Social Credit members. The leader of
the party was a fiery, demagogic automobile dealer, Réal Caouette,
who admits a one-time admiration for Adolf Hitler and Benito Mussolini. While Caouette, unlike most English-Canadian supporters of
the Social Credit Party, is a true Douglasite monetary reformer, his
main electoral appeal was the slogan 'Vous n'avez rien à perdre.' Much
of his party's vote came from people who were disillusioned with the
Conservatives without having been won back by the Liberals. What
the Social Credit vote seemed to exemplify was a rootless, aimless,
poujadiste discontent with the status quo among people whom Premier
Lesage's sophisticated reformers had failed to reach.[10]

Like every other group in present-day Quebec, Réal Caouette's party
soon became afflicted with *nationalisme*. By 1963 Caouette had broken with the English-Canadian leader of his party, forming a separate
Quebec group. While it is not a separatist party, its concern for monetary reform has been largely replaced by rather confused demands for
constitutional reform. It is unlikely that the *créditiste* party will survive
much beyond another election. In the meantime, however, it stands as
an unsettling reminder of the ease with which discontented people can
be attracted to a properly presented slogan.

Both separatism and *créditisme* represent in extreme form the intensity of the nationalist impulse in Quebec and the widespread dissatis-
faction with the social, economic, and political status quo. Although
the source of much of this discontent is in Quebec society itself and can
therefore only be removed by the provincial government, there is an
inevitable tendency to blame Confederation itself. While the vast proportion of Quebecers reject separatism at present, there are very few
articulate French Canadians who are satisfied with the existing position of the French Canadian in Confederation. A host of suggestions to
rectify the situation have been made. Few are very specific, and of
those, most seem impractical or unacceptable from the English-Canadian viewpoint.

Currently a view put forward by several vocal groups in Quebec is that an entirely new constitution should be devised to meet the needs of the 'two nations' in Canada. Under this new constitution each nation would have its own sovereign state, but the two would be associated in a loose confederal arrangement, each represented equally, and each having the right of veto. This theory of 'associate states', though it seems to have won the vague approval of two members of the Quebec provincial cabinet, has very little prospect of acceptance. In the first place, Premier Lesage himself is realistic enough to know, and to have said so publicly, that the time is not ripe for full-scale constitutional revision. English Canada remains largely unconvinced of the need for radical constitutional change. Moreover, there is a committee of the Quebec legislature currently examining a wide range of proposals for constitutional change, and the government will certainly not commit itself before that committee has done its work. Finally, on the basis of the meagre details of the 'associate state' theory that have so far been presented, it is fairly clear that it would create economic chaos and endless political instability. It is, in fact, only a thinly disguised form of separatism.

For the immediate future the present constitutional structure, modified substantially in its workings, offers considerable hope. In the current parlance the new approach is called 'co-operative federalism'. In general this means a commitment by the federal government to the decentralization of responsibilities and revenues and close, almost continuous, consultation between the federal and provincial authorities on nearly every aspect of policy. This even includes federal-provincial meetings on such unquestionably federal responsibilities as international trade. What it means above all is careful, detailed negotiations rather than rhetorical appeals to 'national unity' and 'provincial rights.' Some French Canadians suspect this highly empirical approach as another Anglo-Saxon ruse. But the well-trained civil service that has been built up in Quebec, as well as the highly responsible French-Canadian politicians at both Ottawa and Quebec, recognize that it is the only realistic approach, given the mood of English as well as French Canada. Like most Canadian public policies, 'cooperative federalism' is really another word for compromise. Maurice Lamontagne, one of Prime Minister Pearson' s closest French-Canadian advisers and chief author of the new approach to federal-provincial relations, said recently that 'Confederation ... remodelled to establish a balance of forces which form our country and to satisfy to a greater extent Quebec's aspirations is, I feel, the only real hope of the French Canadians. It is the only way to a mutually acceptable compromise. Co-operative federalism is half way between federalism de tutelle, which existed until 1963 but which is no longer acceptable to French Canadians, and confederative federalism which is no longer satisfactory for present-day problems and which the English Canadians would not accept.'[11]

A second aspect of the new approach to relations between French and English Canadians is a clear commitment on the part of the federal government to improving the status of French Canadians in federal institutions. More French Canadians are being appointed to better civil service posts, and more important, French is gradually becoming a more 'normal' language in the public service. The Royal Commission on Bilingualism and Biculturalism is investigating the whole range of problems relating to French-English relations. The French-speaking co-chairman of this commission is André Laurendeau, one of the most intelligent and respected men in Quebec. As the editor of the nationalist Montreal daily *Le Devoir*, Laurendeau never failed to defend Quebec's autonomy or the rights of French Canadians. But he was also an effective opponent of separatism, the more so, no doubt, since he himself had been a separatist in his youth in the thirties.

The commission has the task of examining the place of French and English Canadians, as well as the role of the numerous ethnic groups or New Canadians, in Canadian society. Its most difficult and at the same time most important task will be to consider the treatment of the French-Canadian minorities outside of Quebec. Here it will be concerned with one of the oldest and most bitter grievances of French Canadians. While the English-speaking minority in Quebec has a completely separate educational system and constitutionally guaranteed bilingualism, the seventeen per cent of French Canadians who live outside Quebec have no such privileges. In some provinces bilingual schools exist in a limited way – in Ontario, New Brunswick, and Saskatchewan – but they are precarious and sometimes impose extra tax burdens on French and Catholic parents. While French Canadians have long asked for more equitable treatment, the response from English Canada, until recently, has been negative. Today many French-Canadian nationalists, particularly those of the separatist variety, advocate the abandonment of the minorities to inevitable assimilation. For many separatists, the opposite side of this coin would be a unilingual Quebec. Most French Canadians, however, remain reluctant to accept this attitude, believing that the minorities are a part of the French-Canadian nation and that it would be immoral to abandon them. As for the minorities, there is no stronger anti-separatist group in Canada than the leaders of the French-speaking Acadians in New Brunswick.

The problem of the minorities will receive a great deal of attention from the Royal Commission. The difficulty will arise, however, when the time comes to implement the commission's recommendations. Many of these recommendations will doubtless relate to educational matters and that is a wholly provincial concern. The fact is that English Canadians have not yet come to accept the view that French Canadians are different from other minority groups and therefore have a right to special treatment. Yet the solution to the present crisis in Canada depends in large part on the practical acceptance of the fact that Quebec is not a province like the others, and that the French-Canadian minorities are not minorities like the others.

The resolution of the current difficulties depends on both the federal and Quebec governments. Perhaps more on the latter than the former, for the source of the problem is economic, social, and educational more than constitutional. But there is always the danger that the more impatient, more ideological groups will force the Quebec government to turn its eyes from practical reforms to constitutional debate. There is also the danger that the anti-French, Canadian voices in English Canada will grow so strong as to convince the moderate people of Quebec that there is no real hope of two nations living peacefully within the bosom of a single state. Both these dangers are increased by the instability of the minority government at Ottawa.

Still, the readjustments that have already been made are reasons for optimism about the future. The Canada that emerges from the present heated debate will be a different country, and probably a better one to live in. And there can be no doubt that the change will be largely the result of the transformation that has taken place in Quebec. René Lévesque summed up that change in an interview just over a year ago when he described his province as 'a nation awake, in full swing, fed up with being seen as a museum, as "the quaint old province of Quebec"; a nation bent on advancing, rising, no longer just content to endure.'[12]

If Quebec nationalism becomes too assertive and self-centred it will undoubtedly stimulate an equally self-centred and assertive response from English Canadians, in which case the country will face a crisis unlike anything it has ever witnessed before. Contrary to the general belief, Canada's problem is one of too much nationalism, not too little. Indeed, the central paradox of the country is that its unity is strongest when its various nationalisms remain muted. 'The Canadian state cannot be devoted to absolute nationalism, the focus of a homogeneous national will,' a distinguished Canadian historian wrote in the 1940s. 'The two nationalities and four sections prevent it.'[13] That is the hard truth that Canadians are trying to relearn today.

[1964]

NOTES

1 André Laurendeau in *Le Devoir*, January 5, 1963.
2 Bruce Hutchison, *Mr. Prime Minister, 1867–1964* (Toronto, 1964), xi.
3 Jean-Noël Tremhlay, M.P. See *Canadian Annual Review for 1961* (Toronto, 1962), 90.
4 Pierre Vadeboncoeur, 'A Break with Tradition?,' *Queen's Quarterly* 65, no. 1 (spring 1958): 92.
5 *Le Devoir*, July 5, 1963.
6 Frank Scott and Michael Oliver, *Quebec States Her Case* (Toronto, 1964), 30.
7 Albert Breton, 'The Economics of Nationalism,' *Journal of Political Economy*, 72, no. 4 (August 1964): 376–86.
8 See, for example, André Major, 'Arms in Hand,' in Scott and Oliver, 73–82.
9 Scott and Oliver, 152–6.
10 Gérard Pelletier, 'Profil d'un démagogue,' *Cité libre*, 14th year, no. 53, January 1963.
11 Maurice Lamontagne, speech to the Club Richelieu de Québec, September 9, 1964.
12 *Le Devoir*, July 5,1963.
13 W.L. Morton, 'Clio in Canadian History,' *University of Toronto Quarterly* 15, no. 3 (April 1946): 234.

TWO

"Au Diable avec le Goupillon et la Tuque": The Quiet Revolution and the New Nationalism

Borduas was the first to break radically ... He risked everything. Modern French Canada begins with him. He taught us the lesson which had been lacking. He let loose the liberty on us.

Pierre Vadeboncoeur, *La Ligne du Risque*, 1963

"La révolution tranquille," the Quiet Revolution, is a phrase that conjures up nothing so much as contradiction. Can a revolution occur silently? Did Quebec experience a revolution in the 1960s? Was Quebec quiet in the 1960s? Only the last question can be answered unambiguously – and negatively. Quebec was a tumultuous and noisy place in the 1960s. Much of the noise was the sound of steam escaping an overheated society: nationalists, students, workers, peace activists, even ecologists. Much the same as elsewhere in the industrialized world. But some of the noise in Quebec was the sound of builders renovating, if not wholly reconstructing, a society. The rhetoric of these renovators was, in many ways, familiar. It was nationalism, a central doctrine of Quebec intellectual and emotional life since the early nineteenth century. But it was not merely the same old nationalism, though it had identifiable roots in the past. Indeed, it was perhaps even more radically new than its exponents realized.

What made the nationalism of the 1960s new and different, even radically different, were the socio-economic changes that had overtaken Quebec and Quebecers since about 1940. A profound change in both the social order and the value system of Quebec was well begun by the early 1950s, moved into a turbulent phase in the 1960s, and gradually settled into the accepted consensus. Out of these changes came a new self-image formulated in a nationalism that, while related to the past, was the expression of a new set of social values, a new public philosophy.

The transformation that Quebec experienced after 1940 can be reduced to the shorthand abstractions, urban and industrial growth. What they meant in human terms can best be seen in Gabrielle Roy's classic *Bonheur d'Occasion* (1945), the tale of Maria Chapdelaine in the city. From the 1880s, when 73 per cent of French-speaking Quebecers lived in the countryside, until 1951, when 67 per cent resided in an urban setting, an inexorable transformation had been taking place. But after 1940 the process accelerated to a rate exceeded only by British Columbia and Alberta, and Quebec rapidly became the most urbanized province in Canada. By 1951, 34 per cent of all Quebecers lived in Montreal. The 1971 census classified the 4,759,000 French-speaking Quebecers as follows: rural farm: 6 per cent; rural non-farm: 16 per cent; urban: 78 per cent.[1]

Despite the continuous character of this socio-economic transformation, neither public authorities nor most of those who defined the society's values willingly accepted the new reality. Or, even if they did, only minimum steps were taken to adjust public policies to new needs – perhaps because some thought the new reality only temporary, or capable of being reversed. In 1927, when more than 60 per cent of Quebecers were already urbanites, Henri Bourassa, still an important nationalist leader and politician, could express the hope that changes in Canadian tariff policy would "put a brake on the orgy of industrialism which disturbs the country and re-establish the preponderance of the rural life, the only guarantee of the health and the *sanity* of peoples."[2]

But in the post-war years the new reality could no longer be ignored, though there was much disagreement about the kind of response required. The nature of the problem was dramatically highlighted in a strike by some 5,000 miners in the asbestos industry lasting for three months in the spring of 1949. There, Quebec workers found themselves arrayed against an American corporation, a provincial government that called itself nationalist, and most of the important voices in a Church that had always claimed to be the front-line defender of French-Canadian interests. The support of Monsignor Charbonneau, Bishop of Montreal, the nationalist daily *Le Devoir*, and a small but important group of younger intellectuals was not enough. The workers lost the battle, though the war was to last much longer, and the outcome was far more complicated. Monsignor Charbonneau's reward was exile in Victoria, British Columbia.[3]

If the Asbestos strike marked the rite of passage of a union movement growing up, it was also a revelation that the old values defended by traditional politicians, traditional churchmen, and traditional nationalists were, at best, ill-suited to the needs of an industrial society and, at worst, merely justification for a reactionary and repressive elite in both state and church. A new society was emerging, one whose size and shape ensured that the old institutions and ideologies could neither define nor confine it.

Even before the workers, the middle class, or for that matter the social scientists, social critics, or politicians realized fully what was transpiring, there was at least one visionary who did. His name was Paul-Emile Borduas, Quebec's most imaginative and radical artist. Because he was a visionary and an artist he was easily dismissed. So he departed first for New York and finally to Paris, never to return to his beloved Sainte Hilaire. But Borduas's life and work epitomize better than any other example what was happening to Quebec: he was the avant-garde, not just as an artist. Borduas, his biographer tells us, was a young French-Canadian painter who, during his youth in the 1920s, deviated in no way from orthodoxy. He wanted to follow a career as a church decorator. His talents were recognized by Monsignor Olivier Maurault, who sent him to study at les Ateliers d'Art sacrés in Paris in 1928. When the economic crisis struck he was forced to give up his studies and return home, where he hoped that his friend, the church artist Ozias Leduc, would help him find work. But the churches, like the economy, were in financial trouble and could not afford new religious art. Eventually Borduas found employment as a teacher in a state-supported art school. Thus, unconsciously, he look the first step along the road to secularism, to a view of the world that led to the creation of his magnificent *automatiste* paintings from which all conventional religious significance disappeared.[4] It led also, in 1948, to his famous manifesto, *Réfus globale*. That revolutionary document, signed by Borduas and fifteen young associates, attacked the values of Quebec society uncompromisingly. Beginning with a capsule history of this *petit peuple* – the rural settlements, the Conquest, the Church, the story of *la survivance*, the fear of modern ideas, of *les poètes maudits* the manifesto rose to a crescendo first as a challenge – "the frontiers of our dreams are no longer what they were," then denunciation "to hell with the holy-water-sprinkler and the tuque," and finally aspiration – "we will follow our primitive need for liberation."[5] *Le goupillon et la tuque* – the holy-water-sprinkler and the tuque, the symbols of traditional culture, the centrepieces of traditional nationalist ideology, these had to be unmasked and rejected. Quebec had to become a modern society like the others – the United States, France, English Canada – just as Borduas and his followers would shift their talents away from crucifixes, stations of the cross, rural landscapes, and habitant families, toward modern, abstract, international art.

To concentrate on one individual, however talented, and to insist that his career symbolizes the transformation of a whole society may seem perverse. But the symbolism is there, one that provides an invaluable insight into what has happened in Quebec and the new self-image, the new nationalism that developed during the years of the Quiet Revolution. Let me explain what I mean.

Traditional French-Canadian nationalism was the dominant ideology of Quebec's leading classes from the second quarter of the nineteenth century until the 1950s. Though its exponents varied somewhat in their outlook, and there were significant challenges to its dominance at least from the 1930s onwards, certain fundamental ideas had a remarkable capacity to endure. Together these ideas and values described an idealized nation, one that had existed in the past, was often threatened in the present, but which, given inspired leadership and correct doctrine, would again materialize in the future. This nation was French in culture (though that meant the culture of pre-revolutionary France, the France "*qui prie*," not the one "*qui blasphème*"), Catholic in religion, and agricultural in socio-economic organization. The Church, the parish, and the family were its essential institutions. The state, the very idea of which implied secularism, played only a marginal role in this conception of the nation, for the society's civilizing mission was much more intimately related to the religious state: the Church.[6] Here was *l'église-nation*, advocated, praised, blessed, and only rarely and softly cursed – in the speeches and writings of nationalist clergy, politicians, journalists, novelists, poets, and educators. It can be found fully and systematically formulated in Monsignor L-F. Laflèche's *Quelques considérations sur les rapports de la société civile avec la réligion et la famille* (1866), most fantastically in Jules-Paul Tardivel's *Pour la Patrie* (1895), oratorically in Monsignor L.-A. Pâquet's frequently reprinted "Sermon sur la Vocation de la Race française en Amérique" (1902), and in the voluminous historical and polemical writings of abbé Lionel Groulx, of which *L'Appel de la Race* (1922) and the essays collected in *Dix Ans d'action française* (1926) serve as the best examples. Even those organs of opinion like the mass circulation daily, *La Presse*, which favoured the industrial development of Quebec, can be found expressing similar stereotypes. On the occasion of the sixtieth anniversary of Confederation in 1927, *La Presse* pointed to Place d'Armes in Montreal as exemplifying Canadian virtues. On one side stood the Church of Notre Dame facing the Bank of Montreal with a statue of de Maisonneuve, the city's founder, in the centre. "It is the image of the Fatherland, with all that signifies. On the one hand, the contribution of the first Canadians, of those who were the first and who have guarded their faith, their virtues and everything which explains their survival and can contribute to the greatness of the nation. On the other hand, the material contribution of our English-speaking compatriots with their eminent practical qualities."[7] Here was a convenient ethnic division of labour that gave spirituality and virtue to the French Canadians, leaving to the English materialism, practicality, and, of course, control of the economy.

This traditional nationalism forged in the crucible of the Catholic religion focused not on politics and economics, but on culture and religion. Usually it was most clearly articulated when cultural and religious rights were threatened: when French-language, Roman Catholic schools were abolished by the provinces of Manitoba or Ontario and when the English-speaking majority attempted to drag French Canadians into the defence of the British Empire.[8] Only occasionally, and ineffectually, did these nationalists concern themselves with the problems created by burgeoning industrialism, which produced the conditions Lord Durham had predicted in the 1840s: the French Canadians were becoming a proletariat in an Anglo-Saxon capitalist world.[9]

This traditional nationalism was expressed lucidly, if somewhat nervously, in the *Rapport de la Commission royale d'enquête sur les problèmes constitutionnels*, or Tremblay Commission, which reported to the Quebec government in 1956. It is the philosophical rather than the constitutional portions of the Report that are relevant here. The definition it gave to French-Canadian culture was traditional, "Christian inspiration and French genius," as was its insistence on the fundamental differences between the French and English "confronting cultures." So, too, its account of the perilous historical conditions through which French Canadians had lived drew on the standard nationalist history as expounded from F.-X. Garneau to abbé Groulx. French and English, the Report observed, "since 1760, live in competition in Canada; with one desiring despite military defeat and political subjection, to preserve its particularism and, with that end in view, seeking to take back into its own hands, and as extensively as possible, the conduct of its own life; the other, resolved to install its institutions and to organize the country according to its ideas and its interests and to have its culture everywhere predominate."[10]

But the Tremblay Report was more than just a systematic statement of conventional wisdom. It recognized that something new had been added to the old French-English equation: industrialism. "If the Conquest put the French Canadians out of tune with the political institutions," the Commission concluded, "the industrial revolution put them out of harmony with the social institutions." Here was a threat of the most demanding character. Now the Commission harked back to earlier nationalists who had warned against urban-industrial society and sang the praises of agriculture. Industrial capitalism, the commissioners warned, "is in complete disaccord with the Catholic French Canadian culture": materialist rather than spiritual, scientific and technical rather than humanist, individualistic rather than communal. Here was the basic challenge: "We have to choose between the Christian concept and materialism, either in its pragmatic or philosophic form" – by which the commissioners meant that both North American capitalism and Marxian communism were antithetical to Christianity.[11]

Having identified the threat of secularism, though the Commission preferred the term "materialism," it could only urge a renewed defence of Quebec's autonomy as a province that, because of its Francophone and Catholic majority, had to be recognized as a province "*pas comme les autres.*" But it only hinted at new strategies that might be required to defend the values that made French Canada a distinct "nation." "The whole institutional system which, up to now has been the broadest and most sympathetic expression of French Canada's special culture, must be completely remade along new lines."[12] The authors of that prophetic sentence little realized how extensive the remaking would prove to be. Nor could they have foreseen how the remaking of institutions would hasten the acceptance of the secular values that were so inimical to the traditional conception of the nation.

During the 1950s Premier Maurice Duplessis's conservative, even reactionary, Union Nationale government managed to dominate Quebec political life through a combination of nationalist rhetoric, a corrupt political machine, a gerrymandered electoral map, and good economic times. But in these same years a vigorous debate about Quebec's past and future developed. In this debate the validity of traditional nationalism was questioned from at least four fairly distinct perspectives. First there were the members of Père Georges-Henri Lévesque's recently founded school of social sciences at Laval University who, having adopted an empirical approach to social analysis, questioned the *a priori* character of social thought in Quebec. These sociologists, economists, and industrial relations experts urged a more inductive, social science approach to the province's social problems. Whether they were professors like Maurice Lamontagne and Maurice Tremblay, or trade union activists like Jean Marchand, they agreed that social thought and social action had to begin by accepting Quebec's urban-industrial condition. Nationalism, at least as traditionally preached, was condemned as an obstacle to a clear perception of Quebec realities.[13]

That view was taken a long step further by the young social scientists, lawyers, journalists, and trade unionists who founded the magazine *Cité libre* in 1950. Led by Pierre E. Trudeau and Gérard Pelletier, both of whom had supported the workers at Asbestos, they developed a forceful and well-documented polemic against traditional national- ists and nationalism generally, arguing for what they called a "func- tional" analysis of social problems and social reform. Like the Laval social scientists, the *citélibristes* argued that nationalism – all national- ism – was unacceptable for it was merely the rhetoric of vested inter- ests who opposed social change. Nationalists identified imaginary ene- mies outside the fortress walls, when the real enemies were within. Home rule was less important than who ruled at home. Nationalist thought, in Trudeau's words, "can only be a timid and reactionary thought." In this critique of traditional ideology, Trudeau and his friends were often sharply anti-clerical, though never anti-Catholic. But their anti-clericalism, or liberalism, and their concern for a more equitably ordered, industrial society led them to insist that the state had to accept a positive role in social and industrial development, for "some state planning has become an absolute necessity ... "[14]

The re-evaluation of the role that the state should play in Quebec was one of the main themes in Quebec social thought in the 1950s. For most, though by no means all,[15] that meant the provincial state. *Le Devoir*, the most important nationalist newspaper, began to advo- cate a more positive role for the state after Gérard Filion and André Laurendeau took charge of the newspaper in the 1950s. These two modern nationalists began to transform the old message preached by Henri Bourassa and his disciples into a new social doctrine that accepted industrial society without any hint of nostalgia for the old agrarianism. *Le Devoir* expounded liberal Catholic social views and argued that the state had responsibility both for social justice and as the defender of French-Canadian society. In 1959 Filion wrote that "French Canadians will remain drawers of water and hewers of wood, small storekeepers and small investors, with a few millionaires here and there, as long as they will not make the only government they have under their control serve in the elaboration and realization of a large-scale economic policy."[16]

More nationalist, focusing almost exclusively on Quebec as the one place where French Canadians had a chance, more controversial than *Le Devoir*, were the views of a new school of historians who came into prominence at the Université de Montréal in the 1950s. The most vis- ible and audible of these young scholar-polemicists was Professor Michel Brunet, son of a small businessman whose post-graduate train- ing had been in the United States, where he was attracted to the eco- nomic interpretation of history. In a series of speeches and essays, in which he developed a thesis originated by his colleague, Professor

Maurice Séguin, Brunet argued that traditional Quebec nationalism was nothing more than a rationalization of French-Canadian economic inferiority and a justification for clerical power. It was not the Church that had ensured French-Canadian survival but rather a high birth rate and isolation in the seigneurial system, away from the Conqueror. The society was nevertheless feeble because its entrepreneurial middle class had been decapitated by the Conquest, leaving the economy in the hands of the British. Whatever the validity of the Séguin-Brunet thesis as history, its contemporary implications were clear. The old clerical nationalism with its emphasis on agriculture, its illusions about French Canada's civilizing mission, and its fear of the state had to be banished. In its place Quebecers should concentrate on building a new entrepreneurial class, make use of the state to defend Francophone interests, and forget about the minorities living outside the province. For Brunet there were Canadians and *canadiens*; the latter group, the minority, being under constant threat of assimilation, had only one, fleeting hope, and that lay in building a strong provincial state into a national state.[17]

Like *Le Devoir*, and utterly unlike *Cité libre*, the Montreal historians were nationalist. But they, like all the other groups considered here, shared the conviction that the old, religion-centred, rural, anti-statist nationalism had outlived its usefulness, if it had ever had any. In its place Quebec needed a new value system, a public philosophy that welcomed the industrial order, assimilated the new social sciences as a replacement for moral exhortation, and willingly used the state for economic and social development, including educational reform. Implicitly or explicitly, each of these groups – and others – were advocating a secular social philosophy, nationalist or non-nationalist.[18] Some attacked the Church for its historic role; others merely concluded that its role in the new society would have to be a diminished one. The Church recognized the threat of these developments. In 1953 the Church hierarchy noted that "a wind of bad-quality liberation seems at present to blow on certain groups. According to these people, it is necessary to free the people from the hold of the Church ... It is, in a new form, pure and simple Protestantism."[19]

The fact is, as Jean Hamelin's recent history of the Church in Quebec demonstrates brilliantly, the Church was already in retreat in the 1950s, though it engaged in a strenuous rearguard action. New recruits declined in number and, of those who entered, fewer stayed the course. The deconfessionalization of some institutions, most notably the Catholic trade unions, was under way. Church attendance declined notably, and by the sixties a declining birth rate demonstrated the ineffectiveness of the Church's teaching about birth control. In 1956 a

Church commission concluded that "our people no longer have a Christian life, they have not even the natural virtues ... Our Christians ignore their religion and the Bible." The urban-industrial order was having exactly the impact on the Catholic population of Quebec that the clerical nationalists had long prophesied. By 1970 a Church-appointed inquiry described the Church as *"en crise"* and documented the claim with statistics such as these: where 2,000 young Quebecers had taken up religious vocations in 1946, only about 100 followed that path in 1970.[20]

The mighty army of the Church, once more numerous in proportion to population than in any country outside of Latin America, had fallen into irreversible decline. It could no longer defend the ramparts against an advancing secularism promoted by a new elite connected with the universities, the mass media, and such social organizations as the trade unions. These were the people who, in Quebec as elsewhere, led the "ethnic revival" that touched many parts of the world by the 1970s. These "secular intellectuals," as Anthony Smith calls them, espoused an "enlightened" rationalism of the sort found in Pierre Trudeau's writings advocating a secular, pluralistic, democratic society in place of the ancien régime. In Quebec the growing acceptance of these new ideas, and the socioeconomic changes they reflected, opened the way for the collapse of Maurice Duplessis's Union Nationale government and the election of Jean Lesage's Liberals with their promise of reform and modernization. That new regime, the product of the socioeconomic and intellectual evolution that had preceded it, gradually brought Quebec's public institutions more fully into conformity with social and intellectual reality. In short, it built a Quebec welfare state accompanied by a new nationalist ideology that defined the society's changed self-image.[21]

Though the Lesage Liberals were elected on a platform that promised both to defend Quebec's autonomy in the Canadian federal system and to make fuller use of provincial powers than Duplessis had done, the party was not explicitly nationalist. Lesage himself had begun his political career in Ottawa and returned to Quebec only after the federal Liberals lost power in 1957. Moreover, the Duplessis regime had given nationalism such a bad name that many of its opponents – except perhaps *Le Devoir* – identified nationalism with reaction. What the Liberals were committed to – reforming education, the public service, the labour laws, and, more generally, the promotion of economic development – had, at least superficially, little to do with nationalism. In the process of implementing these policies, the politicians and their allies

among the new elites found that nationalism was a useful weapon in
the battle to overcome some of the obstacles that stood in the path of
change. Yet it was not the old nationalist rhetoric of Duplessis but
rather a new ideology that focused on, and legitimized, state action.
Three examples, among many, will illustrate this argument: educational reform, the expansion of state control over hydroelectricity, and
the establishment of the Quebec Pension Plan.[22]

The new ideology and its goals are very clearly revealed in the
Report of the royal commission the Lesage government appointed to
examine the province's educational system. Despite its chairmanship –
Monsignor Alphonse-Marie Parent – the thrust of the Report was
unambiguously secular. This is to say that the commissioners argued
that the function of education in a democratic, industrial society was
to equip citizens with the knowledge and skills necessary to achieve
worldly success: "to afford everyone the opportunity to learn; to make
available to each the type of education best suited to his aptitudes and
interests; to prepare the individual for life in society." While the commissioners were aware of it, in failing to include among the goals the
orthodox Catholic claim that education and religion cannot be separated, they simply skirted the issue. Moreover, and this was the main
point of the Report's first volume, they contended that while education
had once been the preserve of private organizations and churches,
"now the state has become the principal agent for organizing, co-ordi-
nating and financing all education." Though the nationalist note was
very muted, the Report did remark that an effective educational system
was "a condition of progress and survival of any country."[23]

From these propositions flowed logically the Commission's first, and
perhaps most important, recommendation: the appointment of a Minister of Education. Since the last Minister of Education had been abolished in 1875 the absence of a political head of the educational system
had always been viewed as a recognition of the Church's primacy in the
field. As the leaders of the Church perceived instantly, the state was
now being called upon to terminate that primacy. The struggle over Bill
60, which the government introduced in 1963 to implement the Parent
Commission's first recommendation, was, on the whole, a decorous
one conducted for the most part behind closed doors. The Church
asserted its traditional position but rather than challenging the principle of the new proposal merely demanded, and obtained, a guarantee
that confessional schools would still be allowed under the proposed
scheme. A new "concordat" was established between church and state,
in Professor Léon Dion's view, but it was one under which the state's
supremacy in education was recognized as a fact. The secular goals of
education would soon be dominant. By 1980 even the Catholic school

committee admitted that schools operated "according to a pedagogical and administrative rationality that is clearly not to be found in the gospel."[24]

At least two conclusions can be drawn from the education reforms implemented during the 1960s. The first is that, since control of education has always been regarded as fundamental to the defence of Quebec's distinctive culture, after 1963 the state, and not the Church, obviously had assumed that onerous responsibility. As the aims of education would now be defined more in relation to the needs of the state than the needs of the Church so, too, the definition of the nature of Quebec's distinctiveness would be altered inevitably. The educational system, and this is the second conclusion, as defined by successive volumes of the Parent Report, was to be centralized, bureaucratized, and, essentially, secular, one designed to prepare young Quebecers for life in the urban-industrial world. As such it would differ only in detail – and language – from the educational systems of New York, California, Ontario, or British Columbia. Insofar as the educational reforms reflected the spirit of the Quiet Revolution and the new nationalism that accompanied it, one of its paradoxical consequences was the replacement of a distinctive educational system by one that was essentially North American in spirit and function.

In the debate over educational reform the nationalist argument was more implicit than explicit. In the almost concurrent debate over a proposal to bring the remaining privately owned power companies under the publicly owned Hydro-Québec system established in 1944, the nationalist theme was utterly explicit. While the economic and administrative advantages of a unified hydroelectric system and the costs and benefits of the heavy expenditures required to complete the takeover were debated, the decisive political issue was expressed in the campaign slogan: *Maîtres chez nous*. René Lévesque, Minister of Natural Resources and chief architect of the nationalization plan, put the case in this manner: "The state must not be absent from the economic scene, for in our particular case that would be equivalent to pure and simple abandonment of the most effective instrument of economic liberation that we possess." And he continued, explaining that while it was not desirable for the state to control the whole economy, it was necessary to "ally the dynamism of private enterprise with the advantages of concerted action by the whole nation." Here, then, the conflict was presented as one between the Quebec state, representing "*la nation entière*," and the Anglo-Canadians who were majority owners of the private power companies. Nothing more graphically reveals the outcome of that struggle than a photograph in Clarence Hogue's celebratory study of Hydro-Québec depicting the strained faces of Shawinigan Water and Power Company employees "attending a French lesson in 1964." Hydro was now completely in the hands of what one of its propagandists called "the national state of French Canada," where the operational language was, quite naturally, French.[25]

Whether the costs and benefits of hydro nationalization were shared equitably by the members of "*la nation entière*" is a controversial question.[26] What is obvious, however, is that the new nationalism used to legitimize the hydro policy emphasized the issue of French-Canadian economic inferiority as the source of cultural weakness. Both hydro nationalization and educational reform were based on that assumption and were designed, in part, to correct it. Moreover, the new nationalism accepted without hesitation the urban-industrial society. Hydro-Québec, and especially the new developments carried out by Francophone engineers, technicians, and workers at places like Manicouagan, came to symbolize the new industrial man who stood at the heart of the new Quebec. The chansonnier Gilles Vigneault turned a prosaic industrial achievement – and ecological calamity[27] – into a popular, nationalist folksong. Where once politicians dreamed that perhaps a school or a bridge would carry their names into posterity, after the 1960s only a power dam sufficed!

The third, and most important, observation is that in this new nationalist ideology the state was again the leading actor. If Church and Nation had once been natural partners, the campaigns for educational reform and hydro nationalization had forged a new partnership of State and Nation, revealed in the growing usage of the phrase "*L'État du Québec*." And state policy in hydro, as in education, meant the centralization and standardization of a system that had once been decentralized and somewhat chaotic. Quebec would now have a hydro system very like that which existed in other Canadian provinces and American states. It would have it because it was necessary, or at least desirable, for the promotion of an industrial economy of the sort found in New York and Ontario.

If the Lesage government's policies in education and hydroelectricity can be seen as an extension of state power where once the Church reigned and over the economy into areas traditionally dominated by Anglo-Canadians, the conflict over pensions brings the struggle to the inter-state level. Since the 1940s the federal government had been developing policies in the social security field that sometimes infringed on provincial jurisdiction or, at least, touched on disputed areas of jurisdiction. The Duplessis government had regularly protested these policies both on grounds of jurisdiction and because the Church in Quebec, viewing social security as a form of charity, opposed state intervention in this area.[28] The Lesage government intended not only to defend provincial jurisdiction but also to devise social security measures that would be run by the state. Consequently, in 1963, when the federal government announced its intention to establish a universal, portable, contributory pension scheme, the Quebec government objected that it intended to implement its own plan. One reason for the Quebec government's decision, in addition to the jurisdictional question, was the scheme devised by a group of talented, nationalistic technocrats to use pension-plan funds for public investments that would assist Francophone participation in the economy. *Maîtres chez nous* had many dimensions.

The struggle between Quebec and Ottawa was dramatic and very public, and both politicians and the media presented it as involving stakes high enough to destroy Confederation. And it is at least arguable that during this conflict Quebec was as close to moving toward independence as it has been at any subsequent rime. In the end the crisis was surmounted. Quebec had a demonstrably superior plan, and a government that was far more determined and clear-minded than Ottawa. Quebec won the battle and thus gained control over its plan and its vast financial resources together with an alteration in federal-provincial tax-sharing agreements that significantly increased Quebec's tax room and revenues. Lesage had insisted that since Quebec was the homeland of the majority of French Canadians it needed a pension plan tailored to its needs. He had used the nationalist argument effectively, flexed the muscles of the Quebec state, and won an impressive, if not total, victory.[29]

From this abbreviated account of a complex issue, a few conclusions may be drawn. First, what might have been a slightly sordid haggle over the division of public funds was converted into a nationalist cause. It was the national homeland of Francophones against Ottawa, where Francophones, always a minority, were hardly visible between 1957 and 1965. Second, the Lesage Liberals had taken a traditional Quebec position and transformed it into a modern cause: it was not the right of the Church in the social field that was being defended, but rather the determination of the Quebec state to move into an area once claimed by the Church and the federal government. Finally, again as in the examples of education and electricity, the new welfare state, of which the pension plan was only one piece, would provide centralized, rationalized, and standardized services to replace the patchwork of haphazardly organized, often patronage-ridden institutions. In this the Quebec government was taking a course already marked out in other industrial societies, though, as the Caisse de Dépôt et Placement illustrated, Quebecers were willing to make important innovations.

The essence of the new nationalism was invoked to justify the developments that have come to be known as the Quiet Revolution. Where traditionally the Quebecer's self-image, his nationalism, focused on language, religion, and the land, the new ideology was articulated by a society for which rural life was only a memory, often a bad one. For members of an urban-industrial society, the concern was with new questions that traditional religious and social teachings seemed incapable of answering. And if traditional socio-religious answers were inadequate, then the Church as an institution was less and less relevant. As new ideas, founded on economics and sociology more than theology and moral philosophy, were explored, so too, a new institution had to be found or created to implement these ideas. That institution already existed: the provincial state provided by Canadian federalism. An *église-nation* became an *état-nation* with the only question being the degree of autonomy that the new *état* might want.

The principal remaining similarity between the old and the new nationalism was language. Yet on closer examination even that similarity is limited. Like the old nationalists, the new were determined to defend the French language as a sheet anchor of Quebec's distinctiveness. But traditional nationalists invariably identified language with religion: *la langue gardienne de la foi, la foi gardienne de la langue.*[30] Language questions often meant purity of language, language as a vehicle of a literary culture, and perhaps above all, language as a medium of education for French and Catholic students everywhere in Canada. Language was protected and preserved by the Church and the educational system and, of course, the two were actually one.

For the new nationalists language came to have a different or at least an additional significance. Indeed, language became even more important than in the past for the simple reason that, as Quebec became more like the rest of North America socio-economically, language became its principal distinguishing characteristic. Thus, during the Quiet Revolution language became a growing preoccupation and a source of increasing tensions as the cry for French unilingualism developed.[31] But the issue was almost totally divorced from religious concerns. Nor was it predominantly a literary or narrowly cultural one. Instead it was socio-economic. Quebecers had come to the conclusion that it was the language of the economy, not the language of the Church, that determined both individual and collective destinies – at least in this world. An economy where corporate managers operated in English was an economy where French Canadians rarely became corporate managers. How could this be changed? The response to this, as to so many other questions, was state intervention. It began, haltingly, with the Lesage government's establishment of a Department of Cultural Affairs. It continued wherever the state moved into the economy and French was made the operational language. It reached its culmination in the work of the Gendron Commission on the situation of the French language in Quebec[32] and in legislation by the Bourassa and Lévesque governments designed to make French the dominant or exclusive language in all sectors of Quebec life. What lay behind these acts, and the surrounding controversy, was expressed very forthrightly in the White Paper on language policy that preceded Bill 101 in 1977. It stated:

The Quebec that we wish to build will be essentially French. The fact that the majority of the population is French will be distinctly visible: at work, in communications, in the country. *It is also a country where the traditional division of powers, especially in matters concerning the economy, will be modified*: the use of French will not be generalized simply to hide the predominance of foreign powers over Francophones; this usage will accompany, will symbolize a reconquest by the Francophone majority of Quebec of the hold which returns to it on the levers of the economy.[33]

Once again, then, the principal characteristics of the new nationalism are crystal clear. In language policy as elsewhere, the state replaced the Church; the values served are secular rather than sacred; the outcome is centralization and homogenization. Though the appeal to traditional values is evident, the thrust is toward the present and future, even at the expense of past distinctiveness.[34]

The rapidity of change in Quebec in the 1960s, and the vigour with which Quebecers asserted their desire for new social and constitutional arrangements, was often startling, especially to English-speaking Canadians and to outsiders. Yet what was happening in that society was far from unique. There has been an "ethnic revival" in almost every part of the world during the last quarter-century. Punjabis, Ibos, Catalans, Basques, Serbs, Croats, Walloons, Occitanians, Bretons, perhaps even Bavarians have, with varying degrees of assertiveness, joined with Québécois in their determination to retain their distinctiveness in an homogenizing world. A variety of hypotheses have been advanced in an attempt to understand this phenomenon. The British social philosopher Ernest Gellner has contended that nationalism is the product of an industrializing society, the glue that holds the society together when old loyalties and obligations based on regions, families, and religion are eroded by socio-economic change. Nationalism imposes a common literacy, what he calls a "high culture," on a society in order to unify it and fit its citizens for the needs of industrial activities. "It means the generalized diffusion of a school mediated, academy supervised idiom, codified for the requirements of reasonably precise bureaucratic and technological communication." While nationalist rhetoric is advanced as an appeal to preserve a society's uniqueness, it is in reality a justification for profound change. "It preaches and defends continuity, but owes everything to a decisive and utterly profound break in human history."[35]

There is much to be said for this hypothesis when applied to Quebec. As I have argued, the new nationalism of the Quiet Revolution, while appealing to certain historic hopes and fears, was in fact the ideological component of a qualitatively different society.[36] So, too, this nationalism legitimated policies whose thrust was toward a more homogeneous, bureaucratized, and centralized society, drawn together by a new educational system, a more centralized economy, and a common welfare and social security system.[37] Thus, Gellner's contention that nationalism propels the transition from a "culture-religion" to a "culture-state" is appealing.

In Quebec in the 1960s there were certainly those who suspected that their nation was being destroyed consciously by the very people who claimed to be saving it. In 1964 abbé Groulx published what he thought would be his last book. Entitled *Chemins de l'avenir*, this was a long lament for a nation suffering "the social sickness of a disruptive industrialism."[38] He pointed to youthful unbelief and moral laxity, a creeping secularism nourished by American materialism, and the anti-clericalism of *Cité libre* and Radio-Canada. For him the Quiet Revolution was a "denial of history, of traditions, a turning of the back on the past; an attack more than cunning against all of the elements that constitute the French-Canadian man, even of the foundations which had until now formed the basis of his life."[39] No wonder he was astonished to receive a letter of congratulations from Premier Lesage, who, evidently not being a very careful reader, was following a quite contrary road to the future.

Yet Lesage's instinct may not have been entirely misguided for he, or his advisers, recognized that not everything about the Quiet Revolution was new. It had connections with the past. Gellner's exclusive emphasis on the relationship between industrialization and nationalism fails to account for nationalism's earlier history in Quebec and elsewhere. Anthony Smith offers a more balanced perspective, one that can fit abbé Groulx and Premier Lesage on the same continuum. The ethnic revival, he writes, is "at one and the same time an attempt to preserve the past, and to transform it into something new, to create a new type upon ancient foundations, to create a new man and society through the revival of old identities and the preservation of the 'links in the chain' of generations."⁴⁰ Nationalism, then, is more than outward symbols; it is also the articulated will of a community to preserve its distinctiveness. That will has a long history in Quebec; it has been persistent and moderate. It has never completely disappeared, though it has changed with the changing needs of society, and especially the changing aspirations of Quebec's leading classes. "Imagined by successive petites bourgeoisies – the liberal professions, the clergy, the new middle class – the nation, as a concept, offers this ideological plasticity that allows it to be associated with the most varied projects," André-J. Bélanger has written. "The nation, like liberty, that of Mme. Roland and others ... what interests can be served in its name!"⁴¹ During the Quiet Revolution, then, a new nationalism evolved that, like the old, expressed the aspirations of Quebec's leading classes. A transformed society required a new self-image: modern, urban, industrial, and secular. Paul-Emile Borduas's angry challenge had been met: the holy-water-sprinklers and the tuques, those relics of traditional Quebec, almost vanished, replaced by micro-computers and hard hats. Borduas might have judged the change a mixed blessing.

[1986]

NOTES

1 These figures are found in Kenneth McRoberts and Dale Posgate, *Quebec: Social Change and Political Crisis* (Toronto, 1980), 51; and Pierre E. Trudeau, ed., *La Grève de l'amiante* (Montréal, 1956), 4–5.

2 *Le Devoir*, 1 juillet, 1927.

3 Trudeau, *La Grève*, 165–212; Renaude Lapointe, *l'Histoire bouleversante de Mgr. Charbonneau* (Montréal, 1962).

4 François-Marc Gagnon, *Paul-Emile Borduas* (Montréal, 1978), 4–64; see also André-G. Bourassa, *Surrealism and Quebec Literature* (Toronto, 1984), 80–155.

5 Paul-Emile Borduas, *Ecrits 1942–1958* (Halifax, 1978), 45–54.

6 Christian Morissonneau, *La Terre promise: Le Mythe du nord québécois* (Montréal, 1978); Maurice Tremblay, "Orientations de la Pensée sociale," in Jean-Charles Falardeau, ed., *Essais sur le Québec contemporain* (Québec, 1953), 193–208.

7 *La Presse*, 1 juillet 1927, cited in Geoffrey Kelley, "Developing a Canadian National Feeling: The Diamond Jubilee Celebrations of 1927" (M.A. thesis, McGill University, 1984), 76. For examples of traditional nationalism, see Ramsay Cook, ed., *French-Canadian Nationalism: An Anthology* (Toronto, 1969).

8 For example, Henri Bourassa, *Que devons-nous à l'Angleterre?* (Montréal, 1915); Henri Bourassa, *Les Ecoles du Nord-Ouest* (Montréal, 1905).

9 Joseph Levitt, *Henri Bourassa and the Golden Calf* (Ottawa, 1969).

10 René Durocher et Michèle Jean, "Duplessis et la Commission royale d'enquête sur les problèmes constitutionels, 1953–1956," *Revue d'histoire de l'Amérique française*, 25, 3 (décembre 1971), 237–64; *Royal Commission of Enquiry on Constitutional Problems, Quebec* (Quebec, 1956): 11: 33, 67, 44.

11 Ibid., 61, 85, 87.

12 Ibid., 65, 72.

13 Robert Parisé, *Georges-Henri Lévesque* (Montréal, 1976); Michael Behiels, "Le Père Georges-Henri Lévesque et l'établissement des sciences sociales à Laval, 1938–1955;" *Revue de l'Université d'Ottawa*, 52, 3 (octobre-décembre 1982): 355–76; Falardeau, ed., *Essais*; Maurice Tremblay, "Reflexions sur le Nationalisme," *Ecrits du Canada français* 5 (Montréal, 1959): 9–44.

14 Trudeau, *La Grève*, 14, 43.

15 Maurice Lamontagne, *Le Fédéralisme canadien* (Québec, 1954).

16 *Le Devoir*, 6 mai 1959.

17 Michel Brunet, *Canadians et canadiens* (Montréal, 1954); *La présence anglaise et les canadiens* (Montréal, 1958); Ramsay Cook, "L'Historien et le Nationalisme," *Cité libre* 15, 73 (janvier 1965): 5–14; Serge Gagnon, "Pour une conscience historique de la révolution québécoise," *Cité libre* 16, 83 (janvier 1966): 4–19.

18 Michael Behiels, *Prelude to Quebec's Quiet Revolution: Liberalism versus NeoNationalism, 1940–1960* (Montreal, 1985)

19 Jean Hamelin, *Histoire du catholicisme québécois: Le XXe Siècle*, Tome 2 (Montréal, 1984), 139.

20 Ibid., 134; *Commission d'Etude sur les Laics et l'Eglise* (Montréal, 1972), 23.

21 Louis-Edmond Hamelin, "Evolution Numérique Séculaire du Clergé Catholique dans le Québec," *Recherches Sociographiques* 2, 2 (1961): 189–242; Hamelin, *Histoire*, 135; Anthony D. Smith, *The Ethnic Revival in the Modern World* (London, 1981), 104; Pierre E. Trudeau, "Some Obstacles to Democracy in Quebec," in Trudeau, *Federalism and the French Canadians* (Toronto, 1968), 103–21; and Trudeau, *Les Cheminements de la Politique* (Montréal, 1970).

22 For a detailed account of the policies of the Lesage government, see Dale C. Thomson, *Jean Lesage and the Quiet Revolution* (Toronto, 1984), and McRoberts and Posgate, *Quebec*, 94–123.

23 *Report of the Royal Commission of Enquiry on Education, Quebec* (Quebec, 1963) 1: 75, 81, 72, 64.

24 Léon Dion, *Le bill 60 et la société québécoise* (Montréal, 1967), 144–45; Thomson, *Jean Lesage*, 310.

25 Clarence Hogue, *Québec un siècle d'électricité* (Montréal, 1979), 269,

386; Paul Sauriol, *La Nationalisation de l'électricité* (Montréal, 1962), 86.

26 Albert Breton, "The Economics of Nationalism," *Journal of Political Economy* 72, 4 (August, 1964): 376–86.

27 Boyce Richardson, *James Bay* (Toronto, 1972)

28 Antonin Dupont, *Les relations entre l'Eglise et l'Etat sous Louis-Alexandre Taschereau 1920–1936* (Montréal, 1972).

29 Thomson, *Jean Lesage*, 184–89.

30 Henri Bourassa, *Réligion, Langue, Nationalité* (Montréal, 1910); Bourassa, *La Langue Gardienne de la Foi* (Montréal, 1918).

31 Raymond Barbeau, *Le Québec Bientôt Unilingue?* (Montréal, 1965).

32 *Rapport de la Commission d'Enquête sur la Situation de la Langue française et sur les Droits linguistiques au Québec* (Québec, 1972), 3 vols. See especially vol. 1, *La Langue de Travail*.

33 "La Politique québécoise de la langue française," *Le Devoir*, 2 avril 1977.

34 William D. Coleman, *The Independence Movement in Quebec* (Toronto, 1984), 182.

35 Ernest Gellner, *Nations and Nationalism* (Ithaca, N.Y., 1983), 57, 125.

36 Charles Taylor, "Nationalism and the Political Intelligentsia," *Queen's Quarterly* 71, 1 (Spring, 1965): 152.

37 In *Entre l'Eden et l'Utopie* (Montréal, 1984), Luc Bureau offers a satirical and humorous account of the failures of planning. See especially 200–03.

38 Lionel Groulx, *Chemins de l'avenir* (Montréal, 1964), 22. The following year the conservative philosopher George Grant offered a similar reflection on Canada as a whole in his *Lament for a Nation* (Toronto, 1965).

39 Lionel Groulx, *Mes Mèmoires* (Montréal, 1974), 4, 298.

40 Smith, *Ethnic Revival*, 25.

41 André J. Bélanger, "Le Nationalisme au Québec: Histoire en Cinq Temps d'un Imaginaire," *Critère*, 28 (printemps 1980), 58. See also Maurice Pinard and Richard Hamilton, "The Class Basis of Quebec's Independence Movement," *Ethnic and Racial Studies* 7, 1 January, 1984): 19–54; Kenneth McRoberts, "The Sources of Neo-Nationalism in Quebec," 57–85.

THREE

Quebec: The Ideology of Survival

'Nobody in French Canada dares to think – at least nobody dares to think out loud,' a young French-Canadian teaching brother wrote in 1960. Soon, well over one hundred thousand copies of the book *Les Insolences du Frère Untel*, in which these lines appeared, had been sold in Quebec. The very response to Frère Untel's strictures was one evidence that a new Quebec, a Quebec eager for the full practice of freedom and democracy, and engaged in self-criticism, was suddenly emerging. 'We are afraid of authority; we live in a climate of magic where under penalty of death we must infringe no taboo, we must respect all the formulae, all the conformisms,' young Brother Jérôme continued. In his mind, freedom was available for the taking in Quebec, but the people were afraid of it. 'My own idea is that we are freer than we think, that it isn't liberty that is lacking, but the courage to use the liberty that we have. We whine about lost liberty, but don't use what we have ... Speaking as a Canadian, I say shall we take the plunge and be free?'[1]

No one better epitomizes the new Quebec [of the 1960s] than Frère Untel, for despite the trouble with his clerical superiors that his unorthodox little book caused him, Brother Jérôme's challenge was taken up by many of his compatriots. Today's Quebec is a society testing the freedom that Brother Jérôme claimed was present but unexercised. Today's Quebec is a society using that freedom to examine every aspect of traditional life, with the result that many standard assumptions have been rejected. The Church, the State, political parties, the educational system, the economy, and even Confederation have been challenged to justify themselves. Under the raucous noise of a Quebec undergoing a siege of self-criticism is a series of related economic and social changes which form the material basis of the new Quebec.

Ten years ago Professor Jean-Charles Falardeau of Laval University wrote: 'The daughter of Maria Chapdelaine who was an ammunition-factory worker at Valcartier during the war now lives with her own family of five children in the Rosemount ward of Montreal. Maria's married brothers are employees of the Aluminum Company at Arvida and Shipshaw after having been workers at the Jonquière pulp plant.'[2] Nothing could more graphically sum up the change that has taken place in the province of Quebec than this imaginary epilogue to *Maria Chapdelaine*. Nor should it pass unnoticed that these perceptive lines were written over a decade ago. Yet it is only in the last three or four years that Canadians outside Quebec and many inside the province, too – have awakened to the fact that the Quebec of Louis Hémon has moved forward to the Quebec of Gabrielle Roy – and beyond.

It is, of course, political events in Quebec that have awakened us, at last, to these changes. But politics in most democratic societies usually fails fully to reflect fundamental shifts in society until long after the most creative writers, artists, and even sociologists have detected these changes. Moreover, there are peculiar reasons why political change has been especially slow in Quebec in the past.[3] What is even more impor-tant, however, is that it is the very slow pace at which politics in Que-bec – and Ottawa – moved to reflect the basic social transformation which explains the present crisis. And the present crisis is more a crisis within Quebec society itself than a crisis of Confederation. The essence of the crisis, a crisis similar to others that afflict newly emergent nations throughout the world, is that the community's political leaders are attempting to formulate a set of public policies to meet the needs of an urban-industrial society at least a quarter of a century after the society has clearly taken shape. Today, Quebec is a society passing through that characteristic revolution of the mid twentieth century – the revolution of rising expectations, with the expectations ranging from modest demands for increased educational opportunity to demands for total, irrevocable national independence.

Here, then, is the essence of the change that has taken place in Que-bec: an agrarian society has been transformed into an urban-industrial one. In this respect Quebec has become more similar to those parts of North America with which it has close geographic relations – Ontario and the north-eastern United States. But this physical transformation has been followed by an equally radical intellectual change: a new view of the role of the state in society has won increasingly wide acceptance. This is so for two reasons. First, in every modern urban-industrial soci-ety, the positive role of the state is a fact of life. The state must act to protect workers and their families against the impersonal harshness of an industrial society, to stimulate and often direct the economy, to ensure that the citizens have access to the types of education and training that are necessary in a technological society. No one, except perhaps those whose knowledge of Quebec stops with *Maria Chapdelaine*, should be surprised that French Canadians, too, have realized the need for this type of public policy. What is surprising is that it took Quebec so long to discover the benefits, and the dangers, of the interventionist state.

Indeed, it is doubly surprising in view of the second reason for the adoption of a new attitude toward the state in Quebec. That second reason rises directly from the dynamic principle of French-Canadian history: *la survivance*. In so far as urbanism and industrialism have made Quebec increasingly similar to its North American neighbours, the dangers of assimilation have likewise increased. The one effective agency over which French Canadians exercise undisputed control, which can be used to counteract the dangers of assimilation inherent in the new society, is the state. This is what Premier Lesage was underlining when he remarked: 'It must be clearly understood that the state of Quebec acts as a fulcrum for the whole French-Canadian community, and at the present time it is the instrument needed for that community's cultural, economic and social progress.'[4]

Again, what is surprising is that it has taken French Canadians so long to face up to the dangers and challenges of industrialism, and to make use of their state creatively. The danger is one that should have been obvious long ago. In 1839 that shrewd analyst Lord Durham argued that assimilation of the French Canadians by the English was desirable because

their present state of rude and equal plenty is fast deteriorating under the pressure of population in the narrow limits to which they are confined. If they attempt to better their condition, by extending themselves over the neighbouring country, they will necessarily get more and more mingled with an English population: if they prefer remaining stationary, the greater part of them must be labourers in the employ of English capitalists. In either case it would appear that the great mass of the French Canadians are doomed, in some measure, to occupy an inferior position, and to be dependent upon the English for employment.[5]

Lord Durham's prediction was a fairly accurate one. The history of Quebec in the latter part of the nineteenth century is the history of a rapidly increasing population. In these years, Quebec had the highest birth-rate in the world, a fact which gave rise to the romantic nationalist notion of *la revanche du berceau*. It was also a community where, by the 1850s, the efficient arable lands were largely occupied. Despite the heroic, but probably misguided, efforts of men like Curé Labelle in the last quarter of the nineteenth century to encourage an effective program of colonization, French Canadians were, in fact, moving more readily in two other directions, both predicted by Durham: about half a million French Canadians emigrated to the United States in the last half of the nineteenth century;[6] then, as the industrial development of the province began to pick up speed, an increasing number of French Canadians became city-dwellers and industrial labourers. Here, briefly, are the figures: in 1901, 40 per cent of the population of Quebec lived in cities; in 1911, the percentage had risen to 48 per cent; another 8 per cent had been added in 1921; the figure was 63 per cent in 1931 and 67 per cent in 1951. And, as Durham had foreseen, both these movements – to the United States and even to the industrial cities of Quebec – threatened the survival of French Canada as a cultural community. But in the long view the industrialization of Quebec will be judged the salvation of the French-Canadian community, for it provided the means whereby the French-Canadian diaspora to the American melting-pot was finally ended. What is new about the 'new Quebec', then, is that French-Canadian leaders have become convinced not only that the French culture can survive in an urban-industrial society but also that that very society, guided by the positive state, can provide a better life than French Canadians have ever experienced. But the critical atmosphere of today's Quebec reflects not only a social transformation but also the recognition by French-Canadian leaders that the new situation contains both potential benefits and potential dangers for the future of French Canada. And it is this tension, a tension inherent in the whole history of French-Canadian nationalism, that underlies the great debates about federalism, autonomism, and separatism; socialism, pragmatism, and conservatism; clericalism and laicism.[8]

Despite the fact that industrialization may now be seen as a means of salvation for French Canadians, it has not always been viewed in such a light. At the end of the eighteenth century, British parliamentary institutions, in a truncated form, were imposed on French Canada in the expectation that they would ultimately encourage the process of assimilation. In fact, French-Canadian leaders soon discovered that these institutions could be used to ensure *la survivance*.[9] By the end of the nineteenth century, industry was being imposed on Quebec, in the sense that it was not a development that French Canadians had asked for or to any large extent participated in at the directing levels. As two economic historians have noted, the 'economic development of Quebec has been financed, directed, and controlled from the outside.'[10] But French Canadians, as in the earlier case of parliamentary institutions,

are gradually learning to use the forces of industrial progress to promote and defend *la survivance*.

The process of learning, however, has been a slow one – perhaps
almost fatally slow. The reasons for the fears and hostilities with which
French Canadians have approached the subject of industrialism have
been explored in at least three careful and provocative studies of
French-Canadian social thought: by Professor Maurice Tremblay of
Laval, and by Pierre Elliott Trudeau and Professor Michel Brunet, both
of the University of Montreal.[11] Although there are important differences in the viewpoints of these writers, they agree on the central argument that the intellectual leaders of French Canada, by virtue of social
background, education, religious assumptions, and, not least important, necessity, were for a century or more both blind to the benefits
that industrialism could provide and foolish in their repeated praises of
the agrarian way of life. In Professor Brunet's words, 'Agriculturalism
is above all a general way of thinking, a philosophy of the life which
idealizes the past and distrusts the modern social order.'[12] Examples of
this ruralist theme are infinite in number, stretching back, as Professor
Brunet has shown, nearly to the Conquest, and forward, as M.
Trudeau has argued, nearly to the present. One fine example, often
overlooked, is Antoine Gérin-Lajoie's novel of 1862. *Jean Rivard: Le
Défricheur* sang the praises of the Arcadian way of life and the educated colonizer. Gérin-Lajoie's objective in writing his book was less literary than consciously propagandist. He told his brother quite frankly
that his book 'would scarcely amuse the young literary people, but I
have composed it with public utility as a goal.'[13] And that goal was to
emphasize *la vocation rurale* of French Canada. Indeed, the whole literary school of 1860, as Abbé Casgrain's critical writings make clear,
was devoted to the glorification, and deification, of the rural mission.[14]

Such an attitude among literary men is perhaps not wholly unexpected, for the late-flowering influence of the European romantic
movement led in an Arcadian direction.[15] It is less understandable, perhaps, in a man who today would probably be described as a social scientist. In his somewhat neglected work *L'Avenir du peuple canadien-
français*, published in 1896, Edmond de Nevers wrote: 'Certainly it
cannot be too often repeated, that the most solid basis for a nation is
the possession of the land; that the question of "repatriation", that is
of the return to the agricultural districts of the province of Quebec,
remains the order of the day. Lay hold of the land, as far as circumstances will permit.'[16]

'Emparons-nous du sol, c'est le meilleur moyen de conserver notre
nationalité,' became the rallying cry of the agrarian school of nationalists who dominated French-Canadian social thought throughout

much of the nineteenth and early twentieth centuries. Jules-Paul Tardivel, the ultramontane separatist editor of *La Vérité*, summed up the position when he wrote in 1902: 'It is not necessary that we possess industry and money. We will no longer be French Canadians but Americans almost like the others. Our mission is to possess the earth and spread ideas. To cling to the soil, to raise large families, to maintain the hearths of intellectual and spiritual life, that must be our role in America.'[17] This was a mission which received the blessing of influential members of the clergy, for the structure of the Church was best adapted to the organization of rural life. Moreover, the rural life placed the French-Canadian Catholic in a position of sharp contrast to the English-speaking Protestant who seemed, in North America, to be more urbanized, more industrialized, more commercialized, and, it was often insisted, more materialistic and thus less Christian. This was the theme of Mgr L-A. Paquet's famous 'Sermon on the Vocation of the French Race in America', delivered in 1902, the importance of which is perhaps measured by the fact that it was republished in 1925 as *The Breviary of the French Canadian Patriot*. 'Our mission', Mgr Paquet proclaimed, 'is less to manage capital than to stimulate ideas; it consists less in lighting the fires of factories than in maintaining and radiating afar the hearth-light of religion and thought.'[18]

There is, of course, no better or more attractive demonstration of the strength and persistence of the theme of agrarianism than the moving little romance of Maria Chapdelaine written by a French emigré, not a French Canadian, in 1914. Everyone knows the tale of how Maria, having lost her first love, the latter-clay *coureur-de-bois* François Paradis, chose to 'dwell on this land as her mother had dwelt and dying thus to leave behind her a sorrowing husband and a record of the virtues of her race' rather than listen to the siren songs of the easy life in a New England mill town. Even better known are the lines:

Three hundred years ago we came and we have remained ... Strangers have surrounded us whom it pleases us to call foreigners; they have taken almost all the power; they have taken almost all the wealth; but in Quebec nothing has changed. Nothing will change because we are a pledge ... That is why it is necessary to remain in the province where our fathers dwelt, and to live as they lived, so as to obey the unwritten commandment which shaped itself in their hearts, which passed into ours, and which we must transmit in turn to our innumerable children. In the land of Quebec nothing must die and nothing must change.[19]

Undoubtedly Hémon's interpretation of the Quebec he saw in 1914 was true in the sense that the struggle for survival is unending *au pays du Québec.* Here he struck a universal theme in French-Canadian life. But, even as Hémon was writing, the life of the Chapdelaines of Péribonka was becoming increasingly untypical. Quebec *was* changing; by 1914 about fifty per cent of the people were urban dwellers. A more accurate picture of Quebec, even the Quebec of 1914, had to await the publication in 1938 of Ringuet's brilliant *Thirty Acres.* In it is chronicled the harsh evolution of Quebec rural society and its impact on the shrewd, yet bewildered, Euchariste Moisan. 'The land was failing her own,' Euchariste, in lonely exile in the United States, was forced to conclude; 'the eternal earth-mother would no longer feed her sons.'[20]

The gap between the disintegrating Moisan family farm and the poverty-stricken family of Azarius Lacasse in the slums of the St. Henri district of Montreal is a narrow one. Gabrielle Roy's Florentine Lacasse is mid-twentieth-century Quebec's Maria Chapdelaine. And a reading of *Bonheur d'occasion (The Tin Flute)* makes the fears that many French-Canadian nationalists entertained about the dangers of urbanization and industrialization more understandable. The dangers were undoubtedly present – dangers of poverty, crime, licence, and above all, perhaps, secularization and anglicization. It is the people who lived the lives described by Gabrielle Roy, Roger Lemelin, and Gratien Gélinas, who became determined that a new Quebec must be created where the lives of French-speaking Canadians could be lived more comfortably and securely, economically, socially, and culturally. Gabrielle Roy gives a hint of this new Quebec in the portrayal of the ambitions of Jean Lévesque. 'Have you ever been up on the mountain [Westmount]?' Jean asks Florentine one night. 'You may not think so, my girl, but I expect to get my foot on the first rung of the ladder pretty soon, and then good-bye to St. Henri for me.'[21]

Yet the transformation from the agricultural illusion to a realistic appraisal of the dangers and opportunities of an urban-industrial society is not something that was achieved overnight, and to speak of the total predominance of the rural philosophy is to leave an unbalanced impression of French-Canadian social thought. Some serious and effective criticisms have been directed against those who have neglected another, though less important, side of the picture. Professor F.-A. Angers has suggested that for at least a century there have been scattered voices in Quebec advocating a more positive approach to economic questions.[22] Moreover, Professors Faucher and Lamontagne have effectively argued that 'agricultural expansion coincided with the teachings of a traditional philosophy of rural life; but it cannot be said that it resulted from these teachings: *there was nothing else to do.*'[23] This argument is useful in redressing the balance, but it neither explains the persistence of the agricultural philosophy after there were other things to do, nor does it take into account the people who, even during the period of agricultural expansion, were pointing to the need for more serious consideration of other aspects of Quebec economic life. It is these people who are, in a sense, the real founders of the Quebec of the 1960s, and their outlook deserves more consideration and credit than it has been given.

In the mid nineteenth century, just about the time that Gérin-Lajoie was establishing Antoine Rivard as a cultural hero, another thinker was attempting to encourage his fellow-Canadians to turn their attention to what he rightly believed was the wave of the future – industrialism. Etienne Parent, one-time editor of *Le Canadien* and veteran of the political battles of the Papineau period, delivered in 1846 an address entitled 'Industry Considered as the Means of Preserving the French Canadian Nationality'. Industry, Parent told his audience, was the basis of social and political power in North America and the leaders of industry were North America's noblemen. (A later generation was to call them 'robber barons'.) French Canadians had to drop their traditional disdain for business if they wished to conserve their nationality. 'In all branches [of industry and commerce],' he said, 'we are exploited; still we let pass into other hands the riches of our country, and part with the principal element of social power. And the cause of this is that the men we place in competition with those of the other origin are inferior to them in education and capital. Those who could have competed disdain business activity and prefer to vegetate or waste the resources that could have been used to their own profit and that of their country.'[24] If French Canadians refused to pay heed to this warning, Parent continued, a future historian would remark upon the group's disappearance and explain it saying: 'That happened in a country where industry was the only source of wealth and where wealth was the greatest, even the only, means of acquiring social importance. The mass of the people had to be abandoned to the denationalizing influence and action of industrial leaders of the rival race, and so in time lost its national character.' Parent had evidently fully understood the implications of Durham's predictions.

For Parent a revised attitude towards industry and changes in education were necessary if French Canadians were to take their proper place in North American society. And surely here he struck upon an important point that deserves further investigation: that is, the attitude of French Canadians, even French-Canadian businessmen, towards business pursuits, and the scale of social values into which business activity must fit.[25] What work has been done in this field supports the view of an American writer who remarked of France that 'the social order in France has in some measure undervalued the very prizes and penalties that have urged on the capitalist process.'[26] It was this type of situation in Quebec that Parent was attempting to modify, for he recognized that if French Canadians wished to survive in a capitalist and industrial society they must do as the capitalists did.[27]

A recent study [1963] of the educational press in nineteenth-century Quebec suggests that Parent was not alone in his concern that commercial education in the province required more emphasis. In 1871 a school of arts and crafts was opened in Quebec City, and the college at Three Rivers began a commercial course. The prospectus of the Collège Masson in 1871 summed up the economic and educational problem of the province in this fashion: 'By raising, with the aid of strong special studies, the industrial and commercial classes to a higher status and to the influence that they have a right and obligation to demand, one can hope that this fortunate foundation will stop the deplorable current which draws almost all our educated young people towards the liberal professions.' And when Laval established courses in applied science in 1871, one newspaper noted: 'Now that the country, and especially our city, has launched itself on the road of manufactures, industry, and railroads, the study of the arts of the applied sciences will be an inappreciable aid to us and will permit us to work a little more for ourselves and by ourselves without being obliged to rely as heavily on assistance from foreigners.' Further examination of Quebec's educational system in the nineteenth and twentieth centuries will have to be carried out before firm conclusions can be reached about the relation of education to industrialization. It would appear, however, from M. Labarrère-Paulé's study, that by the end of the nineteenth century Quebec educational journals, at least, had become less interested in technical education and more interested in the traditional objectives of French-Canadian clerical nationalism: 'To make the province of Quebec the Christian nation replacing faltering France in the role of the eldest daughter of the Church.'[28] It should be added, however, that this situation reflected more than mere clerical influence. It also reflected the fact that Quebec's economy in the last two decades of the nineteenth century rested in a valley between two peaks of industrial activity – the peak of commercialism and shipbuilding of the 1860s, which had passed, and the peak of industrialism based on electricity, which still lay in the future. In the middle period, about 1870 to 1900, coal, iron, and steam were the characteristic elements of industrial advance, and Quebec lacked them.[29]

By 1900, however, as Quebec arrived at the threshold of a new period of industrial advance, a new apostle of industrialism as a necessary component of French-Canadian survival made his appearance. Errol Bouchette, the very title of whose best-known work, *L'Indépen-*

dance économique du Canada français, illustrates his viewpoint, took up the struggle to interest his countrymen in economic problems where Parent had left off. In 1901 Bouchette warned that the industrial revolution was about to break on Quebec, and that unless preparatory steps were taken, the same problems would be created in Quebec as had been created by the emergence of gigantic trusts in the United States. Foreign capital and business should be welcomed, he noted, but 'we must await them in a good strategic position in order to remain, whenever it happens, *maîtres chez nous.*' Like Parent earlier, Bouchette found it necessary to struggle against the indifference, even the disdain, that his compatriots exhibited towards business. His argument was cast in typically nationalist terms: French Canadians had to become involved in industry, for 'it is to do work not only useful but so essential and obligatory that to fail to do it would be antipatriotic.'[30]

Bouchette, who had no desire to see agriculture disappear from Quebec, realized that not even agriculture could survive if French Canadians lost control of the best of their economy. Thus he coined, to set alongside the old slogan, 'Emparons-nous du sol', the new one, 'Emparons-nous de l'industrie'. But he did not fool himself that a mere slogan was a panacea for French Canada's industrial weaknesses. First, the educational system of the province had to be adapted to provide education and training in the techniques of commerce and industry. Here he was particularly successful – though he was by no means satisfied – for 1907 witnessed the establishment of commercial schools at both Montreal and Quebec: L'Ecole des Hautes Etudes Commerciales. More important, and more original, was his view that the province needed a carefully worked out industrial policy. 'In order to defend its frontiers [a people] organizes an army,' he wrote; 'if it is a question of constitutional liberty, it organizes a parliament. That is what we have done. It is now a question of protecting our economic life, on which our national existence depends.' And though he disclaimed any sympathy with a socialist viewpoint, he had no doubt that state action was necessary, not least of all because French Canadians, individually, lacked the economic power necessary to cope unassisted with the requirements of an industrial society. 'In a country like ours, where there is so much to do, and rapidly, if we wish to have an absolute guarantee of our survival as a distinct political entity in America,' he wrote, 'reform cannot be carried out without an impulse, direct or indirect, from the collective will of the citizens, that is, by the state.'[31]

The step from Bouchette's point of view to that of René Lévesque is not a long one. The Quebec Minister of Natural Resources stated in the summer of 1963 that 'our principal capitalist for the moment – and as far into the future as we can see – must therefore be the state. It must be more than a participant in the economic development and the emancipation of Quebec; it must be a creative agent.'[32] But although the step is short, it is a difficult one, for it represents the step from advocacy to action, from intellectual analysis to political activity. In the years when Bouchette did his most effective writing, a group of young men in Quebec were attempting to promote similar ideas at the practical political level. Though the founders of La Ligue Nationaliste Canadienne – Olivar Asselin, Jules Fournier, Armand Lavergne, Omer Héroux – are, like their intellectual father Henri Bourassa, most often remembered for their attitude to the British Empire, they also gave considerable thought to domestic economic problems. Indeed, one-third of the league's program was devoted to *politique intérieure*, the two other sections relating to Imperial problems and Dominion-provincial relations.[33] Moreover, the league's newspaper, *Le Nationaliste*, devoted a substantial amount of space to economic questions and to advocating a positive approach to industrial problems. 'The first duty of the French race is to provide itself with a government which thinks for it and which acts for it,' the league's paper maintained.[34]

One of the most interesting statements of the league's philosophy was formulated by the ardent, individualistic Olivar Asselin in a pamphlet published in 1909 under the title *A Quebec View of Canadian Nationalism*. In this lengthy pamphlet Asselin spoke of all aspects of the nationalist program. But the most interesting section is the one dealing with social and economic affairs, which Asselin, somewhat surprisingly, described as 'possibly the most important article in the Nationalists' program'. Here he called for railway nationalization, remarking that 'it is a well-known fact, outside the fool's paradises, that the contest in Ottawa is not so much between Liberals and Conservatives as between this and that combination of railway interests'. The latter remark is interesting not least of all because it is very similar to the view held by western farmers in the same period. Asselin further advocated legislation to ensure conservation of natural resources, public ownership of hydro-electric power, a labour code, social welfare legislation, and stringent control over limited-liability companies and monopolies. Of course, the Nationalists were Canadian and not simply French-Canadian in their viewpoint, but Asselin explained why his group concentrated its attentions on Quebec. 'The Nationalists', he wrote, 'have selected Quebec as their first battleground precisely because they hoped race hostility would no longer hamper their working for the future greatness of Canada; also because experience has taught them the necessity of educating people to self-government in the smaller spheres first; and thirdly, because they thought that placing the French province of Quebec at the head of Canadian progress should allay the prejudices entertained against the French Canadian as a citizen.'[35]

It is not without interest and significance that Asselin called the Nationalists 'Progressists' in social and economic policy. The name is revealing because the league bears many similarities to the Progressive movement in the United States in the same period: middle-class leadership with its status consciousness, fear of big business but rejection of socialism, emphasis on a non-partisan approach, and, not least of all, nationalism, which in the end proved the league's Achilles' heel.[36] Many of these points were illustrated in a lecture delivered by Henri Bourassa in Toronto in 1907. 'The Nationalist movement in Quebec', he said, 'is not the movement of a political party.' Having insisted on the Canadianism of the movement, Bourassa then remarked that 'the Nationalist movement is equally opposed to monopolism and socialism.'[37] But he continued by making it clear that Nationalists believed that the state had an increasing role to play in the economic life of Canada and Quebec. It is not surprising that Bourassa showed a sympathetic interest in the developing farmers' movement in the west, which he said was working like the Nationalists 'to save the country from the brutalizing yoke of politicians and plutocrats.'[38] Nor is it surprising that in his later career Bourassa showed some sympathy for the CCF and especially for J. S. Woodsworth.[39] But it would be dangerous to try to make Bourassa (or the Ligue Nationaliste) a consistent social radical. He was, as Laurier said, a *Castor-rouge*, an ultramontane, conservative radical, and in that he was very representative of French-Canadian nationalist thinking.[40]

By the time the First World War broke out, Bourassa and the league turned their attention increasingly toward more traditional nationalist questions – Imperial policy and minority schools – and the experimental social thinking began to take a poor second place. The events of the war years, especially the Ontario school controversy and conscription, increased the French-Canadian nationalists' tendency to concentrate on traditional policies. The new nationalist spokesmen in the post-war years followed the young historian Abbé Groulx and his *Action française*. The organization's writers showed little understanding of, or interest in, economic questions, except perhaps for Olivar Asselin, and its traditionalism was well summed up in an article by Antonio Perrault in 1924:

If we defend our French integrity against imperialism and against assimilative federalism, it is in order to safeguard our Catholic integrity and maintain the apostolic vocation of New France ... Without the maintenance of Catholicism, French Canadians would be anglicized; without the conservation of the language and the intimate springs of the French soul, we would greatly risk ending up as Protestants. Catholicism and French genius, such are the forces from which French Canadians can draw the strength to surmount the obstacles opposed to their survival as a distinct race in America.[41]

Yet the reformist strain and the positive approach to economic problems never entirely disappeared.[42] Indeed, it was reincarnated in the program of L'Action Libérale Nationale during the depression period, and had it not been for Paul Gouin's political inexperience and Maurice Duplessis's political finesse, public policies more in touch with the needs of the times might have found their way onto the Quebec statute book before the outbreak of the Second World War.[43] But Duplessis swallowed up L'Action Libérale Nationale and in the process the reform program was lost. Only after the long years of Premier Duplessis's ascendency ended in 1959 did the reform forces once more have their opportunity. And by that date the social changes which had taken place in Quebec made reform irresistible.

The reasons for the triumph of the new reform nationalism are multiple.[44] Gradual changes in the educational system created a new class of social critics who dissected society with the tools of twentieth-century social science. Moreover, the educational system began to produce, in rapidly increasing numbers, young people trained to fulfil the requirements of a technological society. Trade unionism spread, and behind a militant and dynamic leadership, working people demanded expanded educational opportunities and effective social legislation.[45] The attitude of the Church changed, coming increasingly to reflect the altered society which it served and the liberalizing tendencies of the world-wide organization to which it belongs.[46] New nations emerged on the world's stage, encouraging French Canadians to demand a better life for themselves. 'We have survived enough,' Paul Gérin-Lajoie has written. 'The time has come to give this survival a positive sense, to fix a goal for it, and to justify it.'[47]

Somewhere in the hidden recesses of history where sociological changes and intellectual innovations fuse, somewhere around 1959, Quebec began passing through the labour pains that should produce, finally, a more mature, stable society. And supervising that birth or regeneration is the newly discovered state of Quebec. 'We must know how to use this state of ours fearlessly,' Premier Lesage has said. 'It is not a stranger among us, it belongs to us, and it proceeds from our people.'[48] But a birth, even with the aid of such modern medicines as the state provides, is always difficult. And the birth or transformation of a society that uses the stimulant of nationalism to assist the process is an especially dangerous affair, for the stimulant may prove too powerful, thus either slowing up the process or perhaps even contributing to a stillbirth. There is an inherent tension, perhaps even a contradiction, within the structure of French-Canadian nationalist thought. That tension, a tension between liberating and reactionary impulses, the *Castor-rouge* tension, represents a constant threat to *la survivance* itself.

In a brilliant essay entitled 'La Ligne du risque', Pierre Vadeboncoeur summed up M. Duplessis's policy in a sentence: 'to resist assimilation from without, to resist emancipation from within.'[49] Perhaps Vadeboncoeur also, unintentionally, defines here the insoluble dilemma of French Canada: a group of people proud of its traditions, convinced that survival is its first duty, but condemned to minority status in North America – condemned to that status whether as part of the Canadian federal system or separate from it. The dilemma is found in the fact that the threat of assimilation from outside can only be met by a culturally and economically strong French Canada; but at the same time, when energy is used up fighting real or imagined efforts to assimilate French Canada, there is that much less energy left to build a strong Quebec.[50] M. Duplessis, for his own reasons, followed a policy that drew nearly all of Quebec's energies into the battle for provincial autonomy. But as more and more people awakened to the realization that the battle was a sham, nationalism in Quebec became somewhat discredited; it became, as Gérard Pelletier has written, 'associated with the seamiest side of conservatism and corruption.'[51] And it was during the last years of Duplessis's term of office that reform was reborn, often hostile to, or at least suspicious of, nationalism.[52] But since 1960 nationalism, in a multiplicity of forms, has experienced an enormous revival in Quebec, and in this new situation the old dilemma is once more apparent.

To put the dilemma more concretely: the young reforming intellectuals of La Ligue Nationaliste, despite early professions of interest in economic and social questions, found themselves drawn more and more into struggles for the rights of their group's minority status as Canada passed through the First World War. In the end, their cry for domestic reforms, reforms that would have strengthened the place of French Canadians in the economic life of the country, was lost in the struggle against conscription, against Regulation XVII, against Ottawa, against English Canada. The young reforming intellectuals of L'Action Libérale Nationale were carried away in the same direction by M. Duplessis's war against Ottawa. The brief history of the Bloc Populaire is similarly a witness to the struggle of reaction and reform within a single party. And that conflict within the structure of French-Canadian nationalist thought is nearly as old as French Canada itself. Papineau faced it, for in his thought and action the traditionalist and the liberal were at war, and the traditionalist won out. It was in this way, as Fernand Ouellet has suggested, that Papineau fulfilled Garneau's description of him as the 'image of our nation.'[54]

It is this very same dilemma that provoked Pierre Elliott Trudeau to declare, eloquently, in 1961:

Whether or not the Conquest was the origin of all evils and whether or not the English have been the most perfidious occupiers in the memory of man, it remains none the less true that the French-Canadian community holds in its hands, *hic et nunc*, the essential instruments for its regeneration; by the Constitution of Canada the state of Quebec can exercise the most extensive powers over the souls of French Canadians and over the territory where they live – the most rich and most vast of all the Canadian provinces.

Twenty-five years ago, nationalism succeeded in putting to the service of reaction all the energies that had been liberated by the economic crisis of the thirties. It is necessary at any price to prevent the new nationalism from alienating in the same fashion the forces born after the war and which a new unemployment crisis today exacerbates.

Open the frontiers, this people dies of asphyxiation![55]

Today, the dilemma of French Canada remains unchanged. Nationalism can release creative energies in a people; it can also be destructive and reactionary.[56] It can be reactionary because it enforces conformity where individualism and pluralism are necessary if society is to progress. This is the primary danger of the separatist movements and even of the more emotional forms of contemporary French-Canadian nationalism, for both distract the attention of French Canadians from their fundamental problems and turn their energies toward chimeras. M. René Lévesque has remarked: 'If French culture is to spread, if the French language is to be respected, that will depend above all on the vigour, on the economic and political importance of Quebec.'[57] These goals can be achieved, but they are endangered by the very dilemma created by nationalism. 'The tasks that we must undertake at any price,' Professor Léon Dion has said, 'the tasks that we must absolutely resolve, are already sufficiently complex and will demand from us sufficient efforts that we should not take to dreaming of illusory châteaux somewhere other than on the North American continent.'[58]

The real test of the new Quebec and of the new nationalism is easily summed up: can the tension within French-Canadian nationalism be resolved? The answer is by no means clear, but the future not only of

Quebec but perhaps of all Canada is bound up in the resolution of that critical question.

Every Canadian should welcome the emergence of a new, self-conscious, democratic Quebec. The successful resolution of the conflicts within the French-Canadian community depends chiefly on French Canadians themselves, but it also requires a response from English-speaking Canadians – a response to the liberating, non-conformist forces in Quebec. By definition, that response must be imaginative and liberal in character. For English Canadians to ignore the turmoil within Quebec, or to notice only the extremists demanding the balkanization of our common country, would be a tragedy. To respond to Quebec's labour pains in dumb silence or ill-tempered snarls would only strengthen those reactionary tendencies within French-Canadian ideology. Today those reactionary forces are more dangerous than ever, for they could halt a society's natural evolution and lay up store for a future, perhaps fatal, explosion.

In essence, what the French Canadian is asking for is a larger, indeed an equal, place for his culture in Canadian life. More fundamentally, the French Canadian is asking for concrete evidence of the precepts of liberal democracy that Canadians have always claimed provide the basis of their political life. And the French Canadian's yardstick of Canadian liberalism is the yardstick described many years ago by the English historian Lord Acton, when he wrote: 'The co-existence of several nations under the same state is the test, as well as the best guarantee, of freedom.'[59]

Today many French Canadians believe that English Canadians must assist in bringing reality into closer conformity with that ideal. The challenge of the new Quebec is really a challenge to Canada. And that challenge is summed up in one of the most pressing questions that the country must face in the 1960s: can two cultural communities that have as much in common as French and English Canada work out a fruitful partnership within the bosom of a single state? Such a partnership must promote the values of liberty and individual self-fulfilment, and these values must take precedence over the conformist demands of nationalism, English- or French-Canadian. Can we devise the terms of a partnership that will measure up to Lord Acton's yardstick? In a world divided by national boundaries, ideological quarrels, and economic inequalities, but united by the potential benefits and dangers of modern technology, the answer to that Canadian question has a significance that transcends the borders of the Canadian community.[60]

[1965]

NOTES

1 Brother Jérôme, *Les Insolences du Frère Untel* (Montreal, 1960), 55, 67, 83–4.
2 Jean-Charles Falardeau, 'The Changing Social Structures,' in the work he edited, *Essais sur le Québec contemporain* (Quebec, 1953), 111.
3 Pierre-Elliott Trudeau, 'Some Obstacles to Democracy in Quebec,' in Mason Wade (ed.), *Canadian Dualism*, 241–9.
4 *Le Devoir*, March 7, 1963.
5 G.M. Craig (ed.), *Lord Durham's Report* (Toronto, 1963), 149.
6 Gustave Lanctôt, *Les Canadiens français et leurs voisins du sud* (Montreal, 1941), 294–7.
7 Pierre-Elliott Trudeau, La Grève de l'amiante, 4–5.
8 Léon Dion, 'The Origin and Character of the Nationalism of Growth,' *Canadian Forum* 42, no. 516 (January 1964): 229–33.
9 H. Manning, *The Revolt of French Canada* (Toronto, 1962).
10 Albert Faucher and Maurice Lamontagne, 'The History of Industrial Development,' in Falardeau (ed.), *Essais sur le Québec contemporain*, 36.
11 Maurice Tremblay, 'Orientation de la pensée sociale,' in Falardeau, *Essais sur le Québec*, 193–208; Pierre-Elliott Trudeau, 'La Province de Québec au moment de la grève,' in *La Grève de l'amiante*, 1–93; Michel Brunet, 'Trois dominantes de la pensée canadienne-française: l'agriculturisme, l' antiétatisme, et le messianisme,' in *La Présence anglaise et les Canadiens*, pages 113–66.
12 Michel Brunet, *La Présence*, page 119.
13 Louvigny de Montigny, *Antoine Gérin-Lajoie* (Toronto, 1925), 72.
14 H.-R. Casgrain, 'Le Mouvement littéraire au Canada,' in *Oeuvres complètes de l'abbé H.-R. Casgrain* (Montreal, 1896), 1, 353–75.
15 Gérard Tougas, *Histoire de la littérature canadienne-française* (Paris, 1960), 25.
16 Edmond de Nevers, *L'Avenir du peuple canadien-français*, 439.
17 Robert Rumilly, *Histoire de la Province de Québec* (Montreal, 1943), X: 83.
18 L-A. Paquet, 'Sermon sur la vocation de la race française en Amérique,' in *Discours et allocutions* (Quebec, 1915), 187.
19 Louis Hémon, *Maria Chapdelaine* (Paris, 1921), 144, 252–3.
20 Ringuet (Philippe Panneton), *Thirty Acres* (Toronto, 1960), 246.
21 Gabrielle Roy, *The Tin Flute* (Toronto, 1959), 54.
22 Dominique Beaudin, 'L'Agriculturisme, margarine de l'histoire,' *L'Action nationale* 49 (March 1960): 500–30; and, more important, F.-A. Angers, 'Naissance de la pensée économique au Canada-français,' *Revue d' histoire de l'Amérique française* 15, no. 2 (September 1962): 204–29.
23 Faucher and Lamontagne, 'The History of Industrial Development,' in Falardeau (ed.), *Essais sur le Québec contemporain*, 28.

24 J. Huston (ed.), *Le Répertoire nationale* (Montreal, 1893), 4: 18–19.

25 Albert Faucher, 'La Dualité et l'économique: tendences divergentes et tendences convergentes,' in Mason Wade (ed.), *Canadian Dualism*, 222–38.

26 John E. Sawyer, 'The Entrepreneur and the Social Order: France and the United States,' in William Miller (ed.), *Men in Business* (New York, 1962), 16.

27 M. Cadieux and P. Tremblay, 'Etienne Parent théoricien de notre nationalisme,' *L'Action nationale* 13, (1939, March): 203–19, (April): 307–18.

28 André Labarrère-Paulé, *Les Laïques et la presse pédagogique au Canada français au XIXe siècle* (Quebec, 1963), 114, 116, 171.

29 Faucher and Lamontagne, 'The History of Industrial Development,' in Falardeau (ed.), *Essais sur le Québec contemporain*, 24–30. For the development of the Quebec economy in the later period, see John Dales, *Hydro-electricity and Industrial Development Quebec 1898–1940* (Cambridge, Mass., 1957) .

30 Errol Bouchette, 'L'Evolution économique dans la Province de Québec,' *Proceedings and Transactions of the Royal Society of Canada*, 1901, second series, 7: 119, 122.

31 Errol Bouchette, *L'Indépendance économique du Canada français* (3rd edition, Montreal, 1913), 30, 188, 198, 200, 270.

32 *Le Devoir*, July 5, 1963.

33 *Ligue Nationaliste Canadienne, Programme*, 1903.

34 *Le Nationaliste*, June 19, 1904.

35 Olivar Asselin, *A Quebec View of Canadian Nationalism* (Montreal, 1909), 44, 47, 56.

36 See Richard Hofstadter, *The Age of Reform* (New York, 1955).

37 Henri Bourassa, 'The Nationalist Movement in Quebec,' *Proceedings of the Canadian Club, Toronto, for the Year 1906–7* (Toronto, 1907), 56, 58.

38 *Le Devoir*, July 19, 1913.

39 M.K. Oliver, 'The Social and Political Ideas of French-Canadian Nationalists,' unpublished Ph.D. Thesis, McGill University, 1956, chapters 1 and 2.

40 Bourassa was, to some extent, a typical French-Canadian nationalist in his view of the importance of the agrarian way of life. In 1923 he wrote in *Patriotisme, nationalisme, impérialisme*: 'Our race will survive: grow, and prosper in the measure that it remains peasant and rustic.'

41 Antonio Perrault, 'Enquête sur le nationalisme,' *L'Action française* 2 (February 1924): 118. In 1921, *L'Action française* devoted its annual 'enquête' to 'notre problème économique.' Two contributors, Edouard Montpetit and Olivar Asselin, tried to keep the discussion on the level of facts and figures. But in his summing up of the discussion Abbé Groulx strongly emphasized the non-material nature of French Canada's mission, almost as though he was afraid that inquiry into material questions might

sully the purity of the French-Canadian soul. 'If Catholicism remains for us what it must be,' he wrote, 'if we loyally accept its truth, it indicates to us according to what discipline, in what hierarchy of values, the earthly city ought to be constructed.' (*L'Action française* 6, (December 1921): 718)

42 Michael Oliver, 'Quebec and Canadian Democracy,' *Canadian Journal of Economics and Political Science* 23, no. 4 (November 1957): 504–15.

43 H.F. Quinn, *The Union Nationale*. See especially Appendix B, 206–11.

44 Jean-Marc Léger, 'Aspects of French Canadian Nationalism,' *University of Toronto Quarterly* 27, no. 3 (April 1958): 218–22.

45 Gérard Dion and Joseph Pelchat, 'Répenser le nationalisme,' *L'Action nationale* 31, no. 6 (June 1948): 402–12.

46 J. Hulliger, *L'Enseignement social des évêques canadiens de 1891 à 1950* (Montreal, 1957). See also the excellent essay by Jean-Charles Falardeau, 'Role et importance 'de l'Eglise au Canada français,' *L'Esprit*, Nos. 193–4, August-September 1952, 214–29.

47 Paul Gérin-Lajoie, *Pourquoi le Bill 60* (Montreal, 1963), 23.

48 *Le Devoir*, March 7, 1963.

49 Pierre Vadeboncoeur, 'La Ligne du risque,' *Situations*, 4th year, 1, 42. M. Vadeboncoeur's essay is, in reality, a long indictment of traditional French-Canadian nationalism – which he sees as reactionary and conformist – from the viewpoint of an anti-clerical, left-wing socialist who is also a nationalist. Indeed, the development of M. Vadeboncoeur's ideas from the position of an anti-nationalist member of the *Cité libre* group to his present separatist position, a position which he evidently finds best expressed in the radical separatist journal *Parti pris*, is an interesting example of one type of evolution in contemporary Quebec. Whether or not the traditional liberating ideals of socialism can be made to work in tandem with the conformist demands of nationalism is a question which M. Vadeboncoeur and other supporters of Le Parti Socialiste du Québec have attempted to face but have not yet satisfactorily answered. The order of priority in the party's aims would seem to place the national before the socialist goals. (See *Le Peuple, Journal du Parti Socialiste du Québec* l, no. 1, September 1963.) The remark in the leading editorial that 'Socialism has finally begun ... national liberation will follow' brings to mind Durham's comment that 'the French appear to have used their democratic arms for conservative purposes.' (See G.M. Craig, ed., *Lord Durham's Report*, Toronto, 1963.)

50 Of course the separatist argument is that as long as Quebec remains in Confederation the minority status of French Canadians makes it impossible to resolve the tension between liberating and reactionary elements in their nationalism. Therefore they conclude that national liberation must precede reform. This argument ignores the fact that French Canadians

are a minority because of their geographic position, not because of the British North America Act. For two excellent statements of the separatist position, one historical, the other polemical, see Maurice Séguin, 'Genèse et historique de l'idée séparatiste au Canada français' (*Laurentie*, No. 119, June 1962), and Hubert Aquin. 'L'Existence politique' (*Liberté*, No. 21). For a criticism of the separatist position see Pierre-Elliott Trudeau. 'La Nouvelle Trahison des clercs' (*Cité libre*, April 1962).

51 Montreal *La Presse*, November 18, 1961.

52 Pierre Vadeboncoeur, 'La Ligne du risque,' 43; Pierre-Elliott Trudeau, *La Grève de l'amiante*, passim.

53 Mason Wade, *The French Canadians, 1760–1945* (Toronto, 1955), 981.

54 Fernand Ouellet, *Louis Joseph Papineau. Un Etre divisé* (Ottawa, 1960), 24.

55 Pierre-Elliott Trudeau, 'L'Aliénation nationaliste', *Cité libre*, 12th year, no. 33 (new series March 1961): 5.

56 Jean-Marc Leger, 'Aspects of French Canadian Nationalism', *University of Toronto Quarterly* 27, no. 3 (April 1958): 323.

57 *Le Devoir*, July 5, 1963.

58 Léon Dion, 'The Origin and Character of the Nationalism of Growth,' *Canadian Forum* 42, no. 516 (January 1964): 232.

59 Lord Acton, *The History of Freedom and Other Essays* (London, 1922), 290.

60 For a greatly expanded and much more specific statement of some of the generalities expressed in these last few paragraphs, see the important article by Pierre-Elliott Trudeau et al., 'An Appeal for Realism in Politics.' *Canadian Forum* 44, no. 520, May 1964.

FOUR

The Paradox of Quebec

What will finally become of French Canada? To tell the truth, no one really knows, especially not French Canadians, whose ambivalence on this topic is typical: they want simultaneously to give in to cultural fatigue and to overcome it, calling for renunciation and determination in the same breath.

Hubert Aquin, "The Cultural Fatigue of French Canada", 1962

"Canada is not a country," the Quebec poet Jean-Guy Pilon wrote as he crossed the Prairies heading for Vancouver in 1968, "it's a continent washed by three oceans where twenty million people live, about one third of them French ... In these vast stretches of the Anglo-Saxon West I feel the difference inside me. I am definitely not at home and I realize how true it is to say that Quebec is an entity unto itself with its own culture, language, way of life." [1] But having affirmed his distinctiveness Pilon went on to wonder if, and for how long, that difference could be preserved. "What will become of it?" he queried, and suggested that the answer be postponed for another ten years. Twenty-five years and more have passed, but the ambiguity remains.

That very ambiguity about the future has long characterized Quebec and makes French Canadians a paradox for most of us. The same electorate that gave René Lévesque, an avowed *souverainiste*, provincial power on November 15, 1976, gave Pierre Elliott Trudeau, an avowed federalist, even stronger support on February 18, 1980. One of Quebec's greatest artists, Paul-Emile Borduas, declared about twenty years ago, "I hate all nationalisms." [2] Today most Quebec artists and writers would probably insist that nationalism was what inspired their work. Yet even in a society where many of the leading intellectuals are proclaimed *indépendantistes*, two young philosophers recently published a book, *Le Territoire imaginaire de la culture*,[3] rejecting the nationalist identification of state and nation on which the policies of the Lévesque government rested. That the paradox, the ambiguity, is there is readily demonstrated. It has been the most striking result of opinion surveys on the independence question and Parti Québécois support.[4] One nationalist insists that "It is necessary to resolve it now or to resign ourselves to perish."[5] Another, quite accurately seeing sovereignty-association as part of the ambiguity, recently wondered out loud "if the national movement is not irreversibly on the way to disappearance."[6]

In the face of this paradox how can an English Canadian be expected to decipher the riddle on the face of the French-speaking sphinx? For over forty years I have been trying, and I must confess that some of the message still eludes me. Recently several writers have tried to extract the secret by the use of codes supplied by Karl Marx, Albert Memmi, Jurgen Habermas, Nicos Poulantzas, Louis Althusser, among others.[7] The results, to say the least, are confusing. Is the sphinx bourgeois or merely petit bourgeois? Is the class struggle nationalist or anti-nationalist? These are intriguing questions, but until they are settled perhaps there is still some value in an approach that tries to understand what is on Quebecers' minds by listening to what they have had to say over time. Let me begin at a period of severe crisis in French Canada's history.

The year 1840 was grim for French Canadians. Papineau's abortive rebellion and its aftermath left the *canadiens* profoundly pessimistic. Durham's *Report*, recommending assimilation, had an air of finality about it. Union with Upper Canada, as the essential first step, was about to be forced on Lower Canada. So bleak was the future that Etienne Parent, the most brilliant political writer of his generation and editor of the nationalist *Le Canadien*, declared his acceptance of assimilation if that was the price necessary to gain responsible government.[8]

In that depressed atmosphere of 1840, two *canadien* artists set down, one in poetry, the other in paint, their convictions and feelings about the future. In doing so they provided two enduring clues to the wellsprings of nationalism among French Canadians. The poet was François-Xavier Garneau, later to become famous as an historian. In 1840 he published "Le Dernier Huron" ("The Last Huron"), a poem about a people who had been defeated, dispersed, and assimilated.

> Their names, their eyes, their festivals, their history,
> Are buried with them forever
> And I remain alone to speak their memorial
> To the people of our day![9]

The Hurons, of course, stood as symbols for *canadiens* who, Garneau feared, would share the fate of that once proud and powerful Indian nation.

An Indian also served as a symbol of French Canada in Joseph Légaré's 1840 painting entitled *Paysage au Monument à Wolfe*. Here we see the Indian apparently offering to surrender his bow to the statue of the conqueror, General James Wolfe. Yet nearby, hidden behind a tree trunk, is a canoe waiting to carry the Indian away to his freedom. The critics seem agreed that the Indian (a Mercury figure) is more cunning than submissive, and that he is really preparing to escape to the freedom and independence of the forest.[10]

Taken together these two works of art symbolize the psychological dimension of nationalism among French Canadians. The Last Huron syndrome is the nightmare of ultimate extinction. Légaré's deceptively submissive Indian represents the dream of complete freedom. After nearly a century and a half, neither the nightmare nor the dream has come true. But they remain part of the French-Canadian nationalist psyche, as the psychiatrist-turned-politician, Dr. Camille Laurin, has often noted.[11]

Fear of the future, fear of extinction can be traced to at least two sources. The first is historical. Defeat, something shared by Amerindians and *canadiens*, is a central part of the French-Canadian historical experience. In the beginning was the Conquest. Each generation of French Canadians studies, reinterprets, and tries to come to terms with this central fact of their history – and of all Canadian history. Yet it never goes away. Here is a passage from the Quebec government's 1978 statement of policy on Quebec cultural development. It is a lengthy passage but it is a perfect summary of the currently dominant view of the Conquest among Quebec nationalists.

Then the Conquest came. A small population having had at its disposal a relatively brief time to implant itself firmly on its territory, the original Canadians had to turn in on themselves and assure themselves of the foundations of their survival and of their development in a country firmly taken in hand by another people whose language, religion, laws, political institutions and genius were foreign to them. A conquered group, politically and economically dominated, the Canadians little by little developed the sentiments of a minority and became progressively marginalized in a country which was formerly theirs, but whose commanding heights had quickly escaped them. Regrouping themselves, chiefly in the rural areas, they clung to the soil, to their language, to their religion, to their way of life. As a result of the Conquest, they became isolated as businessmen from the great North American trade and have thus been rendered rather impermeable to the great revolutions of the Western world; they have been satisfied to endure, anchored in the solid realities which form the basis of peasant life.[12]

Each of the Parti Québécois's major public documents takes that sense of defeat symbolized by 1759 as its point of departure, once again demonstrating the centrality of the Conquest to nationalist thought.[13]

Consciousness of a second defeat has assumed an increasingly prominent place in the ideology of contemporary Quebec nationalism: the failure of Papineau's rebellion in 1837–38. In the past, Papineau's anti-clerical side lessened his attraction to clerical nationalist writers. But today, in a secular Quebec, he has been rehabilitated and the *patriotes*, even though they failed, have gained a new respectability. "One hundred and thirty years ago," Robert Lionel Séguin has written, "the Patriots at Saint Denis showed us the road to dignity and liberty. Fertile seeds from which we are gathering the fruit now."[14]

To the Conquest and the abortive rebellion of 1837, other familiar defeats are often added: Riel's hanging, Manitoba schools, Regulation 17 in Ontario, conscription in two world wars, even the air traffic controllers' crisis of 1976 when the use of French in the air space over Quebec was prohibited. Victories, when they come, are always too late: the Supreme Court of Canada rejected some restrictions on English in Quebec in less than three years after enactment; a Manitoba law abolishing French waited ninety years for the same result. A history filled with defeats and humiliations must surely stimulate pessimism. "The only issue – a more or less long-term issue," a Montreal historian wrote in the 1950s, "is the assimilation of the weaker culture by the stronger." And yet that pessimistic nationalism was closely linked with the fire of separatism in the 1960s, and its historical interpretation has been part of the official ideology of the Parti Québécois.[15]

Fear of the future has a second underlying cause: numbers. Throughout their history French Canadians have been preoccupied with their minority position. That is hardly surprising. New France was a tiny colony, outnumbered even by its Huron allies in the seventeenth century and constantly overshadowed by the more heavily populated English colonies to the south. While the French outnumbered the English in the Canadas until the 1850s, the pressure of English-speaking immigration was a major influence in the growth of the *parti patriote* in the 1830s.[16] One of the themes that runs constantly through Garneau's *Histoire* is his fear for a future in which the *canadiens* will be a minority. Again and again he refers to "*un peuple peu nombreux*," "*un peuple si faible en nombre*," and so on. "But a people of small numbers," he observed in explaining the French Canadians' attitude during the American Revolution, "cannot control its own destiny, is obliged to act with much care and prudence."[17]

Throughout the latter half of the nineteenth century French-Canadian leaders were extremely conscious of two demographic facts. The first was *la revanche des berceaux*, "the revenge of the cradle." An extraordinarily high birth rate meant that French Canadians fulfilled the Malthusian law: population doubled every twenty-five years. "During the last two centuries," a Quebec demographer wrote in 1957, "world population bas been multiplied by three, European population by four, and French Canadian population by eighty, in spite of net emigration which can be estimated at roughly 800,000."[18] Given those figures even Sir John A. Macdonald's view that the solution to the French-Canadian problem lay in immigration and copulation sounds futile.

But the other half of the demographic picture for French Canadians was emigration, chiefly to the United States. That "national haemorrhage" quite understandably obsessed French-Canadian leaders from the 1840s to the early twentieth century.[19] While some optimists thought that these southbound waves of Roman Catholics would one day restore puritan New England to the true faith,[20] the more frequent reaction was fear – fear that Quebec's population losses would be English Canada's political gain. Abbé J.-B. Chartier put the issue very bluntly when he declared that only "traitors" rejoiced at the sight of Quebecers moving to the United States; keeping them at home was "a question of life or death for the French-Canadian race."[21] The campaigns of Curé Labelle, Arthur Buies, and others to colonize northern Quebec, and Canada, were conducted in the fulsome rhetoric of providential mission, but the goal was a very worldly one: to keep French Canadians at home where their heads could be counted by census takers and vote gatherers.

That preoccupation with numbers has not declined in the slightest. Nowhere in Canada is the decennial census scrutinized more thoroughly than in Quebec. In the last thirty-five years Quebec Francophones have fully absorbed the values and aspirations of urban-industrial people everywhere. That has been accompanied by a dramatic decline in the birth rate. In 1961 Quebec's leading demographer, Jacques Henripin, speculated about population trends in Canada. If existing immigration and birth rates remained constant and French Canadians continued to adopt English at the 1961 rate, he predicted that by 1981 only 23.5 per cent of the Canadian population would be French-speaking, and that percentage would fall to 17 per cent by the year 2011. In 1951 the percentage was 29 per cent.[22] That statement, cautious and careful as it was, set off a chain reaction that led directly to Bill 101, the Charter of the French Language, in 1977. But before that stopping place had been reached the language issue had proven its potency: in

St. Leonard something near communal strife erupted between Francophones and immigrants anxious that their children learn English.
Both the Union Nationale government of Jean-Jacques Bertrand and
the Liberal administration of Robert Bourassa fumbled the issue. And
that played a significant part in the election victory of the Parti Québécois in 1976. In the midst of these events a commission, known as the
Gendron Commission, produced a massive report in which a convincing case was made for making French the working language of the
province. Here was that commission's conclusion:

This policy does not represent a false concern with the problem of numbers. It
is clear the falling birth rate of French speakers, together with the slight attraction that the French language exercises on the non-French-speaking constitutes
a subject of legitimate concern for French-speaking Quebecers. The fear that
French-speaking people will become a minority, if it is unfounded inside Quebec, is much more valid on the Canadian level.[23]

"The fear of becoming a minority": there is the heart of the matter.
It is, in fact, the leitmotif of much Quebec nationalist writing from
Garneau through to successive policy statements of the Lévesque government. It was central to the White Paper on language policy, where
one bold-faced subheading summed up the issue: "If the demographic
evolution of Quebec continues, French-speaking Quebecers will be less
and less numerous." The same point is underlined in the opening pages
of the cultural policy statement and, inevitably, formed a central part
of the argument for sovereignty-association. In the PQ government's
White Paper *La Nouvelle Entente Quebec-Canada* two large graphic
illustrations dramatize the following information: in 1851, 36 per cent
of Canadians were Francophone; in 1971 that figure was 28 per cent
and by 2001 it will drop to 23 per cent. That in turn means that Quebec, which in 1867 held more than one-third of the seats in the Canadian House of Commons, will by 2000 hold less than one-quarter.
"Under these circumstances," the authors of the White Paper argue, "it
would be an illusion to believe that, in future, Francophones can play
a determining role in the government of Canada. On the contrary, they
will be more and more a minority and English Canada will find it
increasingly easy to govern without them. In that respect, far from
being an anomaly, the Clark government is a sign of things to come."[24]

By appealing to "the fear of becoming a minority," to the Last
Huron syndrome, the Lévesque government hoped to convince Quebecers that the time had come to choose independence, to fulfil Joseph
Légaré's vision of freedom. That theme, too, runs deeply in Quebec history. From the resort to arms in 1837 to Lévesque's proposed New

Deal in 1979, the hope for independence always remained alive among small groups of Quebecers. For the most part it has never been much more than a dream to be achieved some day. After Papineau's defeat the dream of separate nationhood lived on in a segment of *le parti rouge*, which opposed Confederation in 1865 (as did a few *bleus*, including the young Honoré Mercier). What the *rouge* favoured in 1865 was not complete independence but a loose form of federalism in which the member states would remain sovereign. When the Quebec Resolutions passed the Canadian Assembly (twenty-seven French Canadians in favour, twenty-two opposed), a newspaper of *rouge* persuasion fulminated: "On this memorable night has been committed the most iniquitous and degrading act which the parliamentary system has witnessed since the Irish deputies sold their country to England for positions, honours and gold."[25]

Like much else in Quebec in the latter part of the nineteenth century, the idea of independence acquired a clerical and conservative tone though its origins with the *rouges* had been secular and liberal.[26] Its chief exponent, Jules-Paul Tardivel (his enemies called him Jules-Paul Torquemada after the head of the Spanish Inquisition), edited a newspaper characteristically called *La Vérité*. In the 1880s, Riel's execution and Macdonald's centralizing policies convinced him that only independence would save Quebec from Anglo-Saxon Protestant domination. In his utopian novel, *Pour la Patrie*, published in 1895, he described the events that, with God's help, led to independence in 1945. One passage, explaining the nationalist goal, is especially interesting:

Our geographical position, our natural resources and the homogeneity of our population enable us to aspire to be ranked among the nations of the earth. It is possible that Confederation offers certain material advantages, but from the religious and national point of view it is filled with dangers for us, for our enemies will certainly manage to wear it away until it is a legislative union in everything but name. Moreover the chief material advantages that are derived from Confederation could be obtained equally well through a simple postal and customs union.[27]

In addition to the obvious similarities to sovereignty-association as devised by the Parti Québécois, Tardivel's projected République de la Nouvelle-France contains some other revealing details. Most notable was the assumed peaceful manner of its achievement – no revolution, no civil war, just a rather heated parliamentary debate, in which a sympathetic English-Canadian Catholic played a crucial role. René Lévesque's plans were postulated on a similar assumption. Canadians, he believed, are sufficiently civilized to be able to work out a division of their country in a federal-provincial conference, presumably carried on prime-time television with suitable commentary.

Those who kept the light of Quebec independence alive during the generations that followed Tardivel were equally reasonable in their expectations. In 1922 abbé Lionel Groulx and his friends in *l'Action française* published an inquiry in *Notre Avenir Politique* that concluded the future was unfolding, as expected, toward independence. But it would come as a natural evolution "as soon as Providence wishes it."[28] French Canadians were called on to prepare themselves, but the timetable was unspecified. So, too, the young separatists who joined with André Laurendeau in *Jeune Canada* in the late thirties spoke only in terms of an undefined future when, by undefined means, "one day a country will be born."[29]

Until the 1960s, then, when Le Rassemblement pour l'Indépendance Nationale and later the Parti Québécois were born, the ideal of independence was simply that, an ideal, more perhaps a state of mind than a concrete political project. Yet it is impossible not to be struck by the degree to which the Parti Québécois fits into this tradition of ambiguity and caution. Independence by steps: *étapisme*. Not even Mackenzie King, that Canadian master of ambiguity, of never doing things by halves that could be done by quarters, could have improved on the Lévesque-Morin strategy. First the removal of the independence issue from the 1976 election by the promise of a referendum. Then a definition of independence that is not independence but sovereignty-association. Next a referendum asking not for approval of sovereignty-association, but merely a mandate to negotiate. Finally a promise of yet another referendum on the outcome of the negotiations. Everything is hedged. Is it any wonder that a muscular separatist like Pierre Vallières, in frustration, pronounced the PQ strategy "as ineffective in liberating Quebec as the improvised result of the Patriots of 1837–38"?[30]

Why is nationalism in Quebec so cautious in tactics, so modest in its demands? Légaré's Indian may be preparing to escape into freedom, for the canoe lies ready. Yet he is also in the act of surrendering his bow to the statue of Wolfe. Perhaps it is not Mercury after all but rather, as the playwright Robert Gurik once contended, Hamlet who is *Prince de Québec*.[31] If, as I have been arguing, French-Canadian nationalism is driven by a fear of extinction, on the one hand, and the dream of absolute freedom, on the other, then it is driven in contradictory directions. Fear of the future and hope for the future come to create indecision, ambiguity, paradox. Is that not Papineau, brilliantly characterized by Fernand Ouellet as *Un Etre Divisé*, and by Garneau as *"l'image de notre nation"*? Caught between the desire to preserve and the desire to liberate, between nationalism and liberalism, he was paralysed, a Franklin without being a Washington.[32]

Garneau himself expressed that same tension, which is at the heart of French-Canadian nationalism. At the conclusion of his great *Histoire*, having surveyed the struggles of his people from the first arrival of the explorers to the union of 1840, he drew one last lesson. It is often quoted, and rightly so, for it catches, as nothing else does, the essential character of nationalism in Quebec:

Let the Canadians be faithful to themselves; let them be wise and persevering, let them not be seduced by the brilliance of social and political novelty. They are not strong enough to follow a career of that sort. It is for great nations to test new theories: they can move freely in their spacious orbits. For us, part of our strength comes from our traditions; we must not stray far from them and alter them only gradually.[33]

That sense of prudence, that belief in the need to tread carefully and to be guided by past traditions, has continued to characterize French Canadians throughout their history. And it is against the background of modest, but persistent, nationalism that the goals of Quebecers can best be understood, whether expressed in the demand for equality of linguistic rights, special powers for the province of Quebec, or sovereignty-association.

Put simply, the goal of French Canadians has always been security, and the strategy for its achievement is the recognition of equality. For a self-conscious minority, both the goal and the means of achieving it are perfectly understandable. By definition a minority is potentially at the mercy of the majority. It lacks security. It must discover a way to maximize its position, to find a mechanism that will allow it to act as an equal or near equal. Consciously, or otherwise, this has always been the strategy of French Canadians anxious to preserve their national distinctiveness. And that includes virtually all French Canadians for, though they have often been divided on means, they have never been divided on ends.

What strategies are possible and available? Papineau tried one route: equality established through independence. That is the tradition of *d'égal à égal*, the Parti Québécois call to arms. But the lesson that many of Papineau's followers drew from the rebellion's failure was that equality would have to be achieved within a political system that they shared with other Canadians. Such equality might never be perfect, but it would be attainable. That was the central message of L.-H. LaFontaine's Address to the Electors of Terrebonne in 1840. He demanded, and received, an equal share of the power within the Union:

that was what the Rebellion Losses Bill demonstrated. But the primary symbol of his success was the repeal of the prohibition against the use of French that had been part of the original union constitution. He practised what Canon Groulx admiringly called *"une politique nationale"*[34] by convincing French Canadians to stand united behind him and thus to maximize their strength. This is the strategy of "French power" practised by every successful French-Canadian federal politician since Cartier: by the concentration of the minority's votes in one party it becomes a near equal.

It is not a perfect strategy and, since it has resulted in defeats as well as victories, critics have devised alternatives. The primary one, historically, might be called "fortress Quebec." It stands between "French power" and separation, taking something from each. It argues that since French Canadians will always be a minority in the federal system, they should concentrate their talents at the provincial level where they are a majority. Quebec, as the homeland of French Canadians, should thus be recognized as a province *pas comme les autres* with powers, at least in some areas, equal to those of the federal government or of all the other provinces combined. This strategy was practised in a limited manner by Mercier in the 1880s, and by Duplessis and Lesage in more recent times. The report of the Tremblay Commission on Constitutional Problems in the late 1950s worked this theory out most completely. And variations on the theme of "fortress Quebec" – though offering fortress status to other provinces, too – can be found in Claude Ryan's 1980 proposal for *A New Canadian Federation*.[35]

Underlying each of these strategies is a conception of French Canada and/or Quebec as a distinctive society, a nation in one of several senses, deserving equality with other nations and particularly with its partner, English Canada. That equality is seen as a necessary condition for the security that alone will banish the Last Huron nightmare, and fulfil, at least in part, Légaré's dream.

Discovering the formula that will guarantee Francophones security through equality has been the persistent quest of Quebecers for nearly two centuries. The very vitality of Francophone culture today is testimony, surely, to the degree of success that French Canadians have achieved. Neither Garneau's fears nor Légaré's hopes have been fulfilled. Both possibilities remain, and so does the riddle on the face of the French-speaking sphinx.

The ambiguity remains because it is an accurate reflection of the reality of Quebec society, its hopes and its fears. But it is more than that. It also reflects the shrewdness of a small, determined people who have discovered over the centuries that in the end survival depends on themselves, and that no single strategy is perfect. Where some see ambiguity as a sign of weakness – "cultural fatigue,"[36] the brilliant novelist, Hubert Aquin, called it – others, and I think correctly, judge it more sympathetically. "The French Canadians' frequent duality of allegiances whereby they elect federal and provincial governments," Michel Morin and Guy Bertrand concluded their dissection of the public philosophy of Quebec, "is sufficient testimony to the natural intelligence of the people, of individuals anxious to guarantee their liberty and their rights by setting the princes who govern them against each other."[37]

[1980]

NOTES

1 Jean-Guy Pilon, "Quebec and the French Fact," in Philip Stratford and Michael Thomas, eds., *Voices From Quebec* (Toronto, 1977), 2–3.
2 François-Marc Gagnon, "Borduas: Father of Quebec Separatism?" *Vanguard* June-July, 1977).
3 Michel Morin et Claude Bertrand, *Le Territoire imaginaire de la culture* (Montréal, 1979).
4 Maurice Pinard and Richard Hamilton, "The Parti Québécois Comes to Power," *Canadian Journal of Political Science* 11, 4 (December, 1978): 739–75.
5 Pierre Vadeboncoeur, *La demiére heure et la premiére* (Montréal, 1970), 7.
6 Pierre Drouilly, "Le paradoxe québécois," *Le Devoir*, 14 février 1980, 5.
7 See, for example, Gilles Bourque et Anne Légaré, *Le Québec, la question nationale* (Paris, 1978); Henry Milner, *Politics in the New Quebec* (Toronto, 1978); and Denis Monière, *Le développement des idéologies au Quebec* (Montréal, 1977).
8 Jacques Monet, *The Last Cannon Shot* (Toronto, 1969), 25.
9 J. Huston, ed., *Le Répertoire national* (Montréal, 1893), 1: 172–75.
10 François-Marc Gagnon, "The Hidden Image of Early French Canadian Nationalism: A Parable," *Arts Canada* (December, 1979–January, 1980): 11–14.
11 Camille Laurin, *Ma Traversée du Québec* (Montréal, 1970), 85.
12 *La politique québécoise du développement culturel* (Québec, 1978), 1: 50–51.
13 *Quebec-Canada: A New Deal* (Quebec, 1979), 3–4.
14 Robert-Lionel Seguin, *La Victoire de Saint-Denis* (Montréal, 1964), 45; Marcel Rioux, *La Question du Québec* (Paris, 1969), 70–71.
15 Michel Brunet, *Canadians et canadiens* (Montréal, 1954), 30. Maurice

Seguin, *L'idée de l'indépendance au Québec* (Montréal, 1968). See also Michael D. Behiels, "Prelude to Quebec's 'Quiet Revolution'; the Re-emergence of Liberalism and the Rise of Neo-Nationalism, 1940–1960" (PH.D. thesis, York University, 1978), 1: 130–91.

16 Fernand Ouellet, *Le Bas Canada 1791–1840* (Ottawa, 1976), 214ff.

17 F.-X. Garneau, *Histoire du Canada* (5th edition, Paris, 1920), 2: 392; Philippe Reid, "François-Xavier Garneau et l'infériorité numérique des Canadiens Français," *Recherches Sociographiques* 15, 1, 31–39.

18 Jacques Henripin, "From Acceptance of Nature to Control: The Demography of the French Canadians Since the Seventeenth Century," *Canadian Journal of Economics and Political Science* 33, 1 (February, 1957): 10–19.

19 Yolande Lavoie, *L'émigration des Canadiens aux Etats-Unis avant 1930* (Montréal, 1972).

20 E. Hamon, *Les Canadiens-Français de la Nouvelle Angleterre* (Québec, 1891), 155–56.

21 Christian Morissonneau, *La Terre Promise: Le Mythe du Nord québécois* (Montréal, 1978), p. 78.

22 Jacques Henripin, "Evolution de la composition ethnique et linguistique de la population canadienne," *Relations* 21, 248 (août 1961): 27–9.

23 *La Situation de la langue française au Québec, 1, La Langue de Travail* (Québec, 1972), 31.

24 "La Politique québécoise de la langue française," *Le Devoir*, 2 avril 1977, 7; *A New Deal*, 29–3.

25 J.-P. Bernard, *Les Rouges* (Montréal, 1971), 265.

26 Fernand Ouellet, "Nationalisme canadien-français et laicisme au XIXe Siècle," *Recherches Sociographiques* 4, 1 (janvier-avril 1963): 44–7.

27 Jules-Paul Tardivel, *For My Country, Pour la Patrie* (1895) (Toronto, 1975), 39. Translation by Sheila Fishman.

28 *Notre Avenir Politique* (Montréal, 1923), 29.

29 André Laurendeau, *Notre Nationalisme* (Montréal, 1935), 5.

30 Pierre Vallières, *Un Québec Impossible* (Montréal, 1977), 71.

31 Robert Gurik, *Hamlet, Prince de Québec* (Montréal, 1968).

32 Fernand Ouellet, *Louis-Joseph Papineau, Un Etre Divisé* (CHA Booklet, Ottawa, 1961), 22.

33 Garneau, *Histoire*, 33.

34 Lionel Groulx, "Un Chef de trente-trois ans," in *Notre Maître, le Passé* (2ième Série, Montréal, 1936), 150.

35 The Constitutional Committee of the Quebec Liberal Party, *A New Canadian Federation*, 1980, 12.

36 Hubert Aquin, "The Cultural Fatigue of French Canada," in Larry Shouldice, *Contemporary Quebec Criticism* (Toronto, 1979), 55–82.

37 Morin et Bertrand, *Le Territoire*, 154–55.

FIVE

The Evolution of Nationalism in Quebec

The nation, it is a little like liberty, the liberty of Madame Roland and of some others, ... what interests can be served in its name!

André J. Bélanger

Hubert Aquin, the brilliant Quebec novelist, was also a political writer of great talent, and perhaps the only nationalist intellectual capable of meeting Pierre Trudeau on his own ground – the logic of historical development. Aquin almost always went to the heart of the matter, even if that meant a certain amount of simplification. In a 1962 analysis of nationalism in Quebec he wrote:

Throughout our history we have confused nationalism and the defence of rights when there is, in my view, opposition between these two attitudes. The defender of our rights is someone resigned to a minority status, while the nationalist wants first of all a nation, wishes the minority condition to be ended. True nationalists want separation and independence, not the perpetuation of a provincial or minority position.

For Aquin a "nation," defined as a culturally homogeneous community, should become a state; for Trudeau, there was no need – indeed, it was undesirable – for cultural nations and political sovereignty to coincide. Each understood the other's logic in a way that was rare in the rather confused debates about Quebec's place in Canada during the 1960s and 1970s.[1]

Yet the confusion of that debate is readily explained: Aquin's logic too easily brushed aside a great deal of French Canada's history. In making the thrust toward political independence the determining criterion of a true nationalist, he cast several generations of cultural and even economic nationalists into outer darkness. Nationalist politics in these terms flickered briefly during the abortive rebellions of 1837–38, then was virtually extinguished until the founding of the small separatist parties, particularly Le Rassemblement pour l'Indépendance

Nationale, in the early 1960s, leading to the foundation of the Parti Québécois in 1968. In fact, however, nationalism defined as the collective will of a distinctive community to survive and grow according to its own cultural imperatives existed, at least among the leadership classes of French Canadians, from the early decades of the nineteenth century. Only occasionally, and even then only in the case of a minority of nationalists, was political sovereignty viewed as the essential means to the end of cultural survival. More often other forms of what might be called "autonomy" were judged realistic and sufficient. Indeed, it can be argued that, with some important differences in detail and especially in timing, nationalism among French Canadians paralleled similar movements in Europe and exhibited the same "mutations" that E.J. Hobsbawm noted in his account of *The Age of Empire*. That is especially true of what Hobsbawm calls the "growing tendency to assume that 'national self-determination' could not be satisfied by any form of autonomy less than full state independence" and the "novel tendency to define a nation in terms of ethnicity and especially in terms of language."[2] Yet, it must be emphatically added that in Quebec those mutations remain, even today, only one tendency among those committed to the survival and growth of the French-speaking culture in Canada.

New France was a child of the *ancien régime*, "a supplement to Europe," in the words of the eighteenth-century geographer Guillaume Delisle. [3] Nevertheless, by the middle of that century, French settlers in North America had developed a sense of distinctiveness from their homeland: they were *habitants*, not *hivernants*, calling themselves *canadiens*. But it was the British Conquest and its aftermath that emphasized that distinctiveness – 65,000 or so French-speaking *colons* separated from their Roman Catholic mother country, part of an English-speaking Protestant empire. But a sense of difference was not nationalism, nor could it be in a society where popular participation in politics was largely unknown and unsought after. It was only during the years of the French Revolution that the first, modest stirrings of liberal and popular unrest were felt. The constitution of 1791 (granted three months before the new French constitution of 1791), which included a representative assembly, drew that discontent into constitutional channels but also, unwittingly, provided the context for the birth of nationalism and nationalist politics. That constitution institutionalized ethnic conflict: the *canadien* majority dominated the elected assembly; the English-speaking minority controlled the appointive legislative and executive councils. And the assembly and other, limited, British freedoms produced political groupings, campaigns, and a relatively free press. If, as many historians contend, modern nationalism was a child of the French Revolution, then French Canadians were among those who witnessed that birth. Yet the revolutionary doctrines of 1789 attracted the interest and sympathy of only a handful of what might be called political intellectuals. It also, of course, attracted the interest and hostility of the leaders of the Catholic Church who were at pains to point out to their flocks the benefits of membership in a Protestant empire, something that had resulted from what the future bishop, abbé J.-O. Plessis, called the *"providentiel"* conquest. "Be faithful," he warned, "or renounce your title as a Christian."[4] By the mid-nineteenth century this theme of the *providentiel* separation of the *canadiens* from France became a dominant note in French-Canadian political thought. Some, like Thomas Chapais, a leading historian and Conservative politician, distinguished between "radical France, conservative France, free-thinking France and Catholic France, France which blasphemes and France which prays," and even most Liberals would have agreed it was that second France, "the France that prays," that was "the true fatherland of our intelligence, as the Catholic Church is the fatherland of our souls."[5]

As the nationalist movement developed in Lower Canada in the 1820s and 1830s it drew on some liberal ideas then current both in France and in the English-speaking world. But it drew even more on the social, economic, and political grievances of French Canadians who increasingly resented the economic and political domination of an English-speaking minority. By the 1830s Louis-Joseph Papineau's *patriote* party claimed to represent *la nation canadienne*, and in 1837–38 a pathetic armed revolt against British domination – a revolt duplicated in English-speaking Upper Canada – was crushed. Papineau's nationalism was founded on a belief that the French-speaking agricultural society, whose members were overwhelmingly Roman Catholic (though Papineau himself was a mild sceptic), was threatened by the English-speaking, commercial Protestant minority backed by the British Colonial Office. The rebellion failed miserably, suggesting, not for the last time, that the concerns of the nationalist elite had made only a superficial impact on the rapidly growing, economically unprogressive rural population.[6] Yet the *patriote* ideology, with one notable revision, established the essential outlines of French-Canadian nationalism for a century.

During the 1840s, when L-H. LaFontaine was working out the political strategy necessary to avoid Lord Durham's recommendation that French Canadians be assimilated, the first systematic statement of French-Canadian nationalism appeared. It was the work of an historian, François-Xavier Garneau. In his *Histoire du Canada*, Garneau hoped to follow the principles of what he called "the modern school of history"; men like Jules Michelet, "who regards the nation as the source of all power." In four large volumes Garneau set out an account of his people that provided them with the essential components of any nationalist ideology: a meaningful past, one with lessons for the present and hopes for the future. It was the story of an heroic struggle by *un petit peuple* for survival – against the Amerindians, the elements, and, finally, the British. Out of that *lutte des races* a nation had been forged, French, North American, agricultural, one where Catholicism was an important, though not a dominant, factor.

Garneau was a nineteenth-century liberal nationalist. He believed in representative government and was thankful that the British had brought it, he disapproved of clericalism and regretted that the Huguenots had been excluded from New France, and he viewed the nation as an essentially secular community. "There is something touching and noble at the same time in the defence of a nationality, a sacred heritage that no people, no matter how degraded, has ever repudiated. Never has a greater and more sacred cause inspired a rightly disposed heart and deserved the sympathy of generous spirits." [7] Implicit in that nationalism was a conservative mood: the need, he emphasized, was defence and preservation, and he urged caution on his compatriots, for change might mean loss of those very characteristics that defined their national being. It was these conservative seeds in Garneau's nationalist garden that bore the most abundant fruit after 1850.

Throughout the European world, and in North America, the failures of the liberal-nationalist thrust of the early decades of the nineteenth century were followed by the triumph of a conservative nationalism. Indeed, as Sir Lewis Namier argued in his *1848: The Revolution of the Intellectuals* (1946), that outcome was almost foreordained. Quebec fell into that familiar pattern. After 1840, the Church, led by the energetic ultramontane prelate, Mgr. Ignace Bourget of Montreal, began a recruitment and ré-organization drive that would gradually give the Church dominant place in Quebec society. As the Church extended and consolidated its control over education and other social institutions in Quebec,[8] so, too, it redefined that society's ideology. Where Garneau had recognized religion as a component of nationalism and the Church as one of the institutions of collective survival, clerical ideologists made religion integral to nationalism and awarded the Church the central role in the defence of the nation. Abbé Laflèche, the most brilliant theoretician of ultramontanism and soon to be Bishop of Trois Rivières, wrote in 1866: "The providential mission of the [French] Canadian people is essentially religious: it is the conversion to Catholicism of the poor faithless people who inhabit this country, and the extension of the Kingdom of God by the formation of a nationality that is above all

Catholic." And if the implications were not obvious, Mgr. Bourget of Montreal made them so in an 1868 pastoral letter: "the true patriot," his priests were to tell their flocks, "is a sincere Catholic. Religion inspires love of country, and the love of country causes love of religion ... Without religion, the national interests are sacrificed; and without the fatherland, religious interests are forgotten and set aside."[9]

When Frenchmen, and others, were celebrating the centennial of the Revolution in 1889, French Canadians, for the most part, recalled other events drawn from their own history. The national holiday of French Canada was not July 14, or for that matter, July 1, the date of Canadian Confederation. Rather it was – and is – June 24, St. Jean Baptiste Day. On that day in 1889 a celebration was held just north of Quebec City at the place where the explorer Jacques Cartier had wintered 355 years earlier, a place that conveniently coincided with the first residence established in 1625 by the Jesuit fathers, including the future martyrs Jean Brébeuf and Gabriel Lalement. That the date marked the 240th anniversary of the destruction of the Jesuit mission to the Hurons was not lost on the celebrating crowds. One of the orators of the day – a day attended by all of the important political and religious leaders of Quebec – summed up the meaning of the Cartier-Brébeuf monument in these words: "Cartier-Brébeuf! It is France and the Church taking possession of the New World."[10] With such ancient and sacred events to commemorate, a mere centennial was hardly worthy of special note!

The changes rung on the theme of this French-speaking, Catholic nation with its rural foundation and spiritual mission in North America – the eldest daughter of the Church, apostate France having abdicated – were infinite in the years before 1960. And, of course, by making religion so central to national identity these clerical ideologists provided themselves and the Church with the principal leadership role in the struggle for survival. "If there is a ruling class here," Henri Bourassa, a leading nationalist spokesman in the early twentieth century, noted approvingly in 1902, "it is certainly the clergy." It should also be observed that having nominated themselves the leaders in the struggle for national survival, churchmen also made themselves a prime target for those who, in the years after World War Two, began to fear that the battle had been lost.[11]

There are, perhaps, two important points that need emphasis about the dominant clerico-nationalist ideology that permeated Quebec's traditional elites before the Quiet Revolution. The first is that it was nationalist in a religious and cultural sense, but rarely in a political or economic manner. Abbé Laflèche's book was written partly as a defence of the Confederation scheme then debated. Bourget had his doubts about Confederation, but he kept them quiet. Only a rare ultra-montane journalist like Jules-Paul Tardivel expressed separatist sentiments and he, like his better-known successor, abbé Lionel Groulx, nationalist historian and activist, postponed independence to a date well into a utopian future.[12] More typical was Henri Bourassa, whose speeches in Parliament and on the public platform, and whose editorials in his nationalist newspaper, *Le Devoir*, all combined an ardent cultural nationalism with a powerful defence of a Canada founded on a federation of autonomous provinces and a compact of two distinct "races" living on terms of equality from Halifax to Vancouver. [13] The nation, being defined culturally, included not only the Quebec Francophones who made up 80 per cent of the population, but also that 20 per cent of the Francophone population that lived elsewhere in Canada. (Indeed, it sometimes also included those hundreds of thousands of Quebecers who had emigrated to the United States.) Moreover, since this definition of nationalism was so deeply infused with religion, its primary focus was on the Church rather than the state. Indeed, the state was sometimes viewed as an instrument of the Church. The French-Canadian nation was, thus, an *église-nation*.

The second and equally important observation to be made is that what clerico-nationalists described was an ideal, not a real nation. This is particularly obvious in economic matters and the persistent description of the French-Canadian nation as having *une vocation rurale*. If Quebec remained predominantly rural through most of the nineteenth century, growing numbers of French Canadians did not. First, there were those hundreds of thousands who emigrated from rural poverty in Quebec to low-paid urban work in the United States – perhaps 900,000 between 1840 and 1930. Then after about 1900, when the industrialization of Quebec began to take off, the movement toward the cities intensified so that by 1921 a slight majority of Francophone Quebecers lived in urban areas. The process had taken place with the encouragement of successive provincial governments more influenced by the need to create jobs and to collect revenues than by the preachments of clerical nationalists. And, indeed, the Church had never been unanimous about the rural virtues and at least some of the clergy recognized the virtues of industrialization – it kept their flocks from emigrating.[14] While the call for increased support for colonization – rural settlement of surplus population – continued to make its impact on Quebec governments until after World War Two, the urban-industrial order had become irrevocable. The rural myth, however, lingered on.

Whatever consensus there was about the nature of the FrenchCanadian nation – and it was never unanimous – began to be shattered in the interwar years. During the 1920s abbé Groulx's *Action française* kept the light of clerico-nationalism aflame, a beacon against the dangers of industrial-urban life. "We need to hold onto the land," the priest-historian wrote in 1924, "attach ourselves to the healthy life which created the vigour of our forefathers, and we crowd insanely into cities where we are decimated by infant mortality and where the level of morality falls sharply."[15] At the end of the decade came the depression – and a paradoxical result. Most obviously, the limitations of clerico-nationalist ideology were harshly revealed; many individuals and groups began to call for a full acceptance of the new industrial order and a re-evaluation of social thought.[16] A collection of dissident young Liberals calling themselves the Action libérale nationale was one such group. Yet it was swallowed up in a new political party, the Union Nationale, which effectively re-imposed traditional nationalist ideas on the province for the next twenty-five years, while presiding over the accelerated industrialization of Quebec society. Appropriately, just at the end of the Duplessis years, a *Royal Commission of Enquiry on Constitutional Problems,* the Tremblay Commission, provided a systematic statement of the ideology that had played so dominant a role in Quebec's intellectual life, one that insisted that the Church "had supplied French Canada with its thought, its way of life and the majority of its social institutions."[17] But that ideology was now under siege.

While the events of World War Two, especially the divisive debate over conscription for overseas service, turned Quebecers in on themselves, the war-induced economic growth had a much more permanent impact. Iron ore, aluminum, pulp and paper, and hydroelectricity together produced the final demise of clerico-nationalism. Out of this new economic order grew a new secular elite that saw its worldly ambitions constrained by an ideology that undervalued economic success and scientific learning, condemned state involvement in social and educational affairs, rejected birth control, and sanctified patriarchy. Gradually these new elites insisted that social and economic problems be subjected to the scrutiny of empirical social science rather than the *a priori* moralizing of Catholic social teachings. Two groups in particular – though they were not alone – characterized this new outlook.[18]

In a society where historical interpretation had always been at the heart of nationalist ideology, it is hardly surprising that a major assault on the old nationalism came in the form of historical revisionism. Abbé Groulx's successors at the Université de Montréal – Professors Maurice Séguin, Guy Frégault, and Michel Brunet – were secular men, two of them trained in the United States. Together they challenged the view that the Church had dominated New France and remained to save the French Canadians after the Conquest. Instead, they argued that New

France, like New England, had been a colony led by a thriving *bour-geoisie* that the Conquest had destroyed, turning the economy over to British merchants. That left the French Canadians excluded from commerce, forced into the rural life. After the Conquest it was not the Church but rather the seigneurial system and a soaring birth rate that had prevented assimilation. The Church, by contrast, in singing the virtues of ruralism, condemning commerce and state intervention, had left the field free for occupancy by the British. Lacking a middle class, the neo-nationalists contended, French Canadians had lost control of the economy even in the one province where they were a majority. The result was a profound crisis: French-Canadian culture was unprotected and often poverty stricken in an urban-industrial order controlled by foreigners. Canadians dominated *canadiens*.[19]

The implications of the Montreal historians' teachings were explicit: French Canadians should set about using the state to promote a new entrepreneurial class in order to regain control over their economic life. Only in this way could they build a modern nation, one that eschewed messianic appeals. This meant concentrating on Quebec as the national state of French Canadians, forgetting the minorities whose fate was assimilation, and unmasking the myth of national unity that merely disguised French-Canadian subordination to the English-speaking majority. Gradually, Canadian federalism would be reformed to reflect the existence of two equal nations. "The government charged with defending and promoting the common good of the French-Canadian nationality is that of the province where the immense majority of the French Canadians live. That is why Quebec cannot be considered simply as one of ten provinces. It has the right to claim a special status."[20] How special became the central issue in the constitutional debates of the 1960s.

Though Brunet and his colleagues never explicitly connected their nationalism with the cause of independence, the implications were there. A second influential historian, Maurice Séguin, in a little book entitled *L'idée de l'indépendance au Québec* (1968), first broadcast over Radio-Canada and then published in the separatist journal *Laurentie*, left little to the imagination. Brunet, himself, developed a theory of so-called "associate states," which was a forerunner of René Lévesque's sovereignty-association – political sovereignty combined with a Canadian common market. With the Montreal historians the concept of *état nation* replaced that of *église-nation*; nationalism was once again viewed as a secular phenomenon.[21]

A second group of thinkers in the 1950s articulated an even more radical criticism of traditional nationalism. This was a loose association of social scientists, lawyers, journalists, and labour leaders who, in 1950, founded a little magazine called *Cité libre*. Pierre Elliott Trudeau became the best known of this group, but he was not alone in his advocacy of a "functionalist" approach to Quebec's problems. His long, documented, and brilliantly polemical introduction to a study of one of Quebec's major post-war labour conflicts, *La Gréve de l'amiante* (1956), dissected traditional clerical and nationalist dogma that, he argued, ignored the realities of French-Canadian life. "Alas," he concluded, "it was the very idealism of the nationalists that most hurt them. *They loved not wisely but too well*; and in their anxiety to obtain nothing but the best for French Canadians, they developed a social thought impossible to put into practice and which to all intents and purposes left the people without intellectual guidance."[22] While this may seem to have been an affirmation of the Montreal historians' viewpoint, Trudeauites did not call for a revised and modernized nationalism. That, they believed, would only substitute old myths with new. Seeing themselves as spokesmen for the working people of Quebec, the *citélibristes* viewed nationalism as a bourgeois ideology; the Montreal historians' formulation was thus merely an ideology for a new business class. Nor did they believe that Quebec needed to construct a nation-state or acquire a special status. Quebec's powers in the Canadian federal system were sufficient; the problem was not the lack of power but rather the failure to use it imaginatively and effectively. While the Montreal historians called for a modernized nationalism and increased provincial autonomy, the *citélibristes* worked toward a modernized social thought and a fully utilized federalism.[23] But each group was preoccupied with the future of French Canada.

The death of Premier Duplessis in 1959 probably removed the cap from the growing frustrations felt by Quebecers, though it is unlikely that even he could have prevented the explosion indefinitely. But with *le chef* gone the "quiet revolution" that had been under way since the end of the war now manifested itself in reforms in education, labour laws, the civil service, the construction of a welfare state, and a pronounced *dirigiste* thrust in economic matters. The state replaced the Church as the principal institution in the collective lives of Quebecers. As the Church had formerly hoped to formulate an ideology to justify its role as the ruling class, so the new bureaucratic ruling class redefined that ideology. The state of Quebec, the national homeland of French Canadians, or as they now increasingly called themselves, Québécois, could no longer accept a status of one province among many. Instead, it must be accepted as a nation, perhaps as not a fully independent one, though that was a future possibility, but at least as *une province pas comme les autres*. *Egalité ou indépendance* became the cry of even so conservative a politician as the Union Nationale's

Daniel Johnson. In Quebec, as elsewhere in the post-colonial world, the process of modernization was a strong stimulus to nationalism, perhaps because change made citizens uneasy about their identities, perhaps because modernizers discovered that nationalist appeals could mobilize the people to support change. In Quebec, as elsewhere, reform, *le rattrapage*, was expensive and nationalist arguments, even threats, proved effective in pushing the central government out of lucrative tax areas in favour of *l'état du Quebec*.[24]

Increasingly, then, the post-1960 Lesage government found Brunet-like arguments appealing and useful. For René Lévesque, the most nationalist of Lesage's ministers and later the leader of the Parti Québécois, Quebec was vulnerable, like "a lobster during shedding season,"[25] its old values and institutions gone and a new shell yet to be grown. That shell would be the state, the Quebec state. Only the state that French Canadians controlled could be expected to assume the task of making Quebecers *maîtres chez nous*: increasing their control over the economy and making their language the dominant one in public and private institutions. If those goals were frustrated by the Canadian constitution, the constitution should be jettisoned and a new one, recognizing Quebec's national status, devised.

During the early 1960s a number of small, often feuding, separatist-nationalist groups were founded. But it was only in 1968 that René Lévesque left the provincial Liberal Party and set about forming the first serious party of national independence since Papineau's disaster. "*Nous sommes des Québécois*" his party statement began, and with astonishing speed he created a movement ready to take power. That was achieved on November 15, 1976. Between then and May 20, 1980, when his party was defeated in a referendum asking for a mandate to negotiate sovereignty-association with the rest of Canada, there was a flurry of activity attempting to legitimize the national project. The Minister of Finance, Jacques Parizeau, *un bon bourgeois* with a Ph.D. from the University of London, provided financial and economic management of a quality that almost quieted the fears of the business community and brought social peace to an unsettled labour scene. Rules concerning party financing were reformed and the problems of the depressed rural economy addressed. Most important of all was Bill 101, the Charter of the French Language. This legislation, designed to end a controversy over language that had grown angrier for a decade, made French the only official language of the province and required its use in both public and private business. Limited language and educational rights were recognized for the Anglophone minority, but not for new immigrants, including "immigrants" from Canada. Though the Anglophones objected, as did leaders of other ethnic groups, and many of those with mobility due to professional skills departed for other parts of Canada, the law was widely accepted as a satisfactory solution to a pressing problem.

Yet the very success of the PQ's language legislation and its overall capacity to provide good government may well have been the cause of its failure to achieve its principal goal: political sovereignty accompanied by economic association with Canada. Of course, the Lévesque government knew that at no time since polls had been conducted on the topic had anything like a majority of Quebecers favoured independence. For that reason the PQ had promised never to act without a referendum. The party had calculated that, once in power, it could convince more people that independence was practical if the new government acted responsibly. In fact, the opposite seems to have happened. The effective promotion of Francophone interests by the provincial government seemed to demonstrate that independence, which would be disruptive, was unnecessary. The fruits of the educational reforms of the sixties came in the shape of a new generation willing and anxious to occupy managerial posts in the private sector – especially since the public sector was full, even bloated. The application of the new language laws to business greatly increased opportunities of this new business-school educated elite. So, too, did the departure of significant numbers of unilingual Anglophones: "the accelerated Frenchification of the Quebec economy," in Dominique Clift's words.[26] With education and social mobility came rising incomes for Francophones. In 1961 Francophones in Quebec had been near the bottom of the province's salary scale. By 1980 French-Canadian ownership of the economy was increasing while Francophone salaries had caught up and even passed those of Anglophones. A confident, new bourgeoisie had emerged, as Michel Brunet had hoped.[27] But its goals were not what he had predicted or hoped for.

Having achieved a status of importance, if not complete dominance, in the new Quebec, this bourgeoisie was not anxious to destabilize the ship by supporting radical constitutional change. Unlike the bureaucratic middle class that had spearheaded the state-building reforms of the 1960s, this new private-sector middle class saw no benefit, and perhaps even some threat, in the further growth of the state. When asked to approve a referendum calling for negotiations on sovereignty-association these people demurred – though the outcome was close enough. Sixty per cent of Quebecers voted "non," 40 per cent said "oui," but the Francophone population divided almost equally. Nevertheless, it was a devastating defeat for Lévesque's état-nation dream. Though his party won re-election in 1981 it was rudderless, and finding it necessary to pay the bills it had run up in the pre-referendum years the government adopted increasingly unpopular policies, especially unpopular with the very people – civil servants and teachers – who formed its most loyal support. And so Quebec's first *indépendantiste* government collapsed, its mission unfulfilled.[28] The new nationalism, then, was a victim of its own success.

Yet if yuppies – or as the French say, *bon chic, bon genre* – are no longer statist-nationalists, that should not be taken to mean that nationalism in Quebec is finally interred. The French-Canadian collective consciousness has roots that are deep and a *vouloir-vivre* too resilient to be destroyed even if the distinctive characteristics of contemporary Quebec are less definite, more North American, than ever before. The ticking time bomb that may set off yet another nationalist upsurge is the threateningly low birth rate that is part of Quebec's modernization.[29] Once French Canada had the highest birth rate in the Western industrial world; today it has the lowest. Quebec is a society where traditional family structures and gender relations, to say nothing of birth control practices, have undergone a radical change. That has resulted in a demographic revolution whose implications are only now being assessed and the "national" consequences contemplated.[30] That is for the future.

For now, then, let me conclude. Nationalism has proven a durable and malleable ideology in French Canada's history. Its content evolved as the society it sought to describe underwent change. But its goal remained consistent: the defence and legitimation of a French-speaking culture in North America. *La survivance* and *l'épanouissement* have been the historic rallying cries of nationalists in Quebec. And that is likely to remain so even in a modern Quebec where *Liberté, égalité et fraternité* are more highly valued than at any time in the past.[31]

[1986]

NOTES

1 Hubert, Aquin, "L'existence politique," in *Blocs erratique* (Montréal, 1977), 57; Pierre Ellion Trudeau, *Le fédéralisme et la société canadienne-française* (Montréal, 1967), esp. 161.

2 E.J. Hobsbawn, *The Age of Empire 1875–1914* (London, 1987), 144.

3 Dale Miquelon, *New France 1701–1744: "A Supplement to Europe"* (Toronto, 1987), 5.

4 Jean-Pierre Wallot, *Un Québec qui bouge* (Montréal, 1975), 264–74.

5 Thomas Chapais, "La Nationalité canadienne-française," *Discours et Conférences* (Montréal, 1880), 34.

6 Fernand Ouellet, *Lower Canada 1791–184: Social Change and Nationalism* (Toronto, 1980), 275–328.

7 François-Xavier Garneau, *Histoire du Canada* (5ème édition, Paris, 1913), xlv, xlviii.

8 Louis-Edmond Hamelin, "Evolution numérique séculaire du clergé catholique dans le Québec," *Recherches sociographiques* 11 (1961): 189–211.

9 L'Abbé L-A. Laflèche, *Quelques Considérations sur les Rapports de la société civile avec la religion et la famille* (Montréal, 1866), 47; Nadia Eid, *Le clergé et le pouvoir politique au Québec* (Montréal, 1978), cited 241.

10 Guy LaFlèche, *Les Saints martyrs canadiens* (Laval, 1988), 281–84.

11 Ramsay Cook, ed., *French-Canadian Nationalism: An Anthology* (Toronto, 1969), 126; Paul-Emile Borduas, *Refus global* (Montréal, 1959); Marcel Rioux, ed., *L'Eglise et le Québec* (Montréal, 1961); Pierre Maheu, "Le Pouvoir cléricale," in *Parti Pris, Les Québécois* (Montréal, 1971), 171–90.

12 Jules-Paul Tardivel, *Pour La Patrie* (Montréal, 1895); Alonie de Lestres (Lionel Groulx), *L'Appel de la race* (Montréal, 1922).

13 Cook, *French-Canadian Nationalism*, pp. 118–52.

14 Yolande Lavoie, *L'émigration des québécois aux Etats Unis de 1840 à 1930* (Québec, 1979), 45; William Ryan, *The Clergy and Economic Growth in Quebec, 1846–1914* (Quebec, 1966).

15 Susan M. Trofimenkoff, ed., *Abbé Groulx: Variations on a Nationalism Theme* (Toronto, 1973), 189–90.

16 Michael Oliver, "The Social and Political Ideas of French Canadian Nationalists" (Ph.D. thesis, McGill University, 1956).

17 *Royal Commission of Enquiry on Constitutional Problems* (Quebec, 1956), 11: 33.

18 Michael D. Behiels, *Prelude to Quebec's Quiet Revolution* (Montreal and Kingston, 1985).

19 Michel Brunet, *La Présence anglaise et les Canadiens* (Montréal, 1958), 113–66.

20 Michel Brunet, *Canadians et canadiens* (Montréal, 1954), 30.

21 Ramsay Cook, *Canada and the French Canadian Question* (Toronto, 1966), 119–42.

22 Pierre E. Trudeau, ed., *La Grève de l'amiante* (Montréal, 1956), 13–14.

23 Trudeau, *Le fédéralisme et la société canadienne-française*.

24 Ramsay Cook, *Canada, Quebec, and the Uses of Nationalism* (Toronto, 1986), chapter 8.

25 René Lévesque, "For an Independent Quebec," *Foreign Affairs*, 54 (1976): 739.

26 Dominique Clift, *Le déclin du nationalisme au Québec* (Montréal, 1981), 165.

27 Alain G. Gagnon and Khayyam Z. Paltiel, "Towards *Maître chez nous*: the ascendency of the Balzacian Bourgeoisie in Quebec," *Queen's Quarterly* (1986): 731–49.

28 Graham Fraser, *René Lévesque and the Parti Québécois in Power* (Toronto, 1984).

29 *L'Evolution de la Population de Québec et ses Conséquences*, Secrétariat de Développement social (Québec, 1984); Marc G. Termote, "Why are Quebeckers dying out even faster than other Canadians?" *Transactions of the Royal Society of Canada*, F, 5th series, 3 (1985), 81–94.

30 Jean-Louis Roy, "Le Nationalisme québécois dans les années 80," *Le Devoir*, 1 juin 1985; Jean-Claude Leclerc, 'L'Effondrement démographique,' *Le Devoir*, 8 novembre 1985.

31 This undocumented assertion would seem to find some support in the survey research that underlies "Les valeurs des jeunes," *L'Actualité* (juin 1989): 28–48. Current attitudes in Quebec to nationalism and/or independence are revealed in *L'Actualité* (mai 199): 7–22.

SIX

Conquêtisme

'History! they shouted. Give us back our History!
The English have stolen our History!'

Leonard Cohen, *Beautiful Losers*

During the autumn of 1965, when Premier Lesage went forth to win
the West, he repeatedly told an anecdote that revealed a great deal
about himself and his people. The anecdote was historical, it was about
the Battle of the Plains of Abraham. 'It was a little battle between two
regiments of regular soldiers from overseas,' he said. 'The French reg-
iment lost the battle and went back to France. The British won, and
stayed, and were assimilated.'[1]

It can be left to a future biographer to explain why Premier Lesage
treated 'the capital fact of French Canadian history' so lightly.[2] For my
purposes the story serves only as a reminder that nearly every French
Canadian, viewing the place of his community in Canada, almost
invariably begins with an interpretation of the meaning of the British
Conquest. No question has more consistently occupied the attention of
French-Canadian historians, intellectuals, politicians, social scientists,
priests, novelists, and newspapermen than the meaning of 1759. And
interpretations of that critical event are almost as numerous as the
classes of people who have examined it. For that reason among others,
the interpretation of the meaning of the Conquest is one of the most
important subjects in the intellectual history of French Canada. Each
generation of French Canadians appears to fight, intellectually, the Battle of the Plains of Abraham again.[3]

Since it is not the Conquest itself but rather what later generations
looking back have thought about it that forms the substance of intellectual history, it is perhaps sensible to begin with the generation of
Garneau and Parent. This choice is not a completely arbitrary one, for
the failure of the Rebellion of 1837 and the imposition of the Union of
1841 were events which, perhaps for the first time since the Treaty of
1763, caused French-Canadian intellectuals to contemplate seriously

the fate of a French-speaking community separated from its Mother-land. As Canon Groulx and others have shown, of course, the search for the meaning of the Conquest began very soon after 1759. But it nevertheless remains true that it was with Garneau's generation, a generation which reflected the birth of French-Canadian nationalism, that the great, acrimonious, and continuing debate about the long-term meaning of the Conquest began its passionate history.[4]

Since the debate appears to have begun in these crisis years, 1837 to 1849, it is not surprising that the graph illustrating its rising and falling intensity runs closely parallel to the graph of political change and crisis in Canada. It has usually been in times of crisis that French Canadians, a most historically-minded people, have turned to the past for the explanation of their plight. And in that past, 1759 has always been the key date. It is the interpretation of the political, cultural, and socioeconomic result of that symbolic year that has formed the core of the continual argument in French Canada about the existing and future state of the nation.

The years between the publication of Garneau's *Histoire* and the First World War represent a formative stage in the debate over the meaning of the Conquest. For Garneau the Conquest was an unmitigated tragedy. In his view the French Canadians' heroic and self-sacrificing past was nothing 'in comparison with the sufferings and humiliations which awaited them and their posterity.' Moreover, the social consequences of the defeat of France were extremely serious, for New France witnessed the exodus of 'the merchants, lawyers, the civil servants, and finally most of the notable people who were still in the country'. As for the great majority, who remained in Canada, 'isolating themselves from their new masters, they gave themselves entirely to agriculture.'[5]

By following an earlier and inferior historian, Michel Bibaud,[6] Garneau thus established one of the great themes in the debate over the consequences of the Conquest: the fate of the leading classes of New France. If the leading classes had, in fact, disappeared after 1763, then the weakness of French Canada's lay leadership and the predominant role of the clergy could be explained. The Garneau view prevailed throughout most of the nineteenth century.[7] The general tendency was to argue that while the lay directing classes had departed, it was in reality good riddance, for they had not been true *Canadiens* anyway. This latter view became especially popular after Judge Baby showed, on the basis of meticulous research, that the number of those who had departed had been greatly exaggerated.[8] For Benjamin Sulte, Baby's work made it plain that 'the true Canadians remained at home.'[9]

Indeed Sulte, who due perhaps to the influence of the Loyalist William Kirby was something of a British imperialist,[10] even argued that the directing class, a noblesse of *Canadien* origin, had remained in Canada and become 'more than ever the leaders thanks to the English regime.'[11] For Sulte, of course, the Conquest was not a tragedy at all, but represented rather a long-run benefit for French Canadians. As the only French-Canadian contributor to a fat imperialist tract published in 1905, Sulte wrote, 'None of the humiliations and annoyances which usually accompany a Conquest were imposed upon them [the French Canadians]. They passed from a reign of absolute subjection under the Bourbons to the free and untrammelled life of a constitutional government.'

By and large, Baby's interpretation, though not necessarily Sulte's Loyalist modification of it,[12] became the conventional wisdom in the decade before the First World War. The view implied that the Conquest had exercised very little effect upon the social structure and the way of life of French Canadians.[13] By the end of the nineteenth century, a growing number of French Canadians tended to discount the importance of the changed political allegiance.

One writer at least, at the end of the nineteenth century, did not accept the view that the Conquest had left the *Canadiens'* way of life unchanged. That writer was the learned and respected sociologist Léon Gérin. Gérin, deeply influenced by the French Catholic thinkers of the school of Frédéric Le Play, believed firmly in the virtues of liberal individualism and free enterprise. He was thoroughly convinced that his compatriots, if they wished to survive in the modern world, would have to acquire the values of modern, liberal, industrial civilization. And to do so, they needed to reform their educational system.[14] The superiority of the English had been demonstrated in their victory over the French in North America, and this he attributed to their self-reliant individualism. In short, the British represented the vanguard of social progress.[15] He was therefore prepared to argue that, from a sociological viewpoint, the British Conquest of Canada was a progressive step since it began the destruction of the old, backward, communitarian order that had been inherited from France. To replace these reactionary values, the Conquest brought the progressive, individualistic values of Britain.[16]

Gérin had both his supporters and his critics. Errol Bouchette, the apostle of industrialization, agreed substantially with his friend's admiration for the virtues of British individualism.[17] On the other hand, writers like Abbé Brosseau, who feared that the implications of Gérin's views threatened French Canada' s spiritual mission, rejected the sociologist' s claims.[18]

Abbé Brosseau's response to Gérin is indicative of an attitude toward the Conquest that was prevalent in the years before the Great War. That attitude stemmed from a belief that French Canada, both before and after the Conquest, was primarily a missionary colony whose goal was to bring the civilizing influence of France and Catholicism to a barbarian North America. If anything, the Conquest had reaffirmed this mission, by strengthening the Church. Accompanying this contention was the further claim that the Church had saved the nation. Garneau, though not especially friendly toward the Church, had noted that 'the religious orders' had remained after 1763.[19] His successors carried the claim a step further. A cleric, J.S. Raymond, in a speech in 1870 in which he explained the recent defeat of France by Germany as a proper chastisement, concluded with what was a standard refrain: 'It is religion which has maintained in us a loyalty, which, in rendering us faithful to our new master, has prevented the absorption of our faith, of our language, of our customs, of our name in the American union.'[20]

But this clerical interpretation of the survival of French Canada went well beyond the simple claim concerning the leading role of the Church. Much more important was the view that the Conquest itself was divinely inspired, for it saved the *Canadiens* from the horrors of corruption, secularism, and revolution that had overtaken France almost immediately after 1763. It was for this reason that Abbé Laflèche, in his defence of the plan for Confederation, rejected the view that the Conquest was a 'national calamity'. Indeed, Laflèche insisted that in the light of 1789 'one will be convinced that the Conquest has not been for us a misfortune, but that it has been the providential means which God used to save us as a people.' Abbé Laflèche then went a step further in his exposition of his people's history. The Conquest had not only cut New France off from the decaying society of France, but it had also grafted it to the healthy British plant. And why was British society so admirable? Abbé Laflèche's response suggests that he learned his British history from rather different books than those volumes of Macaulay that the young Laurier was poring over. The cleric wrote that the British constitution was founded by 'the pious and fervent Catholic Alfred the Great. This man of genius had understood and admired the beauty and the force of the constitution of the government of the Catholic Church. He tried to apply it to the government of the nation that divine Providence had charged him with governing. That is the origin and the model of the English constitution.' Thus, at last, had been revealed the object of Alfred's contemplations while the cakes burned![21]

Abbé Laflèche's view of France and Britain, and therefore of the Conquest, was widely held in French Canada before the First World

War. It was not, however, unchallenged. There were even those who
argued that the role of the Church after the Conquest had been one of
collaboration with the British. Curiously, one of the first writers to suggest this interpretation was a French cleric who had briefly taught at
the Quebec seminary in the 1840s before moving on to Boston. Abbé
Brasseur de Bourbourg's explosive exposé made its appearance in
1852.[22] His charge that the French-Canadian hierarchy had assisted
the British conquerors, as well as his no less unflattering prediction
that the *Canadiens* would ultimately be assimilated into the North
American melting pot, brought a furious and defensive reply of 'hum-
bug' from the respected Abbé Ferland.[23]

The French abbé's book doubtless died a painless death under the
heavy blows of the French-Canadian abbé, but the ideas themselves
died harder, if at all. Indeed, the charge of clerical collaboration was
expressed by a variety of young intellectual *rouges* in the 1890s. It was
a favourite theme of the young men who wrote, unfortunately under
pseudonyms, for the lively but short-lived *Canada-Revue*, published in
Montreal. In one of several excursions into Canadian history, 'Duroc'
wrote in 1893, 'The Catholic clergy made itself the slave of the conqueror, it was its powerful arm thanks to which absolute submission
was assured.' Yet 'Duroc' and his anticlerical friends appear to have
agreed with Abbé Laflèche's estimate of the value of British institutions. Because the Conquest had brought liberal institutions, French
Canadians had survived despite the tyranny of the Church.[24] It was
views like these, and some rather more scandalous ones, that brought
the condemnation of the Archbishop of Montreal down upon the
Canada-Revue. A similar fate, at the hands of Rome, befell L.-O.
David's *Le Clergé canadien* in 1896. Somewhat more moderate in his
views than the contributors to the *Canada-Revue*, David nevertheless
viewed the clergy as the chief beneficiaries of the Conquest. He argued
further that they had misused their predominant position by failing to
support the national cause in 1837 and in 1867 and by contributing to
the economic inferiority of French Canadians through their control
over education.[25]

French-Canadian liberals, or *rouges*, of the nineteenth century were
by no means unanimous in their belief that the Conquest and the consequent establishment of British institutions was beneficial to French
Canada. There were some who believed that the Conquest had been
such a calamity as to demand the most radical steps to erase it. Hector
Fabre, a profound admirer of France, proclaimed in 1871 that 'the
greatest calamity which can strike a growing people is to be separated
from the nationality out of which it comes ...'[26] Twenty years later, in
the midst of economic depression, Louis Fréchette argued that French

Canadians had never accepted the Conquest. 'This feeling,' he wrote in an American magazine, 'is the quiet, unavowed and unconscious but instinctive expectation of some reaction ever cherished, ever dreamed of, and secretly nourished by some undefined hope of future emancipation.'[27] Both Fabre and Fréchette saw the solution to the tragedy of the Conquest in annexation to the United States.

Perhaps the most interesting views of the meaning of the Conquest, interesting because of the men who held them, were those of the three most prominent Quebec political figures at the turn of the century – Mercier, Laurier, and Bourassa. Despite his *nationalisme*, Mercier's view of the Conquest was remarkably conventional. For him the important result of the Conquest was that it brought those parliamentary institutions which had allowed French Canadians to regain their full freedom. 'See what happened to our fathers,' he told the Quebec Société Saint-Jean-Baptiste in 1882. 'Conquered on the Plains of Abraham they remained free and French ...'[28]

Laurier, despite the *rougisme* in his background, held a similar view. In his famous speech on 'Political Liberalism' in 1877, he argued that while French Canadians were a 'conquered race', they had also 'made a conquest: the conquest of liberty.'[29] He returned to these thoughts in the dark days of November 1899 when he had reluctantly acceded to pressure from English Canada to send a Canadian contingent to South Africa. His close friend and confidant, Senator Raoul Dandurand, wrote to him, in a state of depression, arguing that recent events had again proven that 'we are not masters of our destinies.' Laurier's reply was to insist that the Conquest had been erased. 'But who are the conquered in history who, a century after their defeat have been able to show the world, not only that they have conserved their religion, their language, everything which constitutes the distinctive attributes of nationality, but that they are in all things on an equal footing with those who, following your idea, you have been obliged to call their conquerors,' Laurier argued.[30]

Though divided from Laurier on many issues, Henri Bourassa differed very little from the Liberal Prime Minister in his interpretation of the events of 1759. Bourassa, a loyal son of the Church and a temperamental conservative, expressed completely what might be called the traditional interpretation of the Conquest. In his view New France had been primarily a missionary venture, and its people had followed an agricultural calling. The Conquest caused little social dislocation, though there was a small but far from disastrous exodus. 'It may fairly be considered,' he wrote in 1902, 'that the partial exodus of the aristocratic element was an actual loss to Canada, the country being deprived of a large number of its most prosperous and influential inhabitants. But the absence of any other privileged class than the clergy made for a better understanding between the victor and the vanquished, and for the safer protection of the latter.'[31] Moreover, Bourassa's young friends, Asselin, Lavergne, and Fournier, who established *La Ligue Nationaliste Canadienne*, offered a further commentary on the Conquest in the very first sentences of their *Programme*. They declared: 'That it is reasonable to believe that Providence in giving Canada to England wished to familiarize it, by the Conquest, then by the use of parliamentary institutions, with the enjoyment of liberty ...'[32]

Thus by the time of the First World War French-Canadian interpretations of the Conquest had come full circle. What Garneau had seen as a dark and foreboding tragedy had come to be accepted, even by those who suspected Laurier's opportunism, as an event providentially inspired, which had brought as many, if not more, benefits than disadvantages. Yet, in 1919, when the first volume of Thomas Chapais's magisterial *Histoire* appeared,[33] giving the historian's imprimatur to the providential interpretation of the Conquest, a new mood was already present in French-Canadian intellectual circles. That mood was to lead to a profound revision of the revisionists.

After the tensions of World War I, which culminated in the bitter election of December 1917, it is not surprising that some French-Canadian intellectuals began to look at the Conquest from a new perspective. The leader of the revisionists was the recently appointed professor of history at the University of Montreal, Abbé Lionel Groulx. While he was by no means the first writer to contend that eighteenth-century New France had exhibited all the characteristics of a nation, his emphasis was both stronger and different. For one thing he insisted on the essential 'Frenchness' of French Canada. It is true that he suspected the secularism of modern France, but that merely strengthened his view that New France was the true heir of Catholic France. 'Everything which is French comes to us from France,' he wrote in 1912, 'but everything which comes to us from France is not always French.'[34]

Since not everything that came from France was desirable, Groulx admitted that the Conquest had prevented the insidious doctrines of Revolutionary France from undermining French-Canadian values. But that was 'the only compensation'.[35] His chief concern was with the impact of the Conquest on the society of French Canada. In 1921 he stated his view without any equivocation:

This germ of a people was one day profoundly overtaken in its life; it was constricted, paralyzed in its development. The consequences of the Conquest have weighed heavily on it; its laws, its language have been cut into; its intellectual culture was shackled for a long period; its educational system has deviated in some of its parts, sacrificed more than suited it to the English culture; its natural domain has been invaded, leaving it only partially master of its economic forces; by the protestant and Saxon atmosphere its private and public morality has been contaminated. A desolating make-up has gradually covered the physiognomy of our cities and our towns, an implacable sign of the subjection of our souls to the conqueror' s laws.

The most significant step in Groulx's argument was his explicit identification of Confederation with the Conquest. Where earlier writers and politicians, like Chapais and Laurier, viewed Confederation as a giant step in the reconquest of French-Canadian liberty, Groulx's conclusion was quite the contrary. 'The evil of the conquest,' he wrote, 'is aggravated since 1867 by the evil of federalism.'[36]

Groulx perceived, apparently, that the declining power of the British Empire meant that Bourassa's old battles were largely won. Yet, in his view, French Canada was scarcely any nearer to its own freedom, and the achievement of that freedom was, in Groulx's mind, the guiding motive of the French-Canadian nation. 'For the inspiring formula of its life,' he declared in 1937, 'of its politics, it wishes only one: to disengage itself from the embrace of the conqueror, to disengage a little more each day, to increase step by step, its autonomy, to stretch all the tension of its soul, towards the pride of a French destiny.'[37]

Holding views such as these, it was natural that Groulx should question one of the most venerable traditions about the Conquest: its providential character. Despite his clerical calling, and perhaps therefore more authoritatively, he denied firmly that an historian could discern the ways of providence in 'the catastrophe of 1760'. He even hinted that the spokesmen for the Church who, after 1759, had praised the liberality of the British and called upon the people to give their loyal support to the new régime were something very near to betrayers.[38]

In one sense, at least, Abbé Groulx remained a traditionalist. He continued to insist, as most of his predecessors had done, that the Conquest had not altered the most important characteristics of the French-Canadian 'race'. For him, New France had exhibited two primary characteristics: it had an apostolic vocation and an 'agrarian vocation'. He did not deny that there had also been exploration and commerce, but they were secondary. And for French Canadians, the virtues of the past were the virtues for the present. 'In every respect,' he wrote in 1937, 'the agricultural policy remains for French Canada, its vital policy.'[39]

The Second World War, like its predecessor, again stimulated the search for the meaning of the Conquest. For this, the political crises of the period were doubtless partially responsible. But no less important was the accelerated industrialization and urbanization of Quebec. During the war the famous debate over 'why we are divided' was, in essence, a debate over conflicting interpretations of the Conquest. The debate was interspersed with references to Nazi-occupied Europe. Abbé Maheux, rejecting Abbé Groulx's catastrophic interpretation of the Conquest, contended that 'the monstrous conduct of a Hitler, of a Mussolini, the savagery of their war, the oppression that they make weigh on the peoples conquered, invaded, occupied, menaced, makes us see the tableau of the 1758–60 period as an idyl.'[40] Some of this phraseology – 'occupation', 'collaboration', and so on – was to become commonplace in the post-war years. But more important was a striking new concept that was being incorporated into the interpretation of the Conquest. That concept, the concept of the social decapitation of the bourgeoisie, bore a significant relationship to the problems of an increasingly urban and industrial French Canada.[41]

This new interpretation asserted that New France, far from having been an agrarian, missionary colony, was one in which commerce and therefore a bourgeoisie predominated. The most critical result of the Conquest was the destruction of this class and the consequent transformation of the *Canadiens* into an agrarian people dominated by an alien government and an alien commercial class. The survival of French Canada after the Conquest had little, if anything, to do with providence or the clergy. That phenomenon could be explained by a secular socio-economic institution: the seigneurial system.[42]

The implications of the 'social decapitation' thesis are manifold. Most important, in Professor Séguin's words, 'because on the morrow of 1760 commerce and the sources of capital are almost monopolized by the Occupier, the Canadians were not able, for their own territory and in the proportion that their number demanded, to undertake the industrial transformation of Quebec when the time came beginning after the second half of the 19th century.'[43] Secondly, the disappearance of the directing bourgeoisie explains the role of the Church after 1759 and, in turn, 'the three dominant ideas of French-Canadian thought: ruralism, anti-statism, and messianism.'[44] Finally, there is the contention that because of the economic inferiority caused by the Conquest, French Canadians have occupied an inferior 'colonial' status in economic life, education, and politics.[45] It is worth noting, also, that this reinterpretation of the Conquest has been accompanied by a revision of the traditional view of the attitude of French Canadians toward France. The new view rejects the suggestion that the *Canadiens* easily accepted their new British rulers; instead, they passively resisted them. Nor were the conquered people of Canada as hostile to Revolutionary and Napoleonic France as has been traditionally held.[46]

The validity of this new interpretation has not, of course, gone unchallenged. Some scholars doubt the existence of a pre-Conquest bourgeoisie and the question is obviously one that deserves detailed research.[47] Others have questioned the very assumptions upon which the thesis is based.[48] But the view has its supporters, some of whom have used it to develop full-scale sociological interpretations of French-Canadian society.[49] For others it has become the historical underpinning for quasi-radical, radical, and even revolutionary responses to contemporary discontents.[50] Nor should the radically anti-clerical implications of this secular interpretation of the Conquest be left unremarked.[51] Perhaps all that can be said with certainty at this stage is that the continuing controversy about the meaning of the Conquest indicates that it remains a dominant concern of French-Canadian intellectual history.

There remains, now, the problem of attempting an explanation of this dominance. There is, of course, a simple reason. The Conquest happened, and few would deny its significance in the history of French Canada or Canada. Yet that simple explanation is hardly sufficient. Other critical events have taken place in the past – the 1837 Rebellion, Confederation, the Riel affairs, conscription, and so on. Each raises emotions, each has its conflicting interpretations. None has attracted the attention or the emotion of 1759. Indeed, one is repeatedly struck by the frequency with which the later events are discussed in terms of the Conquest and linked with it.[52]

The reason for this obsessive concern with the meaning of the Conquest may be found by looking at the more general question of attitudes toward history itself.

It is often remarked that such slogans as 'Je me souviens' and 'notre maître, le passé' illustrate the French Canadian's consciousness of his past. Would it not be just as true to say that these slogans illustrate the French Canadian's consciousness of the present? For many French Canadians the past, and especially the Conquest, has always been part of the present. It is for this reason that one finds, repeatedly, statements by French Canadians, historians and others, about the 'presentness' of the past, and the usefulness of history to the present. This attitude is well summed up in Canon Groulx's statement: 'History, dare I say it, and with no intention of paradox, is that which is most alive; the past, is that which is most present.[53]

Or in Esdras Minville's revealing remark about 'we who continue history, who are history itself.'[54] This attitude toward history which makes the past part of the present is not, of course, uniquely French Canadian. It bears a marked similarity to the comment of a distinguished Mexican philosopher concerning Hispanic America. 'The past, if it is not completely assimilated, always makes itself felt in the present,' Leopoldo Zea has written, 'Hispanic America continued to be a continent without a history because the past was always present. And if it had a history, it was not a conscious history. Hispanic America refused to consider as part of its history a past which it had not made.'[55] Is it not the failure to 'assimilate' the Conquest, to make it part of French-Canadian history, that explains the endless attempts to interpret it?

There is another element in this explanation. If the past is part of the present, then arguments about the past are, in reality, disputes about the present. As one judges the problems and achievements of the present and the goals of the future, so one interprets the past. If parliamentary government is valuable, then the event that brought it may be admired, or at least accepted. If the leadership of the Church is to be preserved, then the event that allowed it may very well have been providential. If an urban bourgeoisie is necessary, the event that destroyed it must be viewed darkly. If national political independence is the desired goal, then the event that seems to have prevented it is the source of all evil. Professor Brunet, in his usual forthright fashion, has made the point explicitly: 'In every society the interpretation of the past changes frequently,' he has written. 'Is it because men have more freedom in building their past than in shaping their future? On the contrary, it seems that men change the interpretation of their past when they realize that they can give a new orientation to their collective action.'[56]

Thus the young radical nationalist, calling for a destruction of the past, is completely traditionalist when he writes in the preface to his *Petit manuel d'histoire du Québec* that:

This little text book is a programme. A programme for the school of the street, for the man of the street, for the people of the street, for the Quebec people thrown into the street, dispossessed of its home, of the fruits of its labour, of its daily life. This little text book insists on a repossession. The repossession of our history, the first step in the repossession of ourselves, in order to pass to a large step, the repossession of our future.[57]

If Professor Brunet is right, the explanation for the heated debate among French-Canadian intellectuals about the meaning of the Conquest is plain. Since history is looked upon as a tool for shaping the present, the quarrel over the interpretation of the past is a struggle for control over the meaning of the present and the goals of the future.[58] As an American historian has written, in a similar context, 'history becomes a key to ideology, a key to the world view that shapes the programs and actions in the present and future.'[59] It is this attitude toward the past that ultimately explains the central place of the Conquest in French-Canadian intellectual history, and makes the Conquest 'a fourth dominating idea in French Canadian thought' along with agriculturalism, anti-statism and messianism.

[1966]

NOTES

1 Blair Fraser, 'How Lesage Unsettled the West,' *Maclean's Magazine*, vol. 78, no. 22, November 15, 1965, p.57.

2 Michel Brunet, *La Présence anglaise et les Canadiens* (Montreal, 1958), p. 117.

3 It is impossible here to survey the whole field of French-Canadian writing, and I have ignored the field of fiction. But, to choose only two widely separated examples, mention may be made of Octave Crémazie's poem 'Le Drapeau Carillon,' in which he speaks of the French Canadian after 1763 as 'exiled in his own country,' from *Oeuvres Complètes d'Octave Crémazie* (Montreal, 1882), p. 129; and Jean-Charles Harvey's novel, *Marcel Faure* (Montmagny, 1922), p.13, in which it is remarked that after the defeat of Montcalm 'la race était plongée dans une amertume sans fond ... '

4 Abbé Lionel Groulx, *Notre Maître, Le Passé* (Montreal, 1944), 3rd series, pp. 125–78.

5 F.-X. Garneau, *Histoire du Canada*, 5th Edition (Paris, 1920), vol. II, pp. 300, 298, 296.

6 Michel Bibaud, *Histoire du Canada et des Canadiens sous la domination anglaise* (Montreal, 1844), pp. 5, 11–12.

7 J.-B.-A. Ferland, *Cours d'histoire du Canada* (Quebec, 1865), vol. II, p.606.

8 Le Juge Baby, 'L'Exode des classes dirigeantes à la cession du Canada,' *The Canadian Antiquarian and Numismatic Journal*, 3rd series, vol. II, nos. 3 and 4, 1899, pp. 97–14l.

9 Benjamin Sulte, 'L'Exode de 1760–63,' *Mélanges Historiques*, vol. 5 (Montreal, 1919), p. 82.

10 Victor Morin, 'Benjamin Sulte Intime,' *Les Cahiers des Dix*, no. 27 (MontreaI, 1962).

11 Sulte, 'L'Exode de 1760–63,' p.85. See also Abbé A. Couillard Desprès, *Noblesse de France et du Canada* (Montreal, 1916).

12 Benjamin Sulte, 'The French Canadians and the Empire,' in C.S. Gold-
man, *The Empire and the Century* (London, 1905), pp. 420–1.

13 The final word on this subject has probably been said by Robert de
Roquebrune, 'L'Exode des Canadiens après 1760,' *La Nouvelle Revue
Canadienne*, vol. III, no. 1, September-October 1953.

14 See Hervé Carrier, *Le Sociologue Canadien-Léon Gérin, 1866–1951*
(Montreal, 1960), and Jean-Charles Falardeau 'Léon Gérin: Une Introduction à la lecture de son oeuvre,' *Recherches Sociographiques*, vol. 1,
no. 2, April-June 1960.

15 Léon Gérin in *Le Monde Illustré*, 17th year, no. 881, March 23, 1901,
p.780.

16 Léon Gérin, 'L'Intérêt sociologique de l'oeuvre de Garneau,' *La Science
Sociale, Bulletin*, January 1914, p.62; and also Léon Gérin, 'L'Influence
des traditions des quatre principales populations canadiennes dans la vie
privée,' *La Science Sociale*, November 1897, pp. 365–78.

17 Errol Bouchette, 'French Canada and Canada,' *The Canadian Magazine*,
vol. XIV, no. 4, February 1900, pp. 314–16; and Errol Bouchette,
L'Indépendance économique du Canada français (Montreal, 1913), pp.
64 ff.

18 Abbé J.-A.-M. Brosseau, 'Etude critique du livre d'Edmond Demolins *A
Quoi tient la supériorité des Anglo-Saxons*,' *La Revue Canadienne*, vol.
XLVI, March 1904; and Léon Gérin, 'M. Demolins et la Science Sociale',
La Revue Canadienne, vol. XLVI, April 1904.

19 Garneau, *Histoire*, p. 298.

20 J.-S. Raymond, 'Enseignements des événements contemporains,' *La
Revue Canadienne*, vol. VIII, January 1871, p.55. See also Juge A.-B.
Routhier, 'La Religion catholique et la nationalité canadienne française,'
Conférences et Discours (Montreal, 1889), pp. 27–9.

21 Abbé L. Laflèche, *Quelques Considérations sur les rapports de la société
civile avec la religion et la famille* (Montreal, 1866), pp. 73, 74. See also
Philippe Masson, *Le Canada français et la providence* (Quebec, 1875).

22 Abbé Brasseur de Bourbourg, *Histoire du Canada, de son Eglise et ses
missions* (Paris, 1852), 2 vols.

23 J.-B.-A. Ferland, *Observations sur un ouvrage intitulé Histoire du
Canada etc. par M. l'abbé Brasseur de Bourbourg* (Quebec, 1953). See
also Robert Sylvain, 'Un Singulier Historien du Canada,' *Revue de l'Université Laval*, vol. III, no. 1, September 1948.

24 'Duroc', 'Pages d'histoire,' *Canada-Revue*, vol. IV, no. 3, January 21,
1893, p.35; and 'Duroc', 'Le Terrorisme,' *ibid.*, vol. IV, no. 1, January 7,
1893, p. 5. I am indebted to Professor Joseph Levitt of the University of
Ottawa for this reference.

25 L.-O. David, *Le Clergé canadien, sa mission et son oeuvre* (Montreal,
1896), pp. 106–7.

26 Hector Fabre, *Confédération, Indépendance, Annexation* (Quebec, 1871) p. 5.

27 Louis H. Fréchette, 'The United States for French Canadians,' *The Forum*, November 1893, p. 338.

28 Honoré Mercier, *Le Patriotisme* (Quebec, 1882), p.14.

29 Ulric Barthe, *Wilfrid Laurier on the Platform* (Quebec, 1890), p. 55.

30 Public Archives of Canada, Laurier Papers, Dandurand to Laurier, November 2,1899, and Laurier to Dandurand, November 4, 1899.

31 Henri Bourassa, 'The French Canadian in the Empire,' *The Monthly Review*, vol. VII, September 1902, p. 61.

32 *Ligue Nationaliste Canadienne, Programme* (Montreal, 1903), p. 1.

33 Thomas Chapais, *Cours d'histoire du Canada* (Quebec, 1919), vol. 1, p. 21.

34 Abbé Lionel Groulx, *Dix Ans d'Action française* (Montreal, 1926), p. 11.

35 Abbé Lionel Groulx, *Lendemains de Conquête* (Montreal, 1920), p. 233.

36 Groulx, *Dix Ans*, p. 126.

37 Abbé Lionel Groulx, *Directives* (Saint-Hyacinthe, 1959), p. 198.

38 Abbé Lionel Groulx, *Notre Maître, Le Passe*, pp. 162ff.

39 Groulx, Directives, pp. 194, 212.

40 Abbé Arthur Maheux, *Ton histoire est une épopée* (Quebec, 1941), p.28. See also Abbé Arthur Maheux, *Pourquoi sommes-nous divisés?* (Quebec, 1943) and Abbé Lionel Groulx, *Pourquoi nous sommes divisés* (Montreal, 1943). On this dispute, see Archange Godbout, 'Les Préoccupations en histoire et les thèses de M. l'abbé Maheux,' *Culture*, 1943.

41 The first appearance of this thesis appears to have been in the writings of Professor Maurice Séguin in 1946 and 1947. It soon became the central thesis of the so-called Montreal school. It is interesting, however, that no major study of the history of New France has incorporated and fully substantiated the thesis. In *La Civilisation de la Nouvelle France, 1713–44* (Montreal, 1944), Guy Frégault was still a proponent of the traditional view of New France, for he wrote, 'the country, it is the land' (p. 118). By 1954, however, in his pamphlet *La Société canadienne sous le régime français* (Ottawa, 1954), he had adopted the Séguin view. Professor Séguin himself has noted that Frégault was his 'most difficult student', in contrast to Michel Brunet, 'le plus facilement convaincu,' See Michel Lapalme, 'Le Nouveau Groulx s'appelle Séguin,' *Le Magazine Maclean*, April 1966, p. 48.

42 Maurice Séguin, 'Le Régime Seigneurial au Pays du Québec,' *Revue d'histoire de l'Amérique française*, vol. 1, no. 3, December 1947; and *ibid.*, vol. 1, no. 4, March 1948.

43 Maurice Séguin, *La Nation et l'agriculture*, unpublished doctoral thesis, Faculté des Lettres, University of Montreal, 1947, p. 246.

44 Michel Brunet, *La Présence*, pp. 113–66. See also Michel Brunet, *Les Canadiens après la Conquête* (Montreal, 1969).

45 Maurice Séguin, 'La Conquête et la vie économique des Canadiens,' *l'Action nationale*, vol. XXVIII, December 1946.

46 Michel Brunet, 'Les Canadiens après la Conquête – les débuts de la résistance passive', *Revue d'histoire de l'Amérique française*, vol. XII, no. 2, September 1958, and 'La Révolution française sur les rives du Saint-Laurent,' *ibid.*, vol. XI, no. 2, September 1957.

47 Jean Hamelin, *Economie et société en Nouvelle-France* (Quebec, 1960); Fernand Ouellet, 'Michel Brunet et le problème de la Conquêt,' *Bulletin des Recherches Historiques*, vol. 62, no. 2, 1956; Cameron Nish, 'Une Bourgeoisie coloniale en Nouvelle-France,' *l'Actualité Economique*, July and September 1963.

48 Fernand Ouellet, 'L'Etude du XIXe siècle canadien-français', *Recherches Sociographiques*, vol. III, nos. 1 and 2, 1962; Léon Dion, 'Le Nationalisme pessimiste, sa source, sa signification, sa validité,' *Cité libre*, 8th year, no. 20, November 1957.

49 Philippe Garigue, *L'Option politique du Canada français* (Montreal, 1963).

50 The following may be taken as examples of these not very distinct categories: *Le Fédéralisme, l'acte de l'amérique du nord britannique et les canadiens français* (Montreal, 1964); André d'Allemagne, 'L'Etat Laurentien, rêve ou réalité?' *Laurentie*, no. 104, September 1958; Jean-Marc Piotte, 'De l'humiliation à la révolution', *Essais philosophiques*, l'Association Générale des Etudiants de l'Université de Montréal, no. 9.

51 Robert Aubin, 'Pourquoi les clercs ne permettront pas la libération du Québec,' *Liberté* (new series), 4th year, no. 23, May 1962.

52 See, for example, Michel Brunet, *Canadians et Canadiens* (Montreal, 1955), or in a more violent tone, Joseph Costisella, *Le Peuple de la nuit* (Montreal, 1965).

53 Groulx, *Directives*, p.190.

54 Esdras Minville, *Invitation à l'étude* (Montreal, 1959), p.62.

55 Leopoldo Zea, *The Latin-American Mind* (Norman, Okla., 1963), p. 10.

56 Michel Brunet, 'French Canadian Interpretations of Canadian History,' *Canadian Forum*, vol. XLIV, no. 519, April 1964, p. 5. Guy Frégault makes the same point somewhat more cautiously. He writes, 'It is properly one of the functions of history – the principal one in my view – to connect systematically the tradition by which a human group orders its life.' Guy Frégault, *La Guerre de la Conquête* (Montreal and Paris, 1955), p. 459.

57 Léandre Bergeron, *Petit Manuel d'histoire du Québec* (Editions québécois, 1970).

58 No better example of this debate can be found than the recent discussion of the recommendations of the Parent Commission concerning the teaching of history in Quebec schools. The Commission recommended that

history should be viewed primarily as an intellectual discipline. 'It is necessary to dissociate history and patriotic teaching; the goal of teaching history is not in the first place civil, patriotic or religious education.' *Rapport de la Commission Royale d'Enquête sur l'Enseignement dans la Province de Québec* (Quebec, 1964), vol. II, p. 150. The Report's numerous critics have responded that the goal of objectivity is both illusory and dangerous, for it fails to recognize the function of history in shaping the present. See Michel Brunet, 'Le Rapport Parent, notre évolution historique et l'enseignement de l'histoire au Québec', *Bulletin de Liaison de la Société des Professeurs d'Histoire*, no. 3, February 1966; Canon Lionel Groulx, 'Urgence d'un enseignement fervent de l'histoire du Canada français,' *Le Devoir*, May 11, 1966.

59 Warren I. Susman, 'History and the American Intellectual: Uses of a Usable Past,' *The American Quarterly*, vol. XVI, no. 2, pt. 2, Summer 1964, pp. 255–6.

SEVEN

The Historian and Nationalism

English Canadians have an underdeveloped historical consciousness. Neither on the popular nor on the intellectual level does history deeply affect our lives and thoughts. We have no myths and no successful myth-makers. This is merely another way of saying that English-Canadian nationalism is immature, for a consciousness of the past is the stuff out of which nationalism is made. It is no accident that the first Western people with a historical consciousness is also the people whose history provides the archetype of modern nationalism: the Jewish people.[1] Nor is it an accident that, unlike most Western peoples, English Canadians lack a 'national historian', a Bancroft or a Macaulay. This does not mean that our historians have not been nationalists. On the contrary, nearly all of them have been. But none has found the interpretation of our history that can be called *the* national interpretation, though nearly all play some variation on the theme of survival against the threats of the United States.[2]

Whatever nationalism there is in English Canada is based not only on the survival theme but also on the British Conquest in 1760. That event gave English Canadians one very necessary component of nationalism: a sense of superiority. Yet the Conquest has not been presented as a great national event by our historians, probably because it divides Canadians. Also, of course, in the democratic twentieth century, conquest cannot really be unashamedly celebrated. Therefore, English Canadians have usually rationalized the Conquest by insisting that it brought French Canada the blessings of English liberty. The very ambivalence of English Canadians on the subject of the Conquest is an example of an anaemic nationalism.

The explanation of English Canada's lack of a historical consciousness is simple. Our orderly growth from 'colony to nation' has deprived us of the heroic events out of which nationalist myths are made. There is no great, romantic, uniting theme – a revolution or a defence of the fatherland – on which to build a national doctrine. What heroes there are are nearly all French, thus making English-Canadian hero-worship difficult. There is no English-Canadian Dollard or Brébeuf, and most English Canadians are unable to read the language in which these myths are expressed. Only John A. Macdonald comes near to being a national hero of mythical stature, but he is too real to qualify fully. Politicians rarely do, and if they do, it is only because, somehow, they are able to rise above politics; George Washington is a good example. Finally, English Canadians have always been rather uninterested in the past because of their preoccupation with building the present and ensuring the future. While some societies realize the usefulness of historical myths and of national pride in building a nation, English Canadians – perhaps content to live vicariously on others' myths – have been more concerned with railways, tariffs, and settlement. Nationalism is rarely spawned by the prosaic and the practical.

The lack of an inspiring national history in English Canada becomes particularly clear when a contrast is drawn with French Canada. Nationalism and historical writing have always been intimately linked in French Canada. This is only natural for a society that has all the elements of a national mythology in its past: heroes and heroines, wars and adventures, herculean struggles against man and nature, the ultimate tragedy of the British Conquest, and, above all, the sense of mission that all these events combine to foster. With this backdrop, it is little wonder that historians in French Canada have played perhaps the largest single role in developing the nationalist ideology.

The first great French-Canadian historian, the first national historian, was François-Xavier Garneau. Garneau composed his magnificent *Histoire du Canada depuis sa découverte jusqu'à nos jours*, which began to appear in 1845, to refute Durham's claim that French Canadians lacked both history and literature. The *Histoire* disposed of both charges effectively, and in its depiction of the glories of *la survivance* fulfilled yet another purpose. 'I wish,' Garneau revealed to L.-H. LaFontaine, 'to imprint this nationality with a character which will make it respected by the future.'[3]

Garneau's drum-and-trumpet account of the history of his nation dominated French-Canadian historical writing for over half a century. In its later editions, it was emasculated of most of the remarks that had left its author open to the suspicion of anti-clericalism and secularism. Thus, though French Canada's first national historian was a layman, the liberal interpretation that he gave to his people's past was soon transformed by the more conservative and clerical nationalism that triumphed in Quebec during the last third of the nineteenth century. Here

French Canada, as it often does, was reflecting developments in Europe, where the liberal nationalism of 1848 was falling victim to the conservative, Bismarckian type, while the liberal Pius IX was transforming himself into the reactionary Pius IX. Though Garneau had many successors – not the least of whom was the Abbé Ferland – no one immediately replaced him on the pedestal of national historian. Moreover, from the 1870s until the First World War, it was more often clerics like Bishop Laflèche and Mgr L.-A. Paquet who provided the theoretical framework and moral exhortation for French-Canadian nationalists.[4] It is not surprising that the greatest nationalist to emerge in this period was a man whose loyalty to his people was exceeded only by his loyalty to his church: Henri Bourassa.

While Bourassa was not an historian, he recognized the importance of history in the struggle for survival. It was partly as a result of his campaign in Le Devoir that, for the first time since 1865, professors of history were appointed in 1915 at both branches of Laval University. The chair at Quebec went to the temperamentally and politically conservative Thomas Chapais. His great Cours d' histoire du Canada will stand for many years as a model of careful, well-documented political and constitutional history. But Chapais, because of his location in Quebec City, or his temperamental conservatism, or his political realism, or his enormous respect for documents and facts, never developed an all-encompassing 'national doctrine' with which to explain his people's past and present. That task he left to his colleague in the Chair of History at Montreal.[5]

Abbé Lionel Groulx was, and indeed still is, the real successor to Garneau. The first fact about him, obvious but profoundly important, was his clerical training. No trace of the liberal scepticism that had marked Garneau's early work was allowed to creep into his writing. His education in Canada and in Europe came when both religious and nationalist thought were conservative. He reached his maturity and cut his political teeth during the years when the bicultural Canadian nationalism preached by Bourassa was meeting its most serious setbacks in the school and conscription crises. Perhaps the most revealing of all Abbé Groulx's books is the now-almost-forgotten novel he wrote under a pseudonym, L'Appel de la race. The novel took as its background the struggle against the famous Ontario School Regulation XVII and had as its central theme a vendu's recovery of his French Canadianism and the consequent loss of his English-Canadian wife. It is hard to avoid the separatist implications in this Canadian 'mixed marriage.' While Groulx's disciples and admirers have insisted that his use of the word 'race' had little significance, a reading of his novel suggests otherwise. The young historian was doubtless not a member of the racist school of Gobineau and H.S. Chamberlain, but his belief in French-Canadian uniqueness meant that his use of 'race' implied profound and unchangeable characteristics.

In a sense there were two Abbé Groulxs. One was the careful historian whose career was crowned by his *Histoire du Canada français*, in which the glories of survival were celebrated in a fashion both scholarly and lyrical. The other was the speaker, publicist, and pamphleteer, editor of *L'Action française* in the twenties and intellectual mentor of *L'Action nationale* in the thirties and forties. The two roles were never completely distinct. In the essays he collected under the revealing title *Notre maître, le passé*, he used his historical studies to expound his nationalist doctrine. And this doctrine always was that for French Canadians, French Canada came first. French Canada might, he seemed to suggest in the twenties, gradually regain its independence. Or it might, as he later seemed resigned to conclude, remain an autonomous part of a larger Canada. But French Canadians would survive only if they gave their first, indeed only, emotional loyalty to French Canada.[6] It was here that Groulx sought to shift the balance, always delicately poised in Bourassa's thought, toward French Canada. Groulx, in fact, harked back to the tradition of the ultramontane separatist of the late nineteenth century, Jules-Paul Tardivel, with whom Bourassa had debated over the relative merits of Canadian and French-Canadian nationalism.[7] Groulx, like Tardivel but unlike the complex Bourassa, was a French-Canadian, not a Canadian, nationalist.

History, in Groulx's view, was the story of *la survivance*. But more philosophically, it was a play in which two actors participated: man and God. "The more perfect the collaboration between these two, the greater the history."[8] Groulx's examination of the heroic days of New France convinced him that the collaboration was close indeed and that French Canadians were *une race élue*, "a chosen race."[9] The purpose of an awareness of history was explicitly nationalist. 'To reveal the very close identity of blood and its perfect purity, to fasten upon then indicate the moral traits of the race, that is the work of our history, which, in this way, establishes more solidly among us the very foundation of nationality.'[10]

The past was glorious and provided stimulus and motivation in a difficult present. The French-Canadian past was a success story because the people had remained faithful to their religion and their nationality.

Of all the figures of the past whom Groulx set forth as examples for French Canadians to emulate, none took precedence over Dollard, the hero of the Long Sault. In Groulx's view, Dollard epitomized the union of Catholicism and the French tradition that was French-Canadian

nationalism. In 1919, Groulx concluded an impassioned speech entitled 'Si Dollard revenait ...' with the ringing exhortation:

Rise, then, O Dollard, living on your granite pedestal. Call us with your manly
charm and in your heroic accents. We will rise towards you with hands trem-
bling like palms, ardently desiring to serve. Together we will work, we will
rebuild the family house. And for the defence of our Frenchness and of our
Catholicism, if you so command, O Dollard, rapturous and magnetic leader,
we will follow you to the final holocaust.[11]

The religious, messianic tone of this incantation need hardly be
underlined. Where religious conviction nearly always took clear precedence over nationalist ideals (though the two were closely related) in
Bourassa, it would be difficult to make this distinction in Groulx's
thought. And it was the inseparable combination of these elements that
he regarded as the essence of French-Canadian history and nationalism.[12]

While Canon Groulx lives and writes, no French Canadian can
aspire to replace him as 'national historian,' even though his religiously
oriented nationalism grows increasingly anachronistic in the new
atmosphere of Quebec. Moreover, among his successors, history has
become a discipline, at least at first glance, more subject to scientific
investigation and more interesting for its own sake than for the precepts it teaches for today's battles. At first glance, perhaps; but in
actual fact the tradition of history as a fundamental of *la survivance*
and nationalist doctrine remains as strong as ever. Much first-class history has been written, and will continue to be written, by men like
Marcel Trudel, Guy Frégault, and Michel Brunet, as well as other
younger men. Nevertheless, as long as French Canadians remain a
cohesive, national community, proud of their past but insecure in a present dominated by the non-French majority in North America, nationalists will continue to search the past for the weapons of survival. The
best contemporary example is Professor Michel Brunet, director of l'Institut d'histoire of the University of Montreal.

In some superficial ways, Brunet resembles Canon Groulx. He com-
bines research into the past with an enormous interest in the problems
of present-day Quebec. He is nearly as interested in public education
as he is in his university career. His warmth and wit, as well as certain
other qualities, make him one of Quebec's most popular intellectuals.
There is a danger in this type of popularity from which Brunet has not
entirely escaped: the simplification of subtle ideas. But the points of
similarity with Canon Groulx end when Brunet's lay status is noted. 'It
is impossible to understand the new nationalists if one does not first see

them as lay historians; similarly, one cannot understand Groulx if one does not recognize, behind the writer, the cleric,' Léon Dion has written.[13] While the Church stands at the centre of Canon Groulx's analysis of *la survivance*, Brunet is preoccupied with much more secular problems, such as class structure, economic organization, and political power. Nor is the lay historian unwilling to criticize the Church, even cast doubt on its role of guaranteeing French-Canadian survival. All of this suggests, quite accurately, a very different outlook.

As a nationalist historian, Brunet starts from a novel position. Instead of glorifying the past as a 'golden age,' he plays the role of debunker. His national past does not impress him. "It is a past in which heroes and brilliant arts were very rare. A past in which men were only men. They are not less congenial for that. A past in which the *Canadiens*, our ancestors, our grandfathers, and our fathers, knew more defeats than victories. A past in which the failures have been more numerous than the successes. A past without greatness and without flourish to which we are the modest heirs."[14] As for the glorious struggles that guaranteed French Canada's survival, this self-styled enemy of 'wishful thinking' writes: "This survival is not a collective success worthy of astonishment. It was the result of a combination of circumstances which the historian can easily analyse and which owe very little to the clear-sightedness of the *Canadiens* themselves."[15] These icy comments might well come from a writer profoundly hostile to French-Canadian nationalism. But to place Brunet in that category would be wholly misleading; his iconoclasm is the iconoclasm of the true nationalist believer. However, the demythologizing has only just begun.

Without a tear, Brunet condemns the whole corpus of traditional French-Canadian nationalist thought. "Most of the theoreticians of French-Canadian nationalism were mistaken and have badly directed those who gave them their confidence,"[16] he wrote in 1961. This sweeping condemnation is developed in one of Brunet's best and most controversial essays – one of the two essays that established him as an imaginative historian, the other being his account of the economic consequences of the Conquest. In his essay "Trois dominantes de la pensée canadienne française: l'agriculturisme, l'anti-étatisme, et le messianisme,"[17] Brunet analyses and exposes the illusions that he believes have detrimentally dominated French-Canadian thought. Quite characteristically, he uses the bludgeon rather than the rapier. It was this essay that led André Laurendeau, who agreed with its general thesis, to write: "Something tells me that these structures come a little too much from the historian's ideas and not enough from historical facts."[18] This remark could be applied to much of Brunet' s writing; indeed, it is a characteristic of the nationalist school of history. Be that as it may,

Brunet's analysis of the Arcadian ideal, the concept of the spiritual mission of French Canada in North America, and finally the fear of state intervention, is, in general terms, convincing. What, in effect, he is criticizing is the tendency of French-Canadian nationalist thinkers to withdraw from the real world of North American life, the life of an industrial and urban society.

Brunet demands that nationalists accept the facts of North American life and turn their backs on idle talk about the rural vocation and civilizing mission of French Canada. Instead, through the use of the state, a strong community capable of resisting assimilation could be built. Here he presents his view with passion: "Vanquished and conquered, separated from their metropolitan power, deprived of a business class, poor and isolated, ignorant, reduced to a minority in the country that their ancestors had founded, colonized by an absentee capitalism, the French Canadians had an absolute need for the vigilant intervention of their provincial state."[19] Where most earlier nationalists viewed the Church as the primary instrument of French-Canadian survival, the secular-minded Brunet is convinced that a modern nation requires an interventionist state to guarantee its existence.[20] Moreover, he recognizes that Confederation gave the French Canadians a provincial state with substantial powers. But, suffering from worn-out illusions and false spirituality, they failed to use it. The anticlericalism implicit in this view of the state needs no emphasis.

But the question that arises is: why did the French Canadians suffer these illusions so long? The answer is in the central concept of Brunet's thought, the idea that lies at the basis of his whole armoury of sociological generalization, of historical *obiter dicta*, and, above all, of his nationalist doctrine. That concept is the Conquest. It is not that Brunet discovered the Conquest, though he sometimes speaks as though he had; but rather it is the way he interprets its effects that gives his view importance. Naturally the Conquest has always been seen as something of a tragedy for French Canadians, though the more clerical writers never failed to point out that it had saved French Canada from a worse fate – the French Revolution.[21] For Brunet, that is merely a clerical illusion. In fact, the Conquest was the ultimate tragedy and for a startling reason, though not so startling when Brunet's secular assumptions are recalled. The Conquest, says the Montreal historian, brought the downfall of the French-Canadian middle class, leaving Quebec an 'abnormal society' suffering from 'social decapitation'. 'The absence of this directing and lay bourgeois class, whose role has been so important in the evolution of the societies of the Atlantic world, remains the great fact in the history of French Canada since the Conquest.'[22]

It is in his discussion of the consequences of the Conquest that

Brunet the historian becomes Brunet the sociologist who has built a model of what a 'normal society' should be, measures his own society against the model, and finds it wanting. Since the middle class is, according to this model, the backbone of any normal society, it follows readily that French Canada was left nearly powerless when its bourgeoisie, cut off from its metropolitan sources of strength by the Conquest, was gradually replaced by an English middle class. The consequences of the Conquest, then, was a status of economic – and therefore political – inferiority among French Canadians.[23]

Brunet's account of the fate of the French-Canadian middle class has not won unanimous agreement from his fellow historians. One school of economic historians doubts the very existence of any substantial middle class in New France, in the normally understood sense of that term. These writers argue that it was not the Conquest as much as the inefficiency and lack of a real bourgeois ethos that brought about the downfall of the French-Canadian merchants.[24] Indeed, it appears that Brunet, with his profound concern about the present, began by correctly perceiving a contemporary problem that faces French Canada – the lack of a business class – and read it backwards into history to find its source in a traditional French-Canadian nationalist explanation: the Conquest. As so often with Brunet's intoxicating nationalist history, the bottle is new, but the wine fully aged.[25]

The Conquest was, of course, crucial to French Canada. It not only placed New France under a new metropolitan power, but also, through gradual immigration, transformed French Canadians into a minority. Here Brunet advances yet another of his influential hypotheses, perhaps his most influential one. The view is summed up in the title of his first collection of essays, *Canadians et Canadiens*. Briefly the thesis is that not one but two nations inhabit Canada, one Canadian or Anglo-Canadian, the other *canadien* or French-Canadian. Paraphrasing Durham, Brunet writes of 'two nationalisms opposing one another in the bosom of the same state.'[26] Once again, then, in traditional nationalist fashion, Canadian history becomes a struggle of 'races' or nations. But as usual with Brunet, the old idea is given several new twists.

He rejects the old view that English Canadians are merely British colonials. He insists that English Canada is a nation, united by a powerful monolithic nationalism that is British in origin but Canadian in application and the interests it serves. Discussing Canadian involvement in Imperial wars, despite French-Canadian opposition, Brunet observes shrewdly: 'In all justice, it is necessary to say that if someone has sinned through nationalism in Canada, it is not the French Canadians.'[27]

A second implication of the two-nations theory is much more important. Working from a concept (or rather an assumption) of power politics, Brunet argues that when two nations are associated within a single state the majority nation inevitably rules. But in order to have it both ways – that is, the majority rules in Canada but not in Quebec – he formulates his theory in this fashion: 'And, usually, minorities do not govern majorities. Except when the minority has economic control over the area in which it lives.'[28] Thus the minority, the French Canadians, must become reconciled to the fact that in the last analysis the majority, the English Canadians, will rule.

It is a gloomy and pessimistic picture that emerges from Brunet's description of the past and his assessment of the French Canadians' present position. What can a French Canadian do to better the position of his people, or at least guarantee their survival? The answer is that he cannot do very much. Primarily he must be realistic. He must never expect that the minority can lead the majority. For Brunet, there is no possibility that French Canadians might become part of a majority through alliance with like-minded English Canadians because, by definition, there is no such thing as a like-minded English Canadian. Race or nationality usually determines man's viewpoint; most certainly in times of crisis. Of course Brunet cannot deny that French and English politicians can and do work together, and that this co-operation may be of some benefit to French Canadians. Essentially, however, he sees this co-operation (or, in the more derogatory term that he prefers, collaboration) as a means of disguising the naked power of the majority. 'In a state in which two nations coexist, the majority nation must always take care to associate the minority nation with its policy. It is thus less difficult to camouflage it as a common policy, though necessarily it remains no less the policy of the majority nation.'[29] Moreover, the leaders of French Canada 'must never ask from the majority that which it cannot give them. Their objectives ought to be modest but feasible.'[30]

There are two solutions to the problem of relations between Canadians and *Canadiens*. Brunet dismisses these with particular disdain. The first is separatism. In 1954 he wrote that English Canada would never tolerate separatism, and that it possessed the political, economic, and military means to enforce its will. Quebec separatists, he remarked, 'would have an interest in studying the history of the Confederacy.'[31] Equally chimerical for those who wish to preserve French Canada is the belief that Canada can become a bilingual and bicultural nation. 'For some years, the prophets of a new order have been inviting the French Canadians of Quebec to make Canada a bi-ethnic and bicultural country.'[32] 'Those who propose such a program forget – by simple ignorance, because they have the bad habit of mistaking their desires for reality, or with the intention of betraying the good faith of the minority – that Canada is an English country inside of which a French-Canadian province survives as a veritable economic and political colony of the Anglo-Canadian nation.' Indeed, those who advocate this utopian policy of biculturalism and bilingualism have really ceased to be French Canadians.[33] Above all, perhaps, French Canadians must be on their guard against politicians who prate about national unity; for, given the inevitable predominance of the majority, national unity can only mean the suppression of the minority. It is a slogan used by the majority to obtain from the minority something that it would not dare ask for in its own name.[34]

Since national unity is a trap for French Canadians, those who advocate it are in effect the enemies of French Canada. And since it is not only English Canadians but also some French Canadians who favour national unity, Brunet calls forth and subtly broadens the old concept of the *vendu*. Nearly the whole historical leadership of French Canada is condemned for collaboration with the Conqueror and the preservation of the Conqueror's myths. For example, he damns those French Canadians who have dared to suggest that the Conquest may have brought some benefits to French Canadians. 'The *Canadiens* are told', he wrote in 1959, 'that, thanks to the cleverness of their religious and political leaders and their own courage, they have finally successfully overcome all the bad consequences of a foreign domination. The French-Canadian ruling classes – whose accession to a position of pre-eminence has always depended on the willingness of either the British authorities or the English-Canadian leaders – are interested in upholding this historical interpretation.'[35] In short, the traditional leaders of French Canada were Quislings. But the *vendu* category is broadened even further to include those French-Canadian intellectuals, especially the 'social leftists', who find French-Canadian nationalism somewhat stifling and hence reject it or at least seriously criticize it. Finally, there are 'the businessmen, engineers, politicians who make their living with British Canada or need to make friends among English-speaking people. One can easily understand why they speak and act as they do.'[36] The fact of the matter seems to be that all those French Canadians, past and present, who have failed to accept Brunet's particular brand of nationalism have at best been stupid wishful thinkers, at worst traitors. This type of argument is a familiar one, but the familiarity only makes its logical inadequacies more obvious.

If all these activities are suspect, is anything left for French Canadians who 'have long since lost, as a nation, their right to self-determination'?[37] According to Brunet, there is only one possible salvation: vigilant defence of provincial autonomy. Once more the radical turns into the traditionalist, for no political strategy is more marked by the persistent usage of the past than autonomism. But for Brunet, Quebec is the nation-state of French Canada; the diaspora is to be forgotten, doomed to assimilation. Ottawa must be recognized and accepted as the national capital of English Canada, Quebec of French Canada.

For the French Canadians, the government at Ottawa can only be the central government of a federation uniting Quebec and English Canada. A close and harmonious collaboration can and should exist between the federal and the provincial authorities. However, the government charged with defending and promoting the common good of the French-Canadian nationality is the one of the province where the immense majority of the French Canadians live. That is why Quebec ought not to be considered or to consider itself simply as one of ten provinces. It has the right to claim a special status in the Canadian federation since it is the spokesman and defender of the minority.[38]

But provincial autonomy must be more than mere intransigent defence of the constitutional rights of the province. The powers of the province must be used and the old anti-statist illusions rejected.[39] Even the report of the Tremblay Commission, with its voluminous examination and defence of provincial autonomy, Brunet dismisses as 'the summation of traditional nationalism with all its illusions and all its contradictions'.[40] Moreover, he found little to praise in the Union Nationale régime: 'imitating the federal Liberals of the Lapointe-Cardin period, it knew how to exploit with ease the feeling of insecurity, the traditional ideals and the collectivity's instinct for solidarity.'[41] Still, the Union Nationale did defend provincial autonomy and therefore was never severely criticized by Brunet. But the main point is that the time had come for French Canadians to allow their provincial state to play the role they had denied it since the Conquest. A new policy of state intervention, a new 'socialisme royal' such as that practised under the Old Régime by Jean Talon, was necessary if French Canadians were to survive as a twentieth-century industrial and urban society.[42]

Brunet's belief that a form of survival could be ensured through positive autonomy is the one ray of optimism in an otherwise dark picture. His views, and those of the school for which he is the most articulate spokesman, have been given the title of 'pessimistic nationalism.' In some nationalist circles, particularly those still dominated by Canon Groulx's more optimistic and clerical teachings, *brunetisme* won as many enemies as friends. Here is one comment that reveals a good deal about the function of education in a nationalist community: 'In struggling against a style, M. Brunet ends by removing from us the reasons for living and struggling. His irresponsible exaggerations cause incalculable harm to certain young people, and risk killing, by excessive and badly advised criticism, all patriotic education.'[43]

But such criticism, fair as it was, failed to foresee that Brunet's views by their very pessimism could stimulate a reaction more potent than romantic optimism could ever hope to achieve. The criticisms missed the fundamental point that, above all, Brunet too was a nationalist. The historian himself described the function of his iconoclastic analysis: 'National history, gilt-edged and falsified by patriotic emotion, has no educational value. Students, when they have passed the age in which they believed in fairy tales, take a dislike to the study of a history that has no connection with reality and with the present. On becoming adults, the new generations notice that the lives that they are called to live do not correspond to the pastoral idyll that preceding generations have lived. They search in vain to explain to themselves this solution to the continuity between the idealized past and the severely realistic present.'[44] In the new realistic perspective, the past is brought into accurate focus with all its failures and weaknesses. Then it becomes clear that the present can only be reformed by rejecting the old illusions. The world of industrialization and urbanization must be accepted and rural myths forgotten; the spiritual messianism of the past must be replaced by the material needs of the present; the fear of the state must be eradicated, and this instrument of survival allowed to undertake the tasks that all modem societies give it. Thus the old nationalism is denounced to give place to the new.

While these implications of Brunet's history are obvious, there are others that are no less so. Though Brunet himself rejects separatism, his 'national doctrine' could easily, even logically, lead to it. First there is the postulation of two distinct, even opposing, nations. Then there is the theory that the lion necessarily takes the lion's share. What could be more reasonable than to conclude that the only way French Canada can guarantee its survival and live a 'normal' life is to end the political association in which the smaller nation is really nothing more than a 'colony' annexed to the larger nation? In short, the implication of pessimistic nationalism is that, given the Conquest, French Canada is doomed. And if the Conquest lies at the root of the society's problems, and the existing constitutional machinery of Canada rests on that Conquest, then Confederation must be undone and with it the Conquest. In short, whatever other conclusions are possible, there can be no question that separatism is one conclusion that may be drawn from the teachings of the school of Brunet. To the logical young mind, dissatisfied with a status quo so obviously unsatisfactory when judged by the Brunet criteria, separation is obviously preferable to the third clearly implied alternative: assimilation. It is not surprising that the two-nations theory underlies the separatist argument, for separatism is, after all, merely another attempt to undo the decision of 1759. [45]

Obviously the foundation of Brunet's view is found in Durham's 'two nations warring in the bosom of a single state.' The fact that Durham vastly overstated and oversimplified the events that led up to 1837 does not shake Brunet's faith in the theory. It would take a book to disprove the application of the theory, but at least a few questions can be raised now. If 1837 was a 'racial conflict,' how, first of all, can its narrow base be explained; and secondly, how are similar events in 'racially' homogeneous Upper Canada explained? Another example that Brunet chooses as an illustration of his Canadian-*Canadien* dichotomy is the debate over the Canadian contribution to the Boer War.[46] In this debate, he says, Laurier represented the Canadian viewpoint calling for participation, Bourassa the *canadien* viewpoint calling for abstention. If only history were that simple. In fact, Laurier's moderation on the South African question infuriated many English Canadians, as the 1900 election returns showed. As for Bourassa, it is true that his anti-Imperial sentiments found much sympathy in Quebec. It is also true, however, that the Quebec electorate showed no doubts whatever about Laurier in 1900. And, finally, a detail worth noting is that Bourassa himself based his hostility to participation in the Boer War on what he considered a Canadian attitude toward Imperial responsibilities, an attitude defined in the first instance by Sir John A. Macdonald. In nearly every instance, with the possible exception of the conscription crises of 1917 and 1942 (and even these need qualification), the Brunet thesis fails to explain all the facts. In the past, French and English Canadians, beginning with LaFontaine and Baldwin, have in practice rejected Durham's dichotomy.

But Durham's views, which infuriate most French Canadians, exercise a peculiar magnetism on Brunet, who once called the English lord 'the best historian of Canada.'[47] Brunet seems torn between two alternatives: on the one hand is the suspicion that Durham was accurate in his analysis of the causes of the 1837 affair and therefore right in his prescription of assimilation; on the other his nationalist commitment to *la survivance*. Brunet the social scientist attempts to use Durham's analysis without reaching the conclusions that are repugnant to Brunet the nationalist. But the fact that the tension between assimilation and survival remains unresolved in Brunet's own mind explains why his followers, unable to live with the unresolved tension, are forced to choose one of the alternatives – frequently separatism, frequently one of its variants. Had Brunet accepted Durham's analysis and solution, his apparent radicalism would be more convincing. Among many contemporary nationalists, there is a natural demand that radical analysis should produce radical conclusions.[48]

Conclusions more moderate in tone than separatism can also be drawn from Brunet's 'national doctrine'. One such conclusion – though it is really only a separatist variant – has been drawn by the Montreal branch of the Société Saint-Jean-Baptiste, of which Brunet is an officer. The society's submission to the Quebec Legislature's Committee on the Constitution is the distilled essence of *brunetisme*. It rings all the changes on Canadian and *Canadien*, majorities and minorities, conquerors and conquered. 'Will the French Canadians', the submission asks, 'form the last colonized people on earth?'[49]

To this question the old pessimistic Brunet, with his harsh deterministic theory of majorities and minorities, would surely have answered in the affirmative. But a change has taken place in Quebec. A new nationalism, which certainly owes something to the teachings of the Montreal historian, has flowered. Reform has begun, a reform that quite frankly rejects at least the illusions of ruralism and anti-statism, if not messianism. In short, the minority nation is proving that it can do something. Indeed, only the most blindly deterministic two-nations theorist would deny that the so-called minority nation is having a marked impact on the majority nation. These changes have not failed to influence the views of even a social scientist as convinced of his Olympian detachment as Michel Brunet. A note of optimism has appeared that is new, although it grows directly out of his appeal for 'positive autonomism'. The submission of the Société Saint-Jean-Baptiste states: 'Endowed with a self-confidence which they have up to now lacked, French Canadians of 1964, rejecting the fatalistic option of their fathers, seem decided to orient their history by themselves and for themselves.'[50]

The conclusion that the Société Saint-Jean-Baptiste of Montreal drew from its survey of Canadian history, guided by the principles of *brunetisme*, was that Canada needed an entirely new constitution. Two nations require two states that will be associated with one another in a federal structure in which each nation will be equally represented. This submission and its conclusions indicate the extent to which Brunet's theories have become orthodox nationalist assumptions, even in an organization as traditionalist as the Société Saint-Jean-Baptiste.

The widespread influence of *brunetisme* – that combination of iconoclasm and conservatism (or as Laurier said of Bourassa, that *Castor-rouge* mixture that is French-Canadian nationalism) – provides a key to an understanding of contemporary Quebec. And that key is found in the nature and limits of Brunet's debunking attitude towards the past. An insecure society rarely produces debunkers, for it fears most the enemy within. The historical fashions of the United States in the fifties, which down-graded debunking, provide an example. But a society in the process of profound changes, changes that defy the conventional wisdom, seems to produce vigorous criticism of the past. The United States in the thirties is an obvious example.[51]

Brunet's writings coincide with a period of great change in French Canada, a period during which nearly all traditional values are being questioned. Yet Brunet's commitment to debunking is very limited, for he never questions the system of nationalism but only its traditional justification. He is, then, a conservative debunker. An example of radical criticism, a writer who questions the system itself, is Pierre-Elliott Trudeau.[52] This explains an important division in contemporary Quebec. As long as traditionalist nationalism in the form of Maurice Duplessis's Union Nationale held power, all the critics stood together in opposition. But once the Duplessis régime was replaced by a reform administration, the former allies-in-opposition discovered that their ultimate objectives had always been different. For men like Trudeau, nationalism itself lies at the root of French Canada's problems. Therefore they find the new nationalism as deficient in principle, if not in practice, as the old. The other school, which might be called the René Lévesque school, really follows Brunet in rejecting only the traditionalist aspects of nationalism. For them, nationalism is valid if brought into conformity with the social and economic needs of modern society. The Lévesque-cum-Brunet school is currently the predominant one in Quebec, but the Trudeau anti-nationalist (or, more correctly, Actonian multi-nationalist) view is far from having been proven invalid.[53]

The explanation for the popularity of Brunet's austere 'national doctrine' is not far to seek. Despite Brunet's apparent radical iconoclasm, his basic approach to the history of his people is orthodox. History for him, as for previous nationalist historians, is a weapon to be wielded in the unceasing national struggle. Though Brunet is a professional historian, most of his published works are 'sermons for the unsatisfied.' His own research is largely limited to the period immediately following the Conquest, and even here his conclusions have been challenged. As he moves into less familiar areas, his ability to generalize dogmatically grows apace. Indeed, there is even reason to suspect that Professor Brunet aspires to write 'metahistory' in company with Arnold Toynbee, whom the French-Canadian historian has vigorously criticized.[54] But is not Brunet himself something of the 'prestidigitateur' for whom history is a bag of nationalist tricks? Like Toynbee, he is better at diagnosing the ills of society than at prescribing remedies, a fact that may raise doubts about both his diagnosis and the remedies proposed by his followers. 'The time has come for history, in French Canada, to give up the chair of rhetoric, according to the expression of Professor Trudel.'⁵⁵ One wonders if this sound advice can be accepted as long as nationalist objectives dominate the historian's approach.

[1965]

NOTES

1 Page Smith, *The Historian and History* (New York, 1964), page 5.
2 That A.R.M. Lower's *Colony to Nation* (Toronto, 1946) and D.G. Creighton's *Dominion of the North* (Toronto, 1945) are both expressions of Canadian nationalism is obvious. But the difference of viewpoint is almost equally obvious.
3 Abbé Casgrain, "F.-X. Garneau," *Oeuvres complètes* (Montreal, 1885), Vol. II, page 132.
4 Fernand Ouellet, "Nationalisme canadien-français et laïcisme au XIXe siècle," *Recherches sociographiques*, 1963, Vol. IV, pages 47–70.
5 Comparing Chapais and Groulx, Olivar Asselin wrote that "the English of Chapais were men we have never seen except in books; those of Groulx with their Jekyll and Hyde double personality are those that we have known since our childhood." (Cited in Mason Wade, *The French Canadians, 1760–1945*, Toronto, 1954, page 875.)
6 Any of Groulx's casual writings could be used to document this statement. On his near separatist phase see his essays in *Notre avenir politique* (Montreal, 1923). His later, unenthusiastic acceptance of Confederation may be seen in his essay in *Les Canadiens français et la Confédération canadienne* (Montreal, 1927).
7 André Laurendeau, "Sur une polémique entre Bourassa et Tardivel," *L'Action nationale*, Vol. XLIII, No. 2, February 1954, pages 248–59.
8 L. Groulx, "L'Histoire et la vie nationale," *Dix ans d'action française* (Montreal, 1926), page 267.
9 *Ibid.*, page 269.
10 *Ibid.*, page 262.
11 L. Groulx, "Si Dollard revenait ..." *Dix ans d'action française*, page 122.
12 For a brilliant analysis of the nationalism of the Groulx school, see Maurice Tremblay, 'Réflexions sur le nationalisme,' *Ecrits du Canada français*, Vol. V. 1959, pages 9–45.
13 Léon Dion, "Le Nationalisme pessimiste, sa source, sa signification, sa validité," *Cité libre*, 8th year, No. 20, November 1957, pages 4–11.
14 Michel Brunet, *Canadians et Canadiens*, page 45.
15 Michel Brunet, *La Présence anglaise et les Canadiens*, page 196.

16 *Le Magazine Maclean*, March 1961, page 57.

17 Brunet, *La Présence*, pages 113–66.

18 André Laurendeau, "A propos d'une longue illusion," *Le Devoir*, March 19, 1960.

19 Brunet, *La Présence*, page 145.

20 Here, as in many other places, Brunet is much less original in his views than appears on the surface. One writer, who like so many others was a victim of Brunet's criticism, expressed similar ideas on the necessity of state intervention fifty years before Brunet. (See Errol Bouchette, *L'Indépendance économique du Canada français*, third edition, Montreal, 1913.)

21 L. Laflèche, *Quelques considérations sur les rapports de la société civile avec la réligion et la famille* (Trois Rivières, 1866), page 73: "One will be convinced that the Conquest has not been a misfortune for us, but that it bas been the providential means which God used to save us as a people."

22 Brunet, La Présence, page 112. Here too another writer, often criticized by Brunet, expressed a somewhat similar view of the Conquest. See Edmond de Nevers, *L'Avenir du peuple canadien-français*, page 46. A rather different explanation for the dominance of those ideas in French-Canadian thought is presented in Maurice Tremblay, "Orientation de la pensée sociale," in Falardeau (ed.), *Essais sur le Québec contemporain*, pages 193–208, and in Pierre-Elliott Trudeau, *La Grève de l'amiante*, pages 3–90.

23 Brunet, *La Présence*, pages 229–30.

24 Jean Hamelin, *Economie et société de la Nouvelle France* (Quebec, 1961); Fernand Ouellet, "Michel Brunet et la problème de la Conquête," *Bulletin des recherches historiques*, Vol. 62, No. 2, 1956, pages 92–102.

25 Some further discussion may be found in F.-A. Angers. "Naissance de la pensée économique au Canada français." *Revue d'histoire de l'Amerique française*, Vol. XV, No. 2. September 1962, pages 204–29.

26 Brunet, *Canadians et Canadiens*, page 123.

27 *Ibid.*, page 146.

28 *Ibid.*, page 139.

29 *La Présence*, page 277.

30 *Ibid.*, page 292.

31 *Canadians et Canadiens*, page 172.

32 *Ibid.*, page 165.

33 *La Présence*, page 201.

34 *Canadians et Canadiens*, page 13.

35 Brunet, "The British Conquest: Canadian Social Scientists and the Fate of the Canadiens," *Canadian Historical Review*, Vol. XL, No. 2, June 1959, page 106.

36 Brunet, "Co-existence Canadian Style," *Queen's Quarterly*, Vol. LXIII, No. 3, Autumn 1956, page 427.

37 *La Présence*, page 263.

38 *Canadians et Canadiens*, page 30.

39 *Ibid.*, page 169.

40 *La Présence*, page 264.

41 *Ibid.*, page 266.

42 *Ibid.*, pages 142–6.

43 Jean Génest, "Qu'est-ce que le brunetisme?" *Le Devoir*, April 22, 1961.

44 *Canadians et Canadiens*, page 39.

45 See, for example, two books by Raymond Barbeau, *J'ai choisi l'indépendance* (Montreal, 1961), and *Québec, est-il une colonie?* (Montreal, 1962).

46 *Ibid.*, page 138.

47 *Queen' s Quarterly*, Vol. LXIII, No. 3, Autumn 1956, page 430.

48 For an article by a writer to whom Brunet attributes many of his ideas and who makes the separatist implications of pessimistic nationalism clear, see Maurice Séguin. "Genèse et historique de l'idée séparatiste au Canada français," *Laurentie*, No. 119, June 1962, pages 940–96.

49 *Le Fédéralisme, l'acte de l'Amérique du nord britannique et les Canadiens français*, page 93.

50 *Ibid.*, page 96.

51 John Higham, "The Cult of American Consensus: Homogenizing Our History," *Commentary*, Vol. XXVII, 1959, pages 93–101.

52 Pierre-Elliott Trudeau, *La Grève de l'amiante*.

53 Pierre-Elliott Trudeau, "La Nouvelle Trahison des clercs," *Cité libre*, Vol. XIII, No. 46, April 1962, pages 3–16; Albert Breton, "The Economies of Nationalism," *Journal of Political Economy*, Vol. LXXII, No. 4, August 1964, pages 376–86.

54 *Canadians et Canadiens*, page 79.

55 *Ibid.*, page 44.

EIGHT

In the Bourassa Tradition:
André Laurendeau

One argument in favour of bilingualism in Canada is that English Canadians who do not at least read French miss a great deal of vigorous writing in all fields – literature, politics, sociology, and religion. Moreover, they miss the opportunity of reading the most intellectual newspaper in Canada, *Le Devoir*. No English Canadian who has read this serious-minded Montreal daily at any time since its foundation in 1910 by Henri Bourassa can feel anything but regret that we have nothing to compare with it in English Canada. And the most impressive feature of the newspaper has always been its editorial page. It is, of course, a *nationaliste* newspaper and every editorial writer from Bourassa and Omer Héroux, through Georges Pelletier, to André Laurendeau at the present time, has been deeply committed to the cause of *la survivance*. But *Le Devoir* has always been concerned with more than just the negative defence of the rights of *la nation canadienne-française* (though this is the side that English Canadians have usually noticed). Equally important has been its role as the constant critic of life in Quebec. It has fought for higher educational standards, for the purity of the French language, for the rights of trade unions, for social security, and, perhaps above all (because it precedes all these), public morality. For example, in the late fifties it fought Premier Duplessis so vigorously that 'Le Chef' excluded the parliamentary correspondent of *Le Devoir* from his press conferences. The correspondent, M. Pierre Laporte, is today [1965] a leading member of the Lesage government.

Le Devoir has stood for the kinds of things that make a newspaper great and that give it what J.W. Dafoe once called 'personality'. Probably the most important reason for *Le Devoir*'s consistently high quality has been the series of men who have guided it through fifty years' fighting. Henri Bourassa, one of the most impressively intellectual figures in our history, set the standard. Bourassa wanted a journal that would break with the traditional servile party press in Quebec, a paper whose 'duty' would be to defend the rights of French Canadians throughout Canada, the autonomy of Quebec within the federal system, and the autonomy of Canada within the British Empire. Independence from party, but commitment to the religious, political, and cultural interests of French Canada, were Bourassa's watchwords. Today the interpretation and application of those watchwords is the responsibility of a man who, thanks largely to the CBC, is not unknown in English Canada. It is not so many years since the radio program 'Weekend Review' regularly brought to English Canada the gentle accent, penetrating analysis, and unique style of André Laurendeau.

Probably there were few of M. Laurendeau's listeners who were aware of his varied and controversial background. Indeed there would certainly have been some English Canadians who would have abruptly turned off the radio and hoisted the Union Jack had they realized that at various times since 1935 M. Laurendeau had been a separatist, a neutralist, an editor of *L'Action nationale*, a leader of La Ligue pour la Défense du Canada which campaigned against conscription during the Second World War, a founder of the Bloc Populaire, and a one-time Bloc member of the Quebec legislature. In 1944 Blair Fraser told his readers, 'Laurendeau is a man to watch in Quebec politics. A fanatic nationalist, a rabble-rousing speaker, yet a cool, calculating mind ... '[1] In all of his varied activities, M. Laurendeau has attempted to give expression to views that are those of a 'nationalist' and a 'socially conscious Christian'.

But to describe M. Laurendeau as a nationalist is to say very little. Nearly every French Canadian is a nationalist if that amorphous term is taken to mean a belief in French Canada's right to survive as a cultural group. Laurier, Bourassa, Canon Groulx, Duplessis, and Marcel Chaput, to name only a few, are all people who could be fitted into a definition of nationalism. But what these people have in common is probably less significant than their differences. M. Laurendeau, although he shares some qualities with each of them, has gradually evolved his own position. That position contains far more of Henri Bourassa and Canon Groulx than of Laurier or Marcel Chaput.

M. Laurendeau was born into a family that was steeped in the Bourassa tradition. Henri Bourassa's thinking developed in the years between the Boer War and the First World War when the power of the British Empire still seemed to be at its height. He fought hard to convince Canadians that their future lay neither in continuing as a colony with no voice in the determination of Canadian foreign policy, nor in closer integration into an Empire that would speak with a common, co-operative voice in foreign affairs. Bourassa believed that Canada should become a sovereign nation in her own right, within the British family of nations, but with full control over every aspect of her own affairs. He also believed that Canada should be a particular kind of nation formed on the basis of an equal partnership between French and English. One of his greatest fears, a fear shared by Sir Wilfrid Laurier, was that Canadian involvement in Imperial affairs would divide French and English Canadians along cultural lines. In 1902 he set forth his mature thoughts about Canada when he remarked:

A mutual regard for racial sympathies on both sides, and a proper discharge of our exclusive duty to this land of ours, such is the only ground upon which it is possible for us to meet so as to work out our national problems. There are here neither masters nor valets; there are neither conquerors nor conquered ones; there are two partners whose partnership was entered into upon fair and well-defined lines. We do not ask that our English-speaking fellow countrymen should help us to draw closer to France; but, on the other hand, they have no right to take advantage of their overwhelming majority to infringe on the treaty of alliance, and induce us to assume, however freely and spontaneously, additional burdens in defence of Great Britain.[2]

As pressure for Canadian involvement in Imperial and world affairs increased, and as the rights of the French-speaking minorities outside Quebec were gradually whittled away, Bourassa's dream of a bicultural nation seemed to grow less and less attainable. Though Bourassa lived to see his country involved in the Second World War, the peak of his political career was passed by the 1920s.

To many young French Canadians growing up in the late twenties and early thirties, Bourassa was a figure to be respected, but also one who was viewed as something of an exhausted volcano. In his brilliant essay 'Le Nationalisme de Bourassa', M. Laurendeau described his own youthful doubts about the old nationalist chief who had once seemed a true tribune of his people, but who was now either silent, or, worse, openly condemning extreme nationalism.[3] In these same years a new intellectual leader had made his appearance on the Quebec scene, and he was giving nationalism a new, more radical turn. He was Abbé Lionel Groulx, a professor of history. Unlike many French-Canadian historians, Groulx was more interested in what had happened to French Canadians after the British Conquest than he was in painting portraits of the Golden Age of New France, though he did that too. Moreover, he used history to illustrate the unique, unchangeable qualities of French Canadians, a uniqueness he described by the word 'race'. His early books all emphasized the view implied in titles like *L'Appel de la race* and *La Naissance d'une race*. One is inevitably unfair to Abbé Groulx in summarizing his ideas, but his general conception was one that emphasized the rather mystical separateness of French Canadians; his nationalism was characterized by a strongly religious and messianic flavour. Where Bourassa had spoken of a broad Canadianism based on cultural duality, Groulx insisted on French Canadianism, and warned against siren songs of Canadianism. In the early twenties he wrote:

The future and Providence are going to work for us. Joseph de Maistre wrote on the morrow of the French Revolution that God had made such a terrible clean sweep only to lay bare the basis for the future. Let us believe with firm faith that after the vast disorder of the Great War there will be room for marvellous constructions. We make only this prayer to our leaders and to all the chiefs of our race; know how to foresee and to act. Grant that they may no more abandon the development of our life to improvisation and to incoherent action; that for the vanity of a too largely Canadian patriotism they may not sacrifice us to the dream of an impossible unity; that they may know how to reserve the future; that before concluding and deciding our destinies they may take account of the premises of our history; and God will not let perish that which he has conserved by so many miracles.[4]

Abbé Groulx's national doctrine was strongly separatist in its implications. In the twenties, like many other Canadians, he believed that Confederation was falling apart and he hoped to see the establishment of a French and Catholic state on the banks of the St. Lawrence. By the thirties, this dream had slipped into the background. And once the depression came the Abbé's social views began to attract some support. Essentially these views took the form of the traditional conservative nationalist's glorification of the agrarian way of life. But during the depression his remarks took on an anti-capitalist tenor that struck a sympathetic note for the new generation of young, urban intellectuals who all around them witnessed economic stagnation and social dislocation. Groulx's views, especially on economic questions, appealed to young nationalists who saw that the economic transformation of Quebec was taking place under the control of English-Canadian, British, and American capitalists. Here was a transformation that was virtually a new conquest. In 1936 Abbé Groulx declared that because of foreign domination of the Quebec economy, 'with our own property, with our own work, with our own savings we build our economic servitude'.

It was Groulx's teachings that inspired the Jeune-Canada movement. And André Laurendeau, at twenty-four, expressed the sentiments of the movement in a lyrical separatist tract entitled *Notre nationalisme* which he published in October 1935. 'Laurentie reigns over me,' he

declared, 'not as a tyrant of which I would be a slave! Rather as an
ideal freely chosen and passionately served!' Young Laurendeau's ded-
ication of the pamphlet was a shrewd self-analysis of the influence and
weight that he gave to his intellectual seniors: 'To Henri Bourassa and
Abbé Groulx, the one a precursor, the other the craftsman of the doctrine from which these pages proceed.'

The influence of the 'craftsman' Abbé Groulx was deeply imprinted
on Laurendeau when he left to continue his studies in France in 1935.
At the Sorbonne he discovered a new kind of Christian and humani-
tarian influence in the teachings of Jacques Maritain, Nicholas Berdia-
eff, and Emmanuel Mounier. In addition, the writings of Malraux,
Bernanos, and Dostoievski were opened up to him. And in the Europe
of the mid thirties no one as intelligent and sensitive as André Laurendeau could miss observing the dangers of racism in its Nazi and Fascist
forms. In his book *La Crise de la conscription* – 1942, published in
1962,[5] M. Laurendeau wrote of these days in France: 'When the war
in Spain broke out my sympathies did not go to Franco ... at the same
time I felt myself more and more opposed to the Fascist régime, especially Naziism; for I discovered the demands and the greatness of a
democracy purged of capitalist poison.' Clearly the conservative social
teachings of Abbé Groulx were giving way under the impact of the
French Catholic left. In a letter from Paris to *L'Action nationale* in January 1937 he remarked that 'God is not a bourgeois policeman
charged with defending the great properties of nobles and of certain
religious communities, and the shameful expropriation of the poor by
the large capitalists ... '

It was also in France that M. Laurendeau began to learn of the
Canada that existed beyond the borders of the province of Quebec. He
learned from the famous French Protestant sociologist and historian
André Siegfried, at the Collège de France. Siegfried had long been a student of Canada and his book *The Race Question in Canada*, published
in 1907, was one of the most penetrating analyses of Canadian society
ever written. Strangely, it was this Frenchman who set Laurendeau to
thinking about the people with whom he lived without knowing in
Canada. Clearly, when he returned to Montreal his mind had been
opened to a wider Canada and a wider world.

The Canada he returned to in 1937, and especially the Quebec, was
increasingly uneasy about the way of the world. War in Europe seemed
inevitable, and for French Canadians the memory of 1917 and conscription was never far below the surface. It was in this atmosphere
that the twenty-seven-year-old student turned to journalism, assuming
the editorship of the province's most influential nationalist magazine,
L'Action nationale. Once again his attention was turned to *la sur-*

vivance. But Europe had made its mark and Laurendeau wanted it clearly understood that racism had no place in the nationalist movement. Intellectual stimulus still came from the same source as before, as his pamphlet *L'Abbé Lionel Groulx* in the series 'Nos maîtres de l'heure', published in January 1939, made clear. Yet he had determined on returning from France to pursue the interests opened up by Siegfried. He enrolled at McGill in an effort to make contact with English Canadians of his own age. Soon he discovered a left-wing group that seemed to share his anti-imperialism, and by the spring of 1939 he had formed a close association with these students. At this point, he wrote later, 'we dared even to speak of a Canadian nation'. But the university vacation arrived and at the end of the long summer of 1939 came the outbreak of war. Now it became apparent that the assumptions of the French- and English-Canadian student friends had been radically different. The English Canadians, though often reluctantly, chose to support the decision that took Canada into the war. Laurendeau did not. He recalled the repeated promises of the Liberals in Quebec that Canada would not again be involved in a British war. And this was just what the 1939 war seemed to be. Like Bourassa in his opposition to Canadian participation in the Boer War, Laurendeau expressed the deep-felt frustration of finding himself at odds with the majority's commitment to what he was sure was a war that did not directly involve Canadian interests. Surely this was proof of Canada's continuing colonialism. 'In theory,' he recalled later, 'we have been free since the Statute of Westminster; in practice, through the will of the Anglo-Canadians, we cease to be free on important occasions.'

Like so many other French Canadians brought up in the nationalist tradition, Laurendeau believed that the first line of defence for French Canadians was in Quebec. Above all, the province's autonomy must be guarded against the inevitable centralizing temptations that the war effort would present to Ottawa. In a pamphlet published shortly after the outbreak of the war and entitled *Alerte aux Canadiens-français*, he called his compatriots to arms in the defence of their province's autonomy. 'Here we will defend provincial autonomy, the Confederation placed in peril by the centralizing faction, and the existence of French Canada.'

In his little semi-autobiographical study of the war years, *La Crise de la conscription*, M. Laurendeau gives a full and frank account of his efforts to prevent the central government from using the power that above all reminds the French Canadian of his minority status – the power of military conscription for overseas service. Carefully he watched the King government, with its strong Quebec base, retreat from one position after another as it moved slowly but surely towards conscription: from pre-war promises of non-participation to limited participation, from limited participation to full-scale mobilization for overseas service, from conscription for home service to the point in 1942 when Prime Minister King decided to ask the country to release his government from its pledge never to adopt a policy of conscription for overseas service. What annoyed French-Canadian nationalists most about the 1942 plebiscite proposal was that they believed that a bargain or contract had been made in 1939 in Ernest Lapointe's famous pledge to oppose conscription, that the pledge had been renewed in the Quebec provincial election of 1939 which saw Maurice Duplessis defeated, and that for a third time in the federal election of 1940 the promise had been made, whereby French Canadians agreed to support the war on the understanding that participation by individuals would remain voluntary. But in 1942 the whole of Canada, and not just French Canada to whom the pledge had been made, was asked to release the government from its contract. M. Laurendeau and his friends determined to fight against the revocation of the no-conscription pledge.

It is the fight for a negative answer on the plebiscite that M. Laurendeau describes in *La Crise de la conscription*. It is not objective history, but rather an honest attempt to recall the emotions and opinions of the war years. Yet despite the emotion and depth of the crisis, the book is without malevolence or hatred. (How many English Canadians who fought for an affirmative answer in 1942 could say the same of their recollections?) But the central point of the book cannot be missed. M. Laurendeau writes:

During the war many Quebec French Canadians felt that they were living in an occupied country. The English occupied it, it was they who dictated its conduct and prevented the national will from expressing itself effectively; our politicians were collaborators. It was, in comparison to Hitler's Europe, a benign occupation; thanks to King's moderation, the weight was supportable. We risked only our liberties; yet the menace was only occasionally fulfilled. But its existence was enough to poison life.

Despite this feeling of occupation, it is worth emphasizing, a group that formed itself into an organization to fight the plebiscite adopted the title of 'The League for the Defence of Canada' (not French Canada). Though M. Laurendeau does not make much of this point in his book, a re-reading of the league's manifesto would no doubt have reminded him of the strength of the group's belief that their cause reached out beyond the French-Canadian community. The final paragraph of that appeal read:

It is thus not as a province nor as an ethnic group that we take our position. If we refuse to release the government from its engagements of 1939 and 1940, we do it as citizens of Canada, placing above everything the interests of Canada. There exists in this country, we believe, a majority of Canadians for which Canada is the fatherland, and for whom the slogan 'Canada d'abord' or 'Canada first' has never been a simple electoral cry, but the expression of a profound sentiment and of a supreme spiritual conviction. We make our appeal to all those people. We ask them to put their country above the spirit of race or of partisan considerations. Do they wish to take an action that will stop the movement towards the abyss, and which will forcefully attest a majority voice from one ocean to another? To Mr. King's plebiscite, with all the calmness and force of free men, they will reply with a resounding no.

God save our country! Long live Canada![6]

But La Ligue pour la Défense du Canada found little support among English-speaking Canadians, most of whom were convinced that the defeat of Hitler and his allies was the prime interest of Canada. Nevertheless, M. Laurendeau and his friends carried on a vigorous battle despite such obstacles as the refusal of the CBC (on grounds of neutrality) to allow the forces favouring a negative answer to the plebiscite to use the publicly-owned network. When the vote was counted, seventy-one per cent of the Quebec vote was negative, and if the English-Canadian voters in Quebec are subtracted from the provincial total, the French-Canadian 'non' had ninety per cent approval.

Quebec was isolated once more. M. Laurendeau and his friends turned their temporary organization into something more permanent and founded a new nationalist party, the Bloc Populaire. For these men, the old parties were completely discredited and none of the 'new parties', the CCF, the Social Credit, or even the Union Nationale whose leader had betrayed his early reformist allies, was acceptable. M. Laurendeau became secretary of the Bloc, and sat briefly in the Quebec legislature. But the party never achieved any widespread appeal, and soon it found itself divided between its more traditionalist, conservative nationalist supporters and a more radical, almost socialist wing. The latter was M. Laurendeau's wing. Soon M. Duplessis provided a home for the conservative elements, while M. St. Laurent and prosperity removed many French-Canadian grievances and healed old wounds. M. Laurendeau, never happy in politics, returned to journalism. It was, of course, nationalist journalism, with *L'Action nationale* and *Le Devoir*.

But his nationalism was never narrow or fanatical. It was constantly being subjected to self-criticism. Nor, even after the experience of the war years, was he ever seriously tempted to return to his youthful separatist fantasies. Indeed, as he began to travel throughout Canada to talk to English Canadians on CBC radio, and, perhaps most important, as he began to look once more to the outside world with its changing balance of power and its threatening cold war, his vision of Canada broadened again. In a series of articles written for *L'Action nationale* in 1952 and entitled 'Y a-t-il une crise du nationalisme?' he perceptively explored this changed world and Canada's place in it. He found that while the power of both Britain and France had declined, the United States had grown to the status of a super-power. Like so many Canadian nationalists, French and English, he realized that the old battles for Canadian autonomy offered little guidance for a future in which the United States, not Britain, was the threat to Canadian survival. Like all French-Canadian nationalists of the Bourassa school, M. Laurendeau was deeply aware that the power of the United States represented a greater potential threat to French Canadians divided from the rest of Canada than to French Canadians allied to the rest of Canada. French Canadians, while defending their culture and the autonomy of Quebec, would find more security in attempting to forge a new alliance with English Canada than in turning their backs blindly to the outside world.

Throughout the fifties M. Laurendeau was a stout defender of his province's autonomy against the growing power of an Ottawa spurred on by a confident new Canadianism. He was doubtless a little embarrassed in defending the autonomy of the province when he had so little sympathy with the policies of the apparently invincible ruling party, the Union Nationale. Still, by the end of the fifties the province began to develop a new spirit and new energy. The death of Maurice Duplessis in 1959 marked the end of the ice-age in Quebec politics. The very fact that Duplessis's successor, Paul Sauvé, was a reformer indicated that the old order had passed. But neither the brief Sauvé administration nor its successor, the Lesage Liberal régime, has been entirely able to define clearly the shape of the future. But one thing is clear: many of the reforms in public life, in education, and in economic development found echoes in the columns of *Le Devoir* under M. Laurendeau's guidance.

With the birth of reform in the new Quebec has come much turbulence and discontent, which, as always, expresses itself in the language of nationalism. Once more a separatist movement has been born, stronger and more effectively organized than at any lime since 1837 and, on the fringes, talking the same language of totalitarianism and violence that has characterized young nationalist movements in countries suffering the worst excesses of European imperialism. The battle of the sixties, then, is not merely the old one of *la survivance* fought with new weapons, but also a dispute about the future shape of Canada. The main scene of the struggle is in Quebec itself, for, in M. Laurendeau's view, 'at Quebec one does what one wishes; at Ottawa one does what one can.' The French Canadians are a majority in Quebec and there they can decide and implement the changes that are necessary in their society. But they are an important minority in all Canada and they must do what they can to make that position more secure. M. Laurendeau is not a separatist; indeed, he presents the young separatist with the most effective counter-arguments. He is not a separatist because he is a realist. More important, he has grown more and more to appreciate the values of his original mentor, Henri Bourassa. In 1904 Bourassa had a public exchange with J. P. Tardivel, whose journal *La Vérité*, devoted exclusively to the development of French-Canadian nationalism, criticized Bourassa for his 'Canadianism'. Bourassa' s reply was unequivocal:

The fatherland, for us, is the whole of Canada, that is to say, a federation of distinct races and autonomous provinces. The nation that we wish to see developed is the Canadian nation, composed of French Canadians and English Canadians, that is to say, two elements separated by language and religion, and by the legal arrangements necessary for the conservation of their respective traditions, but united in an attachment of brotherhood, in a common attachment to a common fatherland.[7]

Essentially this is M. Laurendeau's position. French and English Canadians must stand together if their common 'fatherland' is to have a future. But he hopes that they will stand together in the Bourassa tradition of mutual respect and equality of rights for French- and English-speaking Canadians from coast to coast. That is why he so frequently called for a positive response from English Canada to the new currents that are running through Quebec society. That is why he advocated the appointment of a royal commission to examine the existing relationships between French and English Canadians. Now that he is co-chairman of that commission the same qualities of understanding and courage, of intellectual clarity and humane urbanity that have characterized his life will ensure an investigation and a report of the most thorough and searching kind.

The *Preliminary Report of the Royal Commission on Bilingualism and Biculturalism* contains many sections that bear the clear Laurendeau imprint. None sums up better the intellectual honesty that lies at the heart of the Bourassa tradition than these lines from the document's preamble: '... the feeling of the Commission is that at this point the danger of a clear and frank statement is less than the danger of silence; this type of disease cannot be cured by keeping it hidden indefinitely from the patient.'[8]

At the end of his essay on Bourassa, M. Laurendeau recalls a remark made to him by an English Canadian: 'The point about Bourassa is that he does not belong to French Canada alone.' It is time that the same remark was made about André Laurendeau. For the editor-in-chief of *Le Devoir* there is no distinction, except Bourassa's distinction, between *Canadien* and Canadian.

[1965]

NOTES

1 Blair Fraser, 'This Is Raymond,' *Maclean's Magazine*, January 1, 1944, page 31.

2 Henri Bourassa, *Great Britain and Canada* (Montreal, 1902), page 45.

3 André Laurendeau, 'Le Nationalisme de Bourassa,' in *La Pensée de Henri Bourassa* (Montreal, 1954).

4 Olivar Asselin, *L'Oeuvre de l'abbé Groulx* (Montreal, 1923), page 90.

5 Les Editions du Jour, Montreal, 1962.

6 'Manifeste au peuple du Canada,' *L'Action nationale*, Vol. XIX, No. 1, January 1942, pages 48–50.

7 André Laurendeau, 'Sur une polémique entre Bourassa et Tardivel,' *L'Action nationale*, Vol. XLIII, No. 2, February 1954, pages 248–59.

8 *A Preliminary Report of the Royal Commission on Bilingualism and Biculturalism* (Ottawa, 1965), page 13.

NINE

The B and B Commission and Canada's "*Greatest Crisis*"/Crise Majeure

It will be for Canadians to decide, mainly through their political parties and their governments, whether to accept or reject the principle of equality. Our task is, first of all, to determine the measure of equality now existing; but it is above all to propose a set of measures which would make this equality possible.

– *Report of the Royal Commission on Bilingualism and Biculturalism,*
vol.1, xxxix

On 20 January 1962 the Montreal nationalist daily *Le Devoir* published an editorial entitled "Pour une Enquête sur le Bilinguisme." Signed by André Laurendeau it set out three specific goals: to discover what Canadians thought about bilingualism, to examine bilingual practices in other countries, and to investigate bilingualism in the federal public service. Such an investigation would establish principles for the formulation of a bilingualism policy for Canada. The time had arrived to replace anecdotal assertions by solid research in order that a rational discussion could be held. "A l'heure actuelle, ce champ est abandonné aux séparatistes: les autres se contentent de dire qu'il y aurait lieu de réformer la Confédération; mais personne ne dit comment et jusqu'où. Il serait temps que prennent action ceux qui croient, á certaines conditions fondamentales, en l'avenir du Canada.[1]" This editorial summarized concerns that had been expressed by *Le Devoir* and many French Canadians at least since the founding of the newspaper by Henri Bourassa in 1910.

The context of this modest proposal was the increasingly aggressive tone of the new Quebec nationalism that both drove "la révolution tranquille" and fed off it, and an apparent indifference in the rest of the country – Laurendeau would have called it "English Canada" – to the grievances of French Canadians. A royal commission, Laurendeau hoped, would provide a forum for a productive dialogue. As it happened – though one must wonder if it was a mere coincidence – Laurendeau's proposal fell on sympathetic ears in a federal Liberal Party scrambling to discover a policy that would appeal to Quebec voters and undermine the *créditistes* without committing Lester Pearson's party to anything that would alienate voters in the rest of Canada. Concrete policy decisions could thus be postponed.[2] That, in somewhat more abstract phrases, could stand as a definition of the political purposes of royal commissions – something that is not necessarily to be deplored.

Once the Liberals were returned to power as a minority government in 1963, Laurendeau demonstrated the courage of his convictions by accepting the co-chairmanship, along with Carleton University president Davidson Dunton, of a royal commission with a broad mandate to examine and report on the state of Canadian "bilingualism and biculturalism" and the status of other ethnic communities. Canada was described as an "equal partnership" between "deux peuples fondateurs" ("founding races" in the unfortunate English version), and eight commissioners – four francophones, four anglophones, and two allophones – were appointed. Since Laurendeau insisted that such a commission had first to establish the "facts" about B and B, he was promised a large research budget. How the rather ambiguous mandate of the commission was formulated, and how the commissioners were chosen, remains unclear though I would suggest, in passing, that neither was entirely satisfactory.[3]

The commission at once became known as the B and B Commission – or the bye, bye commission, as Laurendeau's wife was said to have christened it. It set as its first task a series of cross-country public assemblies: Laurendeau and the other commissioners wanted to know what Canadians thought. He and his fellow commissioners got an earful. In Quebec the meetings were often dominated by youthful separatists, while elsewhere anti-French-Canadian voices – in several languages – were constantly heard. *Un dialogue des sourds* – a dialogue of the deaf.

We know from Laurendeau's revealing *Journal* – on which much of my commentary is based – that the commissioners were often surprised, shocked, and depressed – especially, perhaps, co-chair Laurendeau. Outside of Quebec, they found what he concluded was a combination of ignorance and hostility in discussions of French Canadians, the French language, and Quebec. Laurendeau feared that nationalism in Quebec would continue to intensify, threatening both the commission and the country. In 1965 the commission issued a *Preliminary Report* which declared that Canada, "without being fully conscious of the fact, is passing through the greatest crisis [*crise majeure*] in its history."[4] While most French Canadians probably agreed with the assessment, most other Canadians reacted negatively or at least sceptically to what they saw as over-dramatization. Where was the evidence of "crisis" and, if there was one, why were there no suggested cures? To a generally sympathetic historian who, in his comments on CBC Radio had recalled the earlier Riel and conscription crises, Laurendeau wrote this explanation (while admitting that final judgment should be left to future historians): "Ce qui me frappe, en effet, c'est qu'en 1942, alors qu'il était facile de réunir des foules grondantes et tumulteuses dans le Québec, et que la violence verbale se donnait libre cours, je ne me souviens pas qu'un seul groupe vraiment important soit allé jusqu'à mettre en cause les fondements mêmes de notre pays. Quant á l'époque Riel, Canadiens français et Canadiens anglais se seraient dans [sic] doute plus volontiers sautés à la gorge les uns les autres qu'ils ne le feraient aujourd'hui: mais il s'agissait de deux communautés dans l'ensemble rurales, où par consequent les relations entre les citoyens des deux groupes étaient réduites au minimum." Since these conditions were now radically different – some important Quebecers advocated separatism and contact between French and English took place in an urban-industrial society – "le mot 'majeure' prétend qualifier le type de crise que nous traversons plus encore peut-etre que son intensité."[5]

Though that explanation is convincing as far as it goes, it did not really address the heart of the matter. The focus of the crisis of the 1960s was in Quebec itself, where a profound cultural and social transformation was under way – the noisy Quiet Revolution. And it is now obvious that the B and B Commission had little if any capacity to influence that transformation, which related to education, economic development, demography, religious belief, social mores – in short, modernization and secularization.[6] Though the commission did important socio-economic research (especially the study of income distribution by André Raynauld), it concentrated as a necessary consequence of its federal origin, its mandate, and its membership – on linguistic and, uneasily, constitutional issues.

In the late summer of 1965 – 18 August, to be precise – a somewhat depressed Laurendeau sat down to make a record of his own evolution since the beginning of the commission's work. It is interesting not only as a reflection of this complex man's thinking, but because it previewed many of the conclusions of the first volume of the *Final Report* which appeared more than two years later. He had now decided that the heart of the problem was "les rapports de force" between "les deux groupes" – his view that Canada was composed of only "two groups" remained unrevised even though the commission sometimes realized that the "other ethnic groups" complicated the equation.[7] He expressed his guiding belief in liberal, Actonian terms: "La civilisation commence quand le plus fort s'empêche volontairement d'abuser de sa force; donc quand la majorité reconnait des 'droits' aux minorities."[8] But he admitted that his view of what needed to be done had shifted from an emphasis on French-English language issues to a focus on Quebec's status as a province. He wrote that "le statut particulier du Québec est une exigence première: comment parvenir à intégrer, sans l'étouffer, le nouveau Québec qui se manifeste depuis 1959?" Then he added revealingly: "le 'statut particulier' est, jusqu'ici demeuré une idée ou un slogan."[9] And so it was destined to remain. The "Blue Pages" of the first volume *Final Report* – perhaps the most important pages in the entire *Report* – repeated almost verbatim Laurendeau's earlier private reflection: "How can we integrate the new Quebec into present-day Canada, without curbing Quebec's forward drive and, at the same time, without risking the breaking up of the country?"[10] No formula was offered.

In committing himself to an undefined "statut particulier," Laurendeau, like other so-called soft nationalists in Quebec, hoped that his commission would offer a third option – and indeed the "Blue Pages" pointed in that direction. Otherwise there remained two unacceptable positions represented by his two friends: René Lévesque, who as early as April 1964 had, Laurendeau suspected, "les tripes séparatistes" (separatism in his guts),[11] and Pierre Trudeau, whose anti-nationalist federalism Laurendeau rejected as rigid, abstract, and out of touch. (He accurately judged Trudeau's entry into federal politics in 1965 as seeking "une position de force de laquelle il pourra contre-attaquer un René Lévesque.")[12]

When André Laurendeau died suddenly in the spring of 1968, the concept of "special status" died with him largely because without him – and probably even with him – the commissioners were deeply divided over their responsibility in the area of constitutional reform, F.R. Scott arguing against moving into this field and Paul Lacoste insisting that Laurendeau's vision would be betrayed without radical constitutional proposals. "We can't only not agree," Royce Frith reportedly said, "but we can't agree to say we can't agree."[13] In hindsight I think we can say that Laurendeau's death – any reader of his often agonized *Journal* must conclude that the Royal Commission contributed to that premature departure – left the field open to the necessary political combat between Trudeau and Lévesque that had been emerging since the beginning of the decade.[14]

So what was the contribution of the Laurendeau-Dunton commission to the resolution of "the crisis" that it identified? It certainly fulfilled Laurendeau's three goals as set out in *Le Devoir*: the people's views were canvassed, bilingualism elsewhere was studied, bilingualism in the federal public service was assessed – and more. The work of the commission laid the foundations for the enactment of the Official Languages Act in 1969, and its implementation. Moreover, it nudged some provinces to improve French-language education and other services. It drew documented attention to the socio-economic dimension of cultural relations and even made a small gesture in the direction of multiculturalism.[15]

In addition, I think that the commission made one largely ignored major contribution: its existence and unhurried proceedings provided time for the confused debate about the future of Canada and of Quebec to crystallize and for clear-minded proponents of the two workable options to emerge. In 1968 Pierre Trudeau had his *position de force* and René Lévesque had begun to build one for himself. The real debate was about to begin. In the settlement of fundamental, and therefore divisive, issues in complex democracies, delay is often better medicine than haste.

In 1962 André Laurendeau concluded an editorial with one of his most memorable sentences. "Paris valait bien une messe," he wrote, "le Canada vaut peut-etre une enquête." In 1968 I remarked that the work of the B and B Commission demonstrated that "Canada is worth a Royal Commission but it may still need a mass."[15] That turned out to be the longest Mass on record and even now it may be ready to resume after a short adjournment.

[2003]

NOTES

1 André Laurendeau, "Pour une enquête sur le bilingualisme," *Le Devoir*, 20 Jan. 1962.

2 John English, *The Worldly Years: The Life of Lester Pearson 1949–72*, 2 (Toronto: Vintage 1993), 277–8.

3 See André Laurendeau, *Journal tenu pendant la Commission royale d'enquête sur le bilingualisme et le biculturalisme* (Montreal: 1990), 188–299, for his account of the commission's origins and mandate. See also Sandra Djwa, *The Politics of Imagination: A Life of F.R. Scott* (Toronto: McClelland and Stewart 1987), 384–402, which provides the fullest account of the commission's work. Denis Monière's *André Laurendeau et le destin d'un pueple* (Montreal: Québec/Amérique 1983), 289–346, is also useful though tendentious.

4 *A Preliminary Report of the Royal Commission on Bilingualism and Biculturalism* (Ottawa: Queen's Printer 1965), 13.

5 York University Archives, Cook Fonds, André Laurendeau to Ramsay Cook, 9 March 1965.

6 See E. Martin Meunier and Jean-Phillippe Warren, *Sortir de la 'Grande noirceur'* (Sillery: Septentrion 2002), which provides evidence for my conclusion – which is not necessarily theirs.

7 The mandate spoke of "two founding peoples," and the *Preliminary Report* repeatedly referred to this dualism. In Vol. I of the final *Report* the favoured phrase was "two societies," and, while the "greater complexity of English-speaking society" was admitted, the commissioners nevertheless asserted that "despite these centrifugal influences, the fundamental unity of the English-speaking society appears to us beyond question ..." *Report of the Royal Commission on Bilingualism and Biculturalism*, volume 1 (Ottawa: Queen's Printer 1967), xxxiv.

8 Laurendeau, *Journal*, 345.

9 *Laurendeau, Journal*, 343, 344.

10 *Report*, 2:xlvii.

11 Laurendeau, *Journal*, 153; see also 331.

12 Laurendeau, *Journal*, 346.

13 Djwa, *Scott*, 401.

14 *Report*, 1:xxxix, where the commission recognized that "it will be for Canadians to decide, mainly through their political parties and through their governments, whether to accept or reject the principle of equality."

15 *Report of the Royal Commission on Bilingualism and Biculturalism*, vols. 2, 3, 4 (Ottawa: Queen's Printer 1968, 1969). See C. Michael MacMillan, *The Practise of Language Rights in Canada* (Toronto: University of Toronto Press 1998), chapter 3.

16 Ramsay Cook, "Le Canada vaut une enquête," *International Journal*, 23, no. 2, (spring 1968): 295.

TEN

Bourassa to Bissonnette:
The Evolution of Castor-Rougeisme

... le nationalisme que j'ai toujours préconisé n'est pas le nationalisme sauvage qu'on a mis en œuvre dans tous les pays du monde.

– Henri Bourassa (1923)

Le Devoir, throughout much of its history, has been Quebec's Third Party, humming its own discordant tune, imagining its own nationalist *projet de société*. Its dissent and its imagined community, traditionally, were founded on variable blends of nationalism – Canadian, French Canadian, Quebec ("la patrie canadienne" and "la petite patrie canadienne-française," in Henri Bourassa's words[1]) – and Catholic theology. Its ponderous, signed editorials resembled both a papal pronouncement and a legal brief, hardly fare for those who lacked a classical-college education. Its audience has always been the liberal professions, the francophone bourgeoisie – or part of it: doctors, lawyers, priests, teachers, students. And, in the past, it saw as its function the education of that class in doing its duty – *fais ce que dois* was the masthead motto until it recently disappeared with most of Bourassa's other convictions. It has never had a parallel in the rest of Canada (J.W. Dafoe's *Manitoba Free Press* came closest, at least on the editorial page), unless it was the *Canadian Forum*, but even it had more humour (in the past) and fewer subscribers than *Le Devoir*.

In his elegant "postface" to Robert Lahaise's collection *Le Devoir reflet du Québec au 20e Siècle*, Guy Rocher describes the "class" of people who read *Le Devoir* (later he calls this "class," after Foucault, "une société de discours") as "un ensemble de personnes qui partagent les mêmes orientations ou tendances de pensée, de sentiment, de réaction." These people are fairly well educated (Rocher helped replace the classical college with the CEGEP in the 1970s), serious about politics, concerned about Quebec's future, and possessed of a Quebec nationalist sensibility which may encompass anyone from militant separatists to fatigued federalists who want a federalism "plus respectueux du Québec et des francophones canadiens que le Canada ne l'a été jusqu'à présent." Rocher makes one other remark which helps to explain why people actually pay to read a newspaper that throughout most of its history (and it is not *that* different today) lacked serious international and even Canadian news coverage, disdained sports and comics, and confused the economy with the *caisse populaire*. "À la différence de tout autre journal," Rocher claims, "le directeur ou la directrice du *Devoir* est un personnage public. Il ou elle jouit d'un grand prestige, surtout d'une sorte d'autorité morale, d'une aura au Québec même, peut-être parfois plus encore à l'extérieur du Québec, dans le Canada anglais." Who can forget the durable Claude Ryan as he trudged from conference to conference on "What Does Quebec Want?" in the 1970s? Only those bumper stickers proclaiming that "My Canada Includes Quebec" have covered more miles!

Sociologist though he is, Rocher offers no empirical support for his profile of *Le Devoir*'s readership. But it rings true for it sounds just like him – and me, whom I offer as a further sample of such a reader. Back in the 1950s, Professor Arthur Lower, whose student I was, insisted that at least once a week (he was a Methodist) the members of his seminar on French Canada should read a French-language newspaper. I had heard about *Le Devoir* but I had never read it until I found it in the Douglas Library at Queen's University. The experience was, as Lower had no doubt intended, puzzling but exhilarating. Being from Winnipeg, where freight rates, grain futures, and the threat of Saskatchewan socialism dominated the pages of the local newspapers, I was immediately carried away by the endless discussions of Catholicism, corruption, centralization, and Clarence Campbell. (Naturally, *Le Devoir*'s perspective was nationalist, not athletic.) Soon I discovered that even a hotel named the Queen Elizabeth could excite French Canadians to a degree that the queen had never excited me. It was habit-forming and for the next thirty-five years, often daily but always at least weekly, I had my fix. In the early 1960s I laboriously translated editorials (usually by André Laurendeau) for the *Canadian Forum*. Then, during 1964–65, on the invitation of Claude Ryan, I contributed a weekly column. This privilege especially pleased me because Henri Bourassa had originally intended to have an anglophone columnist, none other than John S. Ewart, but the plan had never materialized. I have no idea whether anyone read my column. I did receive a hilarious denunciatory letter from Jacques Ferron on Rhinoceros Party letterhead, so I asked Ryan if he had had any other reactions. Only a few, he said, and none as negative as the ones he had received after a newsboy with an Irish name had been awarded the prize for signing up new subscribers. Apparently an Irish plot to take over the paper had been suspected!

Over the years I came to know some of the people who ran *Le Devoir*. After his superb Grey Lecture[2] at the University of Toronto in 1961, Laurendeau, a self-described "night person," spent a late night at our apartment in conversation. Seeing my recently acquired PHD scroll hanging in the toilet, he enquired, with mock puzzlement, "And what's this strange Anglo-Saxon custom?" I became a permanent admirer. Claude Ryan was different. Whereas Laurendeau might have been a brother, Ryan could only be an uncle. His stern morality, his courage, and his devotion to work were all worn on his sleeve as he travelled the country with a little black notebook tucked into his back pocket. Somehow he seemed Bourassa reincarnated. A brief encounter with Lise Bissonnette, the current director, failed to hint at her future: when I put her on the train in New Haven in the spring of 1979, she said she was off to spend a few days at the Algonquin in New York. A Quebec Dorothy Parker? Certainly not.

So I think that I fit most of Rocher's qualifications for a *Le Devoir* reader. Moreover, in the course of my research during the 1960s and 1970s, I managed to read most of the editorials in the first decade or so of the paper's existence, examined Henri Bourassa's private papers, and even considered writing a book about him. So the love affair was long, faithful, and rewarding. Then, sometime in the early 1990s, about the time Lise Bissonnette took charge, I broke it off and took up with *L'Actualité*, where you do not have to belong to a *société de discours* and can easily skip over Michel Vastel's articles (or read them to find out what the lumpen *nationalistes* are up to). Still, like Woody Allen, I continue to worry about that past relationship and often, as I browse in bookstores, I pick up the old dear – she's only a loony plus GST. I must admit that it still causes my heart to flutter – though not on the days it prints Daniel Latouche.

The strength of *Le Devoir* was always twofold. First, there was its fierce independence in politics. Secondly, there was its clearly espoused principles about Canada, French Canada, and the social order that were not inflexible and were applied fairly to all – though the period between Bourassa's departure and Gérard Filion's arrival revealed the underside of those principles.

Bourassa insisted on independence from the beginning, though his alliance with the *autonomistes*, and through them with the Conservatives during the 1911 election, aroused suspicions then and since that some tainted money may have gone into the launching of the paper the year before. In the mid-1940s Maurice Duplessis tried to take control of the paper – this well before *Le Devoir* had become a powerful critic of *le chef* – but the plan was fought off and in 1947 that perfect tandem of Filion and Laurendeau took charge. Afterwards, independence meant criticism of all parties but a strong tendency to support "nationalist" politicians at election time – Charles Taylor over Pierre Trudeau, for example. In 1980 the paper carried three separate editorials, signed by three different writers, favouring three different parties. Under Lise Bissonnette, the paper opted, almost unconditionally, for sovereignty, which today means the Parti Québécois (PQ)/Bloc Québécois (BQ) alliance, while the voice of federalism has effectively disappeared.

Bourassa's original principles have also largely disappeared – rejected as irrelevant. The founder set out three basic goals: autonomy for Canada within the British Empire – a battle that was won by the 1920s; autonomy of the provinces within the federal system – a battle that has become front and centre; equality of the French and English cultures from coast to coast – almost won in practical terms but no longer of serious interest at *Le Devoir* even though, in her earlier career, Lise Bissonnette herself wrote many editorials defending the minorities *hors Québec* – Lévesque's "dead ducks." Underlying all of these goals was Bourassa's insistence that *Le Devoir* was a Catholic paper, one where all social, political, and even "national" questions would be examined in the light of the teachings of the church. Bourassa's *projet de société*, an essentially conservative one, included criticisms of both market capitalism and socialism but offered only a vague "corporatism" as an alternative. It also meant a preference for Catholic unions over international ones, and a defence of the role of the church in education, health, and welfare. Finally, Bourassa's *projet* saw a woman's place as being in the home, for to leave that sacred sphere would lead to the masculinization of women, what he termed *hommes-femmes*. And that would undermine what he called the *race*. Finally, the anti-Semitism which marred the pages of the paper under Georges Pelletier in the 1930s was rooted in both religious and ethnic nationalism.

Fundamental to Bourassa's thought was his Catholicism – the *castor* part of Laurier's shrewd assessment of him as a *castor-rouge*. Most significantly, his Catholicism always took precedence over his nationalism, a sentiment that, in him, might better be called *patriotisme*, the word he seems to have preferred. His *petite patrie* was French and Catholic, but the two were distinct. Though he blurred that distinction himself in his famous, brilliant defence of French as the language of Catholicism for French Canadians at the Eucharistic Congress of 1910, he normally kept language and religion separate.[3] On the tenth anniversary of *Le Devoir* in 1920, after the events of the Great War had intensified nationalist feeling in Quebec, Bourassa defined his paper's mission as teaching "le vrai patriotisme gouverné par la foi éclairé, par les leçons de l'histoire."[4] Moreover, it was Bourassa's suspicion that Abbé Lionel Groulx, both in his racist novel *L'Appel de la race* (1922) and in the quasi-separatist essays that Groulx's followers in *L'Action française* published as *Notre avenir politique* (1923), had confused nationalism and religion, which led him to dissociate himself from this new nationalist apostle in a vigorous speech entitled *Patriotisme, Nationalisme, Impérialisme* (1923). For Groulx, religion and ethnicity were integrally united in a nationalism that rested on a particular interpretation of the history of French Canada. One of Groulx's strongest supporters was Antonio Perrault, a young lawyer whose contribution to *Notre avenir politique* verged on the advocacy of an independent *état français*. Perrault, the future father-in-law of André Laurendeau, would bring Groulx and Bourassa together one last time in 1942 to oppose the conscription plebiscite. In the 1960s Laurendeau and Groulx drifted apart, especially after Laurendeau became co-chairman of the B and B Commission.[5]

The great and largely unnoticed irony of nationalism in Quebec is that it was a priest, Canon Groulx, who played the pivotal role in erasing the traditional religious restraints from nationalism, thus letting loose a secular ethnic ideology that would eventually transform Quebec society, leaving the church on the margin. Once religion and nationalism became integral, as they did in Groulx's "doctrine," the next logical step was for nationalism to consume religion, as it always consumes associated ideologies, religious or secular.

At *Le Devoir* the transition from a religious to a secular nationalism was symbolized in the career of André Laurendeau. Together with Gérard Filion, whose background was in agricultural journalism, Laurendeau would bring the paper into the twentieth century. Don Horton's fine *André Laurendeau: French Canadian Nationalist* (1992) skilfully traces Laurendeau's often tortured passage from a youthful anti-Semitic separatist to a mature nationalist whose outlook, like many intellectuals of his generation – Gérard Pelletier and Pierre Trudeau, for example – was infused with that variety of liberal Catholicism formulated by Emmanuel Mounier and the French periodical *Esprit*.[6] For Laurendeau, "personalism" was a humanist halfway house between conservative Catholic orthodoxy and ethnic nationalism on the one hand, and a secular, almost socialist, nationalism on the other. (Laurendeau's brother-in-law, Jacques Perrault, was one of the earliest prominent French-Canadian nationalists to join the CCF.) Here lies yet another irony. When, in 1947, Laurendeau resigned from the leadership of the provincial wing of the Bloc Populaire to join the editorial board of Quebec's leading Catholic newspaper, he was no longer a believer. In one of the most bizarre incidents in Canadian historical writing, Laurendeau's son, Yves, chose the publication of Denis Monière's tendentious *André Laurendeau et le destin d'un peuple* (1983) to reveal quite a lot of family history, some of which Monière had consciously chosen to ignore. Most significantly, Laurendeau-*fils* published parts of a letter written to him by his father in 1964 in which he admitted that his faith had disappeared nearly twenty years earlier. From then, until 1964, he had disguised his agnosticism behind a migraine headache which miraculously struck him every Sunday! No less interesting is the fact that, being a resourceful journalist, Laurendeau took the occasion of his partial coming out to write a fictionalized version of his life as a closet agnostic. Published in *Le magazine Maclean* in 1964 and entitled "Une Société Intolerante, qui Force des athées à devenir les Marguilliers ...," the story revolved around a village churchwarden, really Laurendeau himself. Of this character, Laurendeau wrote with unusual bitterness: "At the time he gave me the impression of a man buried alive. Alcohol helped a little to dull the pain of his spoiled life. The man must have possessed considerable vigour just to be able to keep up appearances when he was such a mess inside. Watching him I had a sense of terrible loss, of an impoverishment of himself and the society he lived in, of a stupid and useless sacrifice. And I wondered how many 'rats' like him were in our French Canadian society." The story concluded, "I have never been able to look at this society in the same way since."[7] The "churchwarden" at *Le Devoir* could explain his long silence to his children only by writing that "personne ne l'a su, rigoureusement personne sauf maman (la vôtre, non la mienne bien sûr). Comment vous confier ce que vous n'auriez pas compris et vous aurait troublé? J'ai pris l'habitude du silence ... Au reste, j'avais peur d'une indiscrétion de jeune homme ou de jeune fille, et, *socialement, j'avais besoin du secret*, car j'étais journaliste à un quotidien catholique."[8]

Yves Laurendeau and Denis Monière provided a number of other surprising details: Uncle Laurendeau's espousal of Lamarckian evolutionism and the consequent condemnation of his book *La Vie: Considerations biologique* (1911); grandfather's purchased freedom from a pregnant young Frenchwoman he had met during his musical studies in France; and André's eleven-year affair with Charlotte Boisjoli. (Marie-Claire Blais is obviously a better guide to Quebec than Abbé Groulx.) But most important in the history of *Le Devoir* and nationalism in Quebec is the window that Laurendeau's agnosticism gives us into the issue of secularism in the once "priest-ridden province." The ease with which the Catholic Church in the 1960s abdicated its once powerful throne in Quebec is surely at least partly explained by the existence of many, many Laurendeaus who *socialement* had need of a secret to keep their children happy, to keep their respectability, to keep their jobs. Perhaps a study of the incidence of migraine headaches among French Canadians would help us better to understand the Quiet Revolution!

Laurendeau's agnosticism was easily enough disguised without compromising *Le Devoir* since Filion held fast to Bourassa's religious tradition. As Jean-Pierre Proulx notes in one of the best essays in Robert Lahaise's celebratory collection (only Jacques Rouillard's essay on *Le Devoir* and the labour movement is equally impressive), Claude Ryan, who succeeded Filion as the paper's editor, was a safe, though independent, Catholic. We are not told whether Laurendeau's "secret" was what prevented him from becoming director, but Proulx notes that a suspicion existed in sections of Quebec's hierarchy in 1962 that, theologically, the paper suffered "d'une nette insuffisance dans l'ordre de la pensée."[9] As a reflection of the increasing secularism of its staff and perhaps of its readership, religion received a declining amount of coverage from the 1970s onwards, until by 1990–91 *La Presse* gave religion four times as much space as *Le Devoir*. In 1990 the new director, Lise Bissonnette wrote: "De ces origines catholiques, *Le Devoir* est passé, comme la société québécoise, a une laïcité institutionnelle. Il ne se sent plus lié, aujourd'hui, aux prescriptions d'une Eglise, et se dissocie même, sur des questions morales, de chemins qu'il suivit autrefois avec assurance autant que soumission." She added that *Le Devoir* remained "foncièrement chrétien," but the *Globe and Mail* would probably say the same, as long as the Sermon on the Mount could be read as advocating market economics! Given his well-known views on women in public life, Bourassa would hardly have been surprised that the ascent of the first woman (and a novelist to boot) to the director's chair would be accompanied by a descent into secularism! And he would certainly have agreed – perhaps angrily – with Jean-Pierre Proulx's conclusion that "l'heritage catholique du journal s'est dorénavant transformé en humanisme séculier."

The shift from Catholic orthodoxy to secular humanism has contributed to virtually every other change that has taken place at *Le Devoir*. If conservative Catholicism combined with nationalism to produce corporatism, anti-feminism, and even anti-Semitism, and liberal Catholicism underlay the socially conscious nationalism of Laurendeau and the liberal *civisme* of Ryan, then the new, secular nationalism of Bissonnette is in tune with the aspirations of the *bon chic, bon genre* generation so splendidly portrayed in Denis Arcand's film *Le déclin de l'empire américain*. Like the BQ/PQ alliance, which the newspaper now favours, *Le Devoir*'s *projet de société* departs in only minor ways from

the hegemonic market liberalism of our freely traded globalized industrial world. Jean-Marc Léger, who already in the 1960s was pro-
pounding an Austro-Hungarian solution for Canada similar to the current Bouchard–Parizeau solution of the early 1990s (which in turn can
be found in Tardivel's *Pour le Patrie* (1896) and in many contributions
by Antonio Perrault in Groulx's *Action française*), recently resurfaced
to speak for this new nationalist project. To those who have been urging that Quebecers should first decide what kind of a society they want
before being asked to choose between federalism and independence,
this voice from the past replied: "On ne peut ésperer mettre en oeuvre
un 'projet de société' que si, d'abord, on a la parfaite mâitrise de ses
choix politiques et ses ressources, et de ses lois et ses impôts, c'est-à-
dire si on dispose de la souveraineté."[10]

Once again, as so often in Quebec's past, the cry of *la nation d'abord*
rings through the pages of *Le Devoir*. The goal is to revive and rein-
force what Jean Paré has called "ce culte d'unanimisme."[11] Once a critical voice of dissent – Quebec's Third Party, with its own *projet de
société* – today's *Le Devoir* has added its chant to the chorus crying for
the Bouchard/Parizeau version of sovereignty – the one with ice cream.

Still, the old love affair dies hard. Next time I pass a news-stand I'll
probably buy *Le Devoir*, newly tarted up, if only to read André's
daughter, Francine Laurendeau, on the movies. Bourassa wouldn't
have agreed to that innovation either!

[1995]

NOTES

1 *Le Dixième Anniversaire du Devoir* (Montreal: *Le Devoir* 1920), 72.
2 Still one of the best analyses of separatism in the 1960s. See Ramsay
  Cook and Michael Behiels, ed., *The Essential Laurendeau* (Toronto:
  Copp Clark 1976), 224–33.
3 Henri Bourassa, *Religion, Langue, Nationalité* (Montreal: *Le Devoir*
  1910).
4 Bourassa, *Le Dixième Anniversaire*, 17.
5 Lionel Groulx, *Mes Mémoires*, vol. 4 (Montreal: Fides 1974), 331–41.
6 John Hellman, *Emmanuel Mounier and the New Catholic Left, 1930–50*
  (Toronto: University of Toronto Press 1981).
7 André Laurendeau, *Ces choses qui nous arrivent* (Montreal: HMH
  1970), 197–201; Philip Stratford, ed., *André Laurendeau: Witness for
  Quebec* (Toronto: Macmillan 1971), 263–70.
8 Yves Laurendeau, "En Guise de Supplément au Laurendeau de Monière,"
  Revue d'Histoire de l'Amérique française, 38, no. 1 (summer 1984): 76.

At about the same time, Francine Laurendeau, André's daughter, also made this letter public. See Francine Laurendeau, "Mon père ce héros au sourire si doux," *L'Incunable*, March 1984, 14

9 Robert Lahaise, ed., *Le Devoir reflet du Québec au 20e Siècle* (Montreal: HMH 1994), 407.

10 Jean-Marc Léger, "Projet de société, expression de la confusion," *Le Devoir*, 23 May 1995

11 Giovanni Calabrese, *Jean Paré* (Montreal: Liber 1994), 77.

ELEVEN

A Country Doctor and His Bishop:
An Incident in the History of Science and
Religion in Quebec

Vis-à-vis de Lamarck et de Darwin, nous sommes ici, dans notre province, au point où en était le monde chrétien au XIVe et au XVe siècles, vis-à-vis Copernic et Galilée.

– Albert Laurendeau, *La Vie: Considérations Biologiques* (1911), 109

In January 1961, as the recently elected Jean Lesage government was taking the first steps in what has come to be called the Quiet Revolution – the modernization of the Quebec state – André Laurendeau published an editorial deploring the continuing influence of outmoded scientific ideas among French Canadians. His comments were inspired by a recent speech in which Cardinal Paul-Émile Léger had expressed similar concerns, thereby signalling, in Laurendeau's view, a new openness "nettement en avance sur plusieurs secteurs de notre milieu." In passing, Laurendeau paid hommage to an uncle who, he said, had suffered "une solide condamnation épiscopale" for having supported the theory that man had descended from the monkey.[1]

The editor of *Le Devoir* was no doubt surprised, a few days later, when he received a telephone call from Monsignor Édouard Jetté, bishop of Joliette, who pointed out that the Catholic Church's condemnation of Doctor Albert Laurendeau in 1912 had not mentioned "evolution" but rather had concentrated on "les erreurs philosophiques et théologiques." The younger Laurendeau reportedly replied by thanking the prelate, telling him that "l'affaire singe" was a widely believed family tradition.[2] Given the fragility of André Laurendeau's own religious faith, he probably found the bishop's distinction a rather fine one.[3] He certainly should have, if he knew anything more about his uncle's controversial career.

Albert was the son of Dr Joseph-Olivier Laurendeau, a prominent citizen of Saint-Gabriel-de-Brandon, a village north east of Joliette. Of five sons and two daughters, only Albert, born in 1857, followed his father's footsteps into the medical profession; the daughters married, while Fortunat entered the Jesuit order, J.-T.-R. became a financier, Clovis a furniture dealer, and Arthur a musician – maître de chapelle de la cathédrale de Montréal. Following his early schooling in Saint-Gabriel, Albert entered the École Normale Jacques Cartier in Montreal in 1872 and then graduated in 1879 from the École de Médecine et de chirurgie de Montréal, also known as the Victoria Faculty of Medicine because of its affiliation with the Methodist university in Cobourg, Ontario. This somewhat unusual educational background – he attended neither *collège classique* nor the French-speaking, Catholic Université Laval – perhaps helps to account for Laurendeau's subsequent unorthodoxy in scientific and educational matters. In the same year as he graduated he married Georgiana Mérizzi, the daughter of a Napierville notary. Their only son, Aldéric, continued the family medical tradition in Saint-Gabriel. Of their three daughters, two married, one to Sir William Van Horne's private secretary, and the third remained at home.[4]

Albert, who gradually took over his father's practice in Saint-Gabriel-de-Brandon, gained a reputation as a devoted, energetic practitioner with strong views about his profession's responsibilities, status, and need for reform. A public-spirited man, he served as mayor of his village between 1889 and 1892 but subsequently devoted himself to the politics of the medical profession. Following the first Congrès des Médecins de Langue Française de l'Amérique du Nord in Quebec City in 1902, Laurendeau led in the founding of the Société médicale du district de Joliette, which became one of the most active associations in the province. He was the perennial secretary-treasurer of the Joliette association, and from 1904 to 1920 he was an elected governor of the Collège des Médecins et Chirurgiens de la Province de Québec, becoming vice-president in 1918.[5] As a member of the college's committee on legislation, he played a leading role in persuading the provincial legislature to enact the new medical act in 1909 which significantly increased the autonomy and jurisdiction of the college and standardized admissions, examinations, and curricula, though humanistic studies still weighed more heavily than scientific. The new law's goal, Laurendeau believed, was "relever la qualité et abaisser la quantité des disciples d'Hypocrate dans notre province."[6] Laurendeau, though a strong supporter of cooperation among the various provincial medical associations in Canada and an advocate of a federal ministry of health,[7] insisted that the federal government respect the autonomy of the provincial medical associations in order that French-speaking doctors could "garder intact notre langue, nos usages et coutumes, notre organisation nationale, nos droits en un mot."[8]

Laurendeau's determination to reform the medical profession, to professionalize it, included demands for stricter enforcement of medical ethics (déontologie médicale), the regulation of professional misconduct by the college, the exclusion of bone-setters and other nonprofessionals ("charlatans") from practice, and improved control of patent medicines. In order to raise the standards of medical practice and the status of Quebec doctors, he believed that two general problems had to be addressed: overcrowding in the profession and inadequate "formation morale, intellectuelle et scientifique." The first problem, he argued, was so severe that many doctors were forced to take on other work to supplement their incomes. In Saint-Gabriel-de-Brandon, he reported, "deux se font une rude concurrence dans le commerce de pharmacie et moi-même pendant longtemps, j'ai tenu un comptoir d'escompte."[9] This Darwinian "struggle for life," as he called it, resulted from cut-throat competition, inadequate fees, and resulting low incomes. One solution, adopted by the Joliette association in 1913, was a uniform fee schedule: home visit, 1 to 2 dollars; simple fracture, 5 to 10 dollars; appendectomy, 40 to 60 dollars. Improved incomes were necessary because "le médecin doit occuper une position élevée dans la hiérarchie sociale, et il ne peut tenir son rang, commander la confiance, le respect du public, sans avoir des revenus convenables."[10]

Better incomes were only the first step. At least as important were educational reforms that would raise standards and lower the number of new medical graduates. The 1909 Medical Act had made a beginning in raising standards of certification. But more was needed. Quebec, Laurendeau contended, had too many *collèges classiques* and not enough technical, agricultural, industrial, and commercial colleges. The result was an excess of priests and members of the liberal professions in a society where "étrangers" increasingly dominated the economy.[11] Worst of all was the lack of respect for science among French Canadians, and that, too, resulted from an educational system that was unsuited to the needs of a modern people. The classical curriculum taught dead languages rather than live ones, Latin and Greek instead of English, which, Laurendeau believed, "pourrait être le levier de notre succès," though French would retain its prior place "à cause de sa supériorité sur les autres idiomes." And for those intending to become medical doctors, classical philosophy required replacement by a new one that "enseignerait à nos jeunes gens les principes généraux des sciences positives et naturelles – en s'appuyant uniquement sur les procédés et des faits naturels guidée seulement par la raison."[12]

During the decade before the First World War, Laurendeau achieved a position of some prominence, even notoriety, in the Quebec medical profession through speeches to professional organizations and frequent contributions to such medical publications as *L'Union Médicale du Canada* and *La Clinique*. His association with the latter publication is especially interesting since it was founded by Dr François-Xavier Le Moyne de Martigny, who, like his brother Adelstan, another medical man, was a leading member of the Freemasons, an organization that was closely watched by the clergy. Laurendeau was certainly acquainted with the founder of *La Clinique* since he had served with him on the committee of the Collège des Médecins et Chirurgiens concerned with reforming the province's medical act. Though Laurendeau seems never to have joined the Masons, he often expressed views about science and education that were shared by members of the dreaded *loges*. In Quebec, in those years, association was often enough to suggest guilt.[13]

Laurendeau's views on the importance of science had developed over a number of years and were based on a substantial knowledge of the scientific and religious debate over evolutionary theory. In Quebec, where Sir William Dawson, the Presbyterian principal of McGill University, and Abbé Léon Provancher and other Catholic scientists had firmly rejected Darwinism, Laurendeau was venturing onto dangerous ground. In March 1907 he informally addressed the Joliette medical association on the topic of biological evolution. Monsignor Joseph-Alfred Archambault, who had been appointed the first bishop of Joliette in 1904, having already served as vice-rector of the Montreal branch of the Université Laval, demanded an immediate explanation, including proof that Laurendeau submitted "à l'autorité suprême et infaillible de l'Église." The doctor replied that he had expounded "le Darwinisme" not as a dogma but only as a theory so widely accepted among biologists that educated men, especially medical doctors, should be familiar with it. He disclaimed any hostility to religion, denied that any conflict existed between God as creator and modern science, and argued that these discussions should not be left to freethinkers alone.[14] Rather than withdrawing in the face of this formidable foe, Laurendeau decided to prepare a more formal presentation of his views and to invite the bishop to hear them at a public meeting where the cleric would have an opportunity to "exposer les doctrines chrétiennes sur ces questions."[15]

In this speech, which the bishop did not attend, Laurendeau appealed to the authority of a number of European Catholic writers, including Monsignor J. Guibert in France and Sir G.J. Mivart in Great Britain, who claimed that religion and evolution were not in conflict.[16] Though Laurendeau's defence was moderate, another member of the

association, Dr Bartolet, took the podium to attack his colleague's
"materialism." To this Laurendeau replied that "l'homme, son origine
et sa fin matérielles, sont strictement du domaine de la médecine."[17]
The question of God's existence, and the immortality of the soul,
belonged to a different order, one that was separate from science. Here
was the essence of Laurendeau's position, one that to Bishop Archambault was the heresy of modernism: the separation of religion and science and, by implication, the existence of an autonomous, secular
sphere of thought. "L'humanité ne peut rien perdre, elle ne peut que
gagner, au point de vue intellectuel et moral, par la diffusion de la science et de la vérité,"[18] Laurendeau asserted. He hardly helped his case
by citing Haeckel, Voltaire, Kant, Lacordaire – and attacking the
Inquisition!

Archambault had a different view of "la vérité." He invited the doctor to attend the cathedral on the following Sunday where the bishop
"en chaire" would explain the "erreurs du modernisme," and again
demanded Laurendeau's submission.[19] The doctor once more vigorously denied either that his defence of evolution contravened Catholic
teaching – "le catholicisme peut admirablement se concilier avec la
vraie science" – or that he adhered to any of the sixty-five propositions condemned by the papacy. In matters of faith and morals he
accepted the church's infallibility while reaffirming the scientific truth
of evolution.[20]

The bishop demanded more; there could be no reservations. He
insisted that his parishioner specifically accept six propositions: five
declared God's precedence over material existence and the sixth stated
that scientific truth could not contradict religious truth as proclaimed
by the church. There could be no separation of science and religion.
When Laurendeau temporized, the bishop gave him eight days to
choose between submission and condemnation. The full submission
came in two days – though it was not abject. Surely, after Louis Agas-
siz and Jean-Louis Armand de Quatrefages, no serious scientist could
defend the fixity of species or the claim that the earth was created in
4004 BC. And he concluded: "Par deux fois, publiquement, j'ai répété
que les conflits entre la science et la foi, proviennent non de la science
ni de la religion, mais des savants qui interprètent mal les faits, ou des
théologiens qui ne pénètrent pas le sens des Écritures." The bishop
refused to be drawn into further argument. He accepted the submission
with "la joie dans l'âme" and declared that "l'incident est clos."[21] The
cleric would soon realize that he had been too sanguine.

At Quebec in July 1908 Laurendeau took advantage of his position
as president of the Third Section of the Congrès des Médecins de la
Langue Française to restate in blunt terms his radical critique of the

province's educational system, particularly the backwardness of scientific teaching which resulted in a conservative, even reactionary medical profession. He claimed that external control – church control – of appointments to medical faculties detrimentally affected professional standards. The problem, he insisted, was philosophical: deductive idealism remained dominant over empirical investigation. "... la philosophie doit avoir pour base la raison fondée sur nos sensations; hors de là, nous tomberons dans la métaphysique, le mysticisme, le transcendant, toutes choses que doit repousser le médecin, lequel doit étudier et traiter l'homme et ses maladies, par les procédés naturels."[22] True scientific reasoning, Laurendeau maintained, meant the rejection of natural law and, by implication, traditional Christian teaching about creation. "La croyance à la fixité des espèces conduit à l'inertie intellectuelle," he argued; "la foi en une essence humaine physique, différentielle des autres animaux, mène à l'anthropolâtrie: dogmes opposés à la raison et antiscientifiques."[23] After some reflections on the need for better sanitary laws (he especially insisted on the inclusion of "temples réligieux" in the application of these laws), the need for careful isolation of tuberculosis patients, the prohibition of alcoholic beverages, and action again prostitution to prevent the spread of syphilis, he concluded with an affirmation of his faith in science as the only certain road to social and moral progress.[24]

Laurendeau was proud to hold and express what he believed were "advanced" ideas. His colleagues did not share his satisfaction – or his ideas. "Le sentiment général de l'assemblée," *L'Union Médicale* reported after the speech, "ne lui a pas permis de terminer l'exposé de son travail."[25] Laurendeau, nevertheless, had the text of his speech printed and distributed. When this new statement of scientific naturalism came to the attention of Bishop Archambault in the autumn of 1910, he pronounced it "un scandale." He demanded a retraction or at least Laurendeau's agreement that the 1907 correspondence, including the doctor's submission to the authority of the church, be published. Laurendeau first agreed to publication but then offered "une retraction directe" of anything that contradicted Catholic teachings.[26] Once more the matter seemed closed, the troublesome doctor having returned to orthodoxy. Or so the bishop may have believed, or at least hoped.

In fact, it is likely that, by the date of this second retraction in October of 1910, Laurendeau was already planning publication of *La Vie: Considérations Biologiques*, which appeared early in 1911. He must have known that this book, which included all the letters he had earlier exchanged with the bishop, and which carried neither a publisher's imprint nor an ecclesiastical imprimatur, would reopen and intensify the earlier controversy for it was going to "briser des vieilles traditions,

secouer d'antiques préjugés, et par-dessus tout, troubler la quiétude de
la masse de la hiérarchie."[27] He pleaded for his work to be judged only
by scientific, not religious, standards, again insisting that science
existed autonomously. He doubtless knew that this appeal was futile
for he now intended to state frankly and explicitly his commitment to
scientific naturalism, the view that life could be explained by a combination of Lamarckian and Darwinian evolution. Against what he
called the puerile doctrine of creation taught in Quebec classical colleges, Laurendeau asserted that "la vérité réside dans l'évolution de
Lamarck, de Darwin et de la pléiade de savants qui ont assis cette doctrine sur les bases solides."[28] Evolutionary theory or "le trans-
formisme," the Lamarckian term often preferred by Laurendeau,
applied equally to man and the rest of nature. How else could the differences between lower and higher races be explained, or the virtual
disappearance of such peoples as the Huron, the Iroquois, and the
Abenaki?[29]

Though Laurendeau's reading on the subject of evolution was extensive and certainly included Lamarck's *Philosophie Zoologique* (1809),
it is doubtful whether he had read Darwin's *On the Origin of the
Species* (1859). If he had read it, he failed to grasp the essential difference between the French writer's contention that evolution was verti-
cal, a response to environmental challenges and the inheritance of
acquired characteristics, and the English naturalist's theory of branch-
ing evolution through natural selection. Laurendeau, like Lamarck and
unlike Darwin, believed that evolution was progressive.[30] The Quebec
doctor's views were doubtless influenced by French neo-Lamarckians,
who, for linguistic, ideological, and nationalist reasons, insisted that
Charles Darwin's work complemented rather than superseded the earlier evolutionary theories of Lamarck. Moreover, the forthright Laurendeau found Darwin's well-known caution unappealing.[31]

Having set out his concept of evolution, the Saint-Gabriel contro-
versialist turned to the practical implications of his views. Science, he
maintained, held the key to the future, but French Canadians were
being denied that key. "Au XVIIIe siècle, il a fallu une langue
philosophique, au XIXe siècle, une langue poétique, au XXe siècle il
faudra une langue scientifique."[32] And scientific knowledge, by which
Laurendeau meant evolution, was not necessary only to guarantee
good science for it also explained the moral, intellectual, and social
evolution which ensured that "l'utopie d'aujourd'hui deviendra la réalité de demain."[33] No people were in greater need of a scientific outlook
and culture than the French Canadians, whose future would be bleak
unless their outmoded philosophy and values were set aside in favour
of "les grandes lois de l'évolution."[34]

Laurendeau had good reason to expect a quick response from Bishop Archambault for the churchman seemed to pay the closest attention to the doctor's every word.[35] On 19 March 1912 the bishop issued a circular to his clergy condemning *La Vie* and prohibiting the faithful from reading it. Ten days later the same message was published in *L'Étoile du Nord*. In vigorous, unambiguous prose, Archambault declared:

J'y ai constaté des erreurs assez nombreuses en matière de philosophie chrétienne et de théologie catholique; en outre, des injures toutes gratuites à l'adresse de la hiérarchie, de notre clergé canadien-français, des professeurs de nos universités et de nos collèges, des éloges exagérés des savants et des philosophes athées et matérialistes, des insinuations regrettables au sujet des guérisons miraculeuses, de la confiance des fidèles dans le pouvoir d'intercession des saints, un mépris évident de l'enseignement scholastique, etc. Parmi les graves erreurs doctrinales, que contient le livre *La Vie*, il y en a même plusieurs au sujet de la liberté humaine, de la nature de notre intelligence, de l'autorité de l'Église en matière scientifique, des relations de la science et la foi, de la puissance de la raison humaine de connaître l'existence de Dieu et l'immortalité de l'âme; erreurs qui ont été formellement condamnées soit par le Concile du Vatican, soit par le décret *Lamentabili*, et par l'encyclique *Pascendi*.[36]

No mention was made of the theory of evolution, for the bishop recognized that the issue was a more fundamental one: the primacy of religious authority.

Urged to recant, Laurendeau once again insisted that he was not hostile to religion, he claimed a conscientious right to express his views, and he stated his intention to continue to study these great questions, speaking publicly only if provoked. Finally, as in the past, he denied that science claimed any authority in matters of religious belief and teachings. "À la suite de ces déclarations de principes," he concluded, "il vous appartient, Monseigneur, de juger si je puis encore faire partie de la société religieuse, ou si je dois en être définitivement et pour toujours exclu. Toute autre déclaration me déshonorerait à mes yeux; je croirais commettre une infamie en affirmant ce que ma conscience répudie. Je puis vous affirmer que mes convictions sont aussi profondes et sincères que les vôtres. Vous êtes maintenant juge et je m'en rapporte à vous."[37] The bishop was ready to judge: either Laurendeau submitted in writing or he faced denial of the sacraments, including a Christian burial in case of death.[38]

The doctor held firm for nine months. There is no record of the discussion that he must have held with his family, including his Jesuit brother, or friends. The pressure must have been intense, his medical practice and livelihood perhaps jeopardized. On 4 March 1913 he visited the bishop and the following day surrendered. "J'accepte l'enseignement de l'Église catholique, je regrette les erreurs que ce livre peut contenir; au point de vue de la doctrine chrétienne, les erreurs proviennent sans doute de ce que mon instruction religieuse est insuffisante; aussi, désirant la paix, ayant donné à mon activité un but autre que celui d'atteindre aux sommets scientifiques – j'ai résolu de ne plus écrire." He asked that the matter be quietly closed, expressing repugnance at the prospect of any publicity that would deny him "la paix et la quiétude mentale."[39] Nevertheless, the following day, the "Bulletin Religieux" in *L'Étoile du Nord* announced the doctor's "soumission à l'autorité ecclésiastique" and his retraction of all the doctrinal errors contained in *La Vie*.[40] The bishop believed that this discreet public notice was a necessary part of the agreement. He congratulated his defeated opponent "d'avoir, sous l'action de la grâce divine, accompli son devoir."[41]

Once again the incident was closed, the faithful people of Joliette safe from scientific naturalism, the doctor silenced. Laurendeau returned to his normal routine, visiting his patients, teaching hygiene in the local schools, advocating temperance, and being continuously re-elected to office in the medical associations. Obviously, many still admired his energy and intelligence even when they disagreed with his radical scientific views. Some of his time and energy was devoted to business interests, including a wood-fibre plant and a potash venture which failed during the war years. He was apparently successful in developing and patenting at least one improved surgical instrument.[42] Doubtless, too, he took notice of the unexpected death of Monsignor Archambault in April 1913, only two years after their last confrontation.[43]

During these less eventful years, Laurendeau continued to think about his evolutionary convictions and his humiliation by the church. Once the bishop was gone, perhaps he looked for an appropriate opportunity to raise the old questions again. Late in 1918 the occasion arrived almost by accident, when he was invited to join the editorial board of the medical journal *La Clinique*, another sign of the continuing esteem in which he was held by his colleagues. But, if he was thought to have mellowed, it was a misjudgment. He declined the invitation, saying, half-jokingly perhaps, that he was born in the woods and remained uncivilized. "Bref, je pourrais être un trouble-fête, comme je l'ai été déjà," he wrote, repeating, summarily, his evolutionary views.[44] The following month he expanded on his beliefs, pointing out that he had been misrepresented by the journal's editor. On the very day that the armistice was achieved in Europe, 11 November

1918, Laurendeau fired a new intellectual rocket in an explanation of his condemned book, *La Vie*. Clearly unrepentant, he claimed that he had been threatened with excommunication without being allowed to explain himself. Now he wanted to state again his continuing belief in the theory of evolution and to insist that, without freedom of thought, genuine science would never flourish in Quebec's universities. The time had arrived to appoint freethinkers, Protestants, and Jews, as well as Catholics, to university posts and to allow them autonomy in their teaching. His liberalism, if anything, had strengthened: "Quelle leçon de tolérance ce serait – de cette tolérance, mère de la concorde et du progrès."[45] A brief controversy followed, just enough to cause the exasperated rural doctor to repeat his long-held belief that, in Quebec, "nous en sommes encore à l'âge médiéval."[46]

Now in his early sixties, Laurendeau continued his heavy schedule of medical practice, medical politics, and writing. At the end of the Great War, Joliette, like many other parts of Canada, was struck by an influenza epidemic. Laurendeau worked harder than ever and, as in the past, reported on his sometimes innovative treatments to his colleagues. He cared for about five hundred cases, three hundred in Saint-Gabriel alone. Only a dozen died. He was rightfully proud of his achievement.[47] Perhaps it was overwork or a life of action, controversy, and tension that contributed to his sudden death from heart failure on 19 August 1920. The previous week had, as usual, been filled with professional meetings. Then, returning from visiting a patient in the neighbouring parish of Saint-Cléophas, he died at the wheel of his automobile near his office in Saint-Gabriel-de-Brandon. On 23 August the funeral Mass, held in his parish church, was sung by his brother Fortunat.[48] His would not be the fate of Joseph Guibord, a-mouldering in a deconsecrated grave.

Summing up the tumultuous life of this remarkable country doctor, his colleague Dr Joseph Gauvreau struck the right note when he wrote that Laurendeau's "originalité consistait surtout à n'être pas souvent de l'avis de tout de monde."[49] For that reason, his life provides several insights into the career of a country doctor and into the professionalization of medical practice in Quebec. In the latter field Laurendeau was a leader who attracted powerful, though not unanimous, support.[50] More significantly, perhaps, Laurendeau's life reveals something about the state of scientific and religious values in Quebec culture in the early twentieth century. Here he found few to join in his crusade in favour of scientific progressivism. The conflict between Dr Laurendeau and Msgr Archambault demonstrated the church's determination to protect its flock against the errors of modernism, of which the most important was the idea that science existed separate from religion.

Though the initial victory went to the bishop, Laurendeau's ideas were apparently tolerated, or at least ignored, by the end of the Great War. The battle was a long one, but, beneath the apparent calm of rural Quebec, new ideas and influences were at work that would slowly and profoundly change that society. That was what Dr Albert Laurendeau hoped for. "Ce n'est pas une révolution que je prêche," he wrote in one of his last polemics, "c'est l'évolution de notre grande institution canadienne-française [Université Laval] dans son intérêt and dans l'intérêt de notre race."[51] The pace of evolutionary change, he fully realized, could be glacial.[52]

[2001]

NOTES

Father François Lanoue generously provided me with copies of documents in the Archives de l'Évêché de Joliette relating to the conflict between Bishop Archambault and Dr Albert Laurendeau. I am greatly indebted to him and to Xavier Gélinas, who carried out indispensable research for me in Quebec medical journals. Jean Hamelin and Yvan Lamonde carefully read and commented on the completed version of this study.

1 *Le Devoir*, 31 Jan 1961, 4.
2 Archives de l'Évêché de Joliette, "Extrait du livre de procès-verbal de la Société historique de Joliette," vol. 2, 1947–68, 125–6 (hereafter *Joliette*).
3 Yves Laurendeau, "En guise de supplément au Laurendeau de Monière," *Revue d'Histoire de l'Amérique française*, 38, no. 1 (summer 1984): 76. André Laurendeau's decision to keep his own religious doubts confidential may have been at least partly the result of the family tradition about Uncle Albert's fate.
4 *L'Étoile du Nord*, 20 Aug. 1920; *La Clinique*, 8 (August 1917): 157; on l'École Normale Jacques Cartier, see Thérèse Hamel, "Hospice-Ardhelme-Jean-Baptiste," *Dictionary of Canadian Biography*, vol. 13 (Toronto: University of Toronto Press 1994), 1049–52; on l'École de Médecine, see Denis Goulet, *Histoire de la Faculté de Médecine de l'Université de Montréal, 1843–1993* (Montreal: vlb, 1994), 40–9.
5 *L'Union Médicale du Canada*, 49, no. 9 (September 1920): 463
6 *La Clinique*, 1, no. 1 (April 1910): 4; *La Clinique*, I, 10, janvier 1911, 331. On the 1909 legislation, see Goulet, *ibid.*, 128–29; Goulet, Denis, et André Paradis, *Trois siècles d'histoire médicale au Québec: Chronologie des institutions et des pratiques (1639–1939)* (Montréal: vlb, 1992), 368–69; *SPQ* (1909), ch55

7 *L'Union Médicale du Canada*, 43, 10 (October 1914): 438.

8 *La Clinique*, 1, no. 2 (May 1910): 38.

9 Ibid., 1, no. 10 (June 1911): 329.

10 Ibid., 5, no. 1 (April 1914): 5–9, 10.

11 Ibid., 1, no. 10 (January 1911): 331.

12 Ibid., 8, no. 5 (August 1917): 159, 160.

13 Roger Le Moine, "Le Grand Orient de France dans le context québecois (1896–1923)," in Yvan Lamonde, ed., *Combats Libéraux au tournant du XXᵉ siècle* (Montréal: Fides 1995), 154; Roger Le Moine, *Deux Loges montréalaises du Grand Orient de France* (Ottawa: Les Presses de l'Université d'Ottawa 1991), 130; *La Clinique*, 2, no. 1 (April 1910): 1; A.-J. Lemieux, *La loge l'Emancipation* (Montréal: La "Croix" 1910). Xavier Gélinas drew this connection to my attention.

14 *Joliette*, Archambault to Laurendeau, 20 March 1907, and Laurendeau to Archambault, 21 March 1907.

15 *Ibid.*, Laurendeau to Archambault, 29 August 1907.

16 Albert Laurendeau, *La Vie: Considérations biologiques* (n.p. 1911), 169–94.

17 *Ibid.*, 197.

18 *Ibid.*, 212.

19 *Joliette*, Archambault to Laurendeau, 16 December 1907 and 19 December 1907.

20 *Ibid.*, Laurendeau to Archambault, 20 December 1907.

21 I*bid.*, Laurendeau to Archambault, 28 December 1907, and Archambault to Laurendeau, 30 December 1907.

22 Albert Laurendeau, *L'Avenir de la Médecine* (Discours Prononcé au Congrès des Médecins de la Langue Française à Québec en juillet 1908), 8.

23 I*bid.*, 9.

24 I*bid.*, 17, 24.

25 *L'Union Médicale du Canada*, 37, no. 12 (December 1908): 607.

26 *Joliette*, Archambault to Laurendeau, 19 October 1910; Laurendeau to Archambault, 20 October 1910 and 25 October 1910. Professor Marcel de Grandpré generously provided me with the text of Doctor Laurendeau's *L'Avenir de la Médecine* and also allowed me to read his unpublished study of Laurendeau, entitled "Un Moderniste en Possession de la Vérité," which helped me to understand the 1910 incident.

27 *La Vie*, 35. Laurendeau would later claim (*Joliette*, Laurendeau to Archambault, 20 June 1912) that he had meant to write "la hiérarchie *sociale ...*"

28 *La Vie*, 65.

29 *Ibid.* 145; on "transformism," see Ernst Mayr, *One Long Argument: Charles Darwin and the Genesis of Modern Evolutionary Thought* (Cambridge, Mass.: Harvard University Press 1991), 187.

30 See Mayr, *One Long Argument*, 17, 21, 43; François Jacob, *La Logique du Vivant: Une Histoire de l'Hérédité* (Paris: Gallimard 1970), 142–52. On Quebec science, see Luc Chartrand, Raymond Duchesne, and Yves Gingras, *Histoire des sciences au Québec* (Montreal: Boréal 1987), 159–200, and Richard A. Jarrell, "L'Ultramontanisme et la Science au Canada français," in Marcel Fourner, Yves Gingras, and Othmar Keel, *Science & Médecine au Québec: Perspectives sociohistoriques* (Institut Québécois de Recherche sur la Culture 1987), 41–68; Carl Berger, *God and Nature in Victorian Canada* (Toronto: University of Toronto Press 1983); Peter R. Eakins and Jean Sinnamon Eakins, "Sir John William Dawson," and Jean-Marie Perron, "Léon Provancher," *Dictionary of Canadian Biography*, 12 (Toronto: University of Toronto Press 1990), 230–37 and 868–70.

31 Yvette Conry, *L'Introduction du Darwinisme en France au XIXe siècle* (Paris: Librairie Philosophique J. Vrin 1974), 308–12; *La Vie*, 107. In *Charles Darwin the Man and His Influence* (Cambridge, U.K.: Cambridge University Press 1996), Peter Bowler notes that "the decades around 1900 saw a growth in the popularity of non-Darwinian mechanisms of evolution and an increased willingness among scientists to proclaim themselves openly hostile to Darwinism" (209). During this period, Lamarckianism won new approval.

32 *La Vie*, 97.

33 *Ibid.*, 158.

34 *Ibid.*, 163.

35 *Joliette*, Archambault to Laurendeau, 19 August 1910 and 25 August 1910.

36 *L'Étoile du Nord*, 28 March 1912, 4.

37 *Joliette*, Laurendeau to Archambault, 20 June 1912.

38 *Ibid.*, Archambault to Laurendeau, 26 June 1912.

39 *Ibid.*, Laurendeau to Archambault, 5 March 1913.

40 *L'Étoile du Nord*, 6 March 1913, 6.

41 *Joliette*, Archambault to Laurendeau, 7 March 1913.

42 *La Clinique*, 11, no. 6 (September 1920): 94; *La Presse*, 20 August 1920, 10.

43 *La Semaine Religieuse de Montréal*, 5 May 1913, 290–304.

44 *La Clinique*, 9, no. 8 (November 1918): 257.

45 *Ibid.*, 9, no. 9 (December 1918): 282–3.

46 *Ibid.*, 10, no. 1 (April 1919), 27.

47 *Ibid.*, 9, no. 10 (January 1919): 297–300; *L'Union Médicale du Canada*, 48, no. 1 (January 1919): 24–30.

48 *L'Étoile du Nord*, 26 August 1920, 1.

49 *L'Union Médicale du Canada*, 49, no. 9 (September 1920): 463.

50 *La Clinique*, 1, no. 1 (April 1910): 1–5; *L'Union Médicale du Canada*, 39, no. 8 (August 1910): 464–70; *La Clinique*, 5, no. 6 (September 1914): 244–50.

51 *La Clinique*, 9, no. 9 (December 1918): 283

52 For a general discussion of the acceptance of Darwinian evolution in Quebec, see Chartrand, Duchesne, and Gingras, *Histoire*, 179–200. The subject needs further investigation.

TWELVE

The Meaning of Confederation

As the fiftieth anniversary of Confederation approached, in 1917, a Canadian historian faced with the task of explaining the meaning of Confederation might have concluded that his country's founders intended to build a nation capable of assisting Great Britain and her allies in their magnificent effort to make the world safe for democracy. Ten years later, the historian, basking in the glories of the Balfour Declaration, might well have replied that the objective of Confederation was to lay the foundations of a nation capable of winning full autonomy within the British Commonwealth. Another historian, in the midst of the Great Depression, would probably have insisted that the intention of the founders was to establish a nation with a central government strong enough to guarantee all Canadians a reasonable standard of living and social welfare. At the end of the Second World War, yet another practitioner of this sensitive craft might have claimed that the far-seeing statesmen of 1867 had intended to build a nation capable of interpreting Europe to America, and vice versa. A decade ago [1957] the answer would certainly have been that the great object of Confederation was to build a nation in the northern half of the North American continent strong enough to resist annexation to the United States. Perhaps in the 1970s some particularly perceptive reader of the *Confederation Debates* will be able to conclude that the real intention of those serious, if not always sober, Victorian gentlemen who sat around the tables at Charlottetown, Quebec, and London was to build a nation scientific enough to launch a bilingual astronaut on his travels to the moon.

Each of those historians, it should be noted, would be English-speaking. A French-speaking historian would in some cases have given those same answers. But he would also have insisted that there was another objective equal to if not prior to the ones emphasized by his English-speaking colleagues. The French-speaking historian would have maintained, at each of the dates mentioned, that the objective of Confederation was to guarantee the survival of *la nation canadienne-française*. He would then have gone on either to defend or to criticize Confederation according to his view of how fully this objective had been served.[1]

While each of these interpretations, in its French and English variations, is based with a greater or lesser degree of accuracy, the answer of the mid 1960s must place the emphasis on yet another interpretation. This interpretation stems from the most permanent theme in Canadian history: the relations between French- and English-speaking Canadians. Among the several objectives of the architects of the Canadian constitution, none was more important than the effort to accommodate the needs of the two cultural communities that had been made co-inhabitants of British North America by the Seven Years' War and the American Revolution. In the minds of the men of 1867 that accommodation was to be achieved by the founding of a new nation. But the important question relates to their definition of the form of that nation.

Several years ago [1961] a young French-Canadian intellectual began his explanation of his position as a Quebec separatist with some lines that go directly to the heart of the meaning of the word 'nation' in the context of Confederation. In his tract *J'ai choisi l'indépendance*, Raymond Barbeau wrote:

The national thought of French Canadians has always seemed ambiguous to me; most of those who defend our interests remain undecided before the following question: does the French-Canadian nation exist? According to the response that we give, our political and patriotic activity will be centred on the state of Quebec or, inversely, on Canada and the federal government. If the Canadian 'nation' exists, the French-Canadian 'nation' has never existed, or exists no longer, either in theory or in practice.[2]

That claim represents the fundamental assumption of the separatist thesis in the current debate over the future of Confederation. It is that a nation must express itself through a sovereign state. A nation that lacks a state of its own is a colony and therefore must, like other colonies, win its independence.[3]

The view that state and nation must be coterminous represents a form of political orthodoxy that finds its roots in the French Revolution, was nurtured by the accidental alliance of liberals and nationalists in the nineteenth century, and flowered under the warm sun of Wilsonianism at Versailles in 1919. That the plant has now clearly produced bitter, even poisonous, fruit has not greatly decreased its apparently habit-forming attractions.[4] Indeed, in the 1960s ideological nationalism, with its emphasis on cultural homogeneity and the right of self-determination, is perhaps more alive and more inebriating than at any time since 1848.

Yet despite the nineteenth-century origins of what is perhaps best called the ideal of the nationalist-state, it was a different ideal that motivated the founders of the Canadian nation. That is why any answer to the question of the meaning of Confederation must be both exceedingly simple and extremely complex. If it were just one or the other we would almost certainly not have had that apparently endless search for the elusive Canadian identity, and French-Canadian identity, which has characterized so much writing about Canada. Nor would we have had the ever-repeating debate about the functions of the various levels of government in Canada if the men of 1864–7 had given us a statement of intention either so simple that every schoolboy could grasp it or so complex that only a philosopher-king could interpret it. But Sir John A. Macdonald's merry men did neither. Hence the debate and hence also the fascination of Canadian history.

The meaning of Confederation was, first, simple. There cannot be the slightest doubt that the intention of the Fathers of Confederation was, in Macdonald's words, the 'founding of a great nation.'[5] Here on the northern half of the North American continent 'a new nationality' was being founded. Not one of the supporters of the scheme, English- or French-speaking, contended otherwise. The opponents of the scheme, from whatever part of British North America they came, recognized the nation-building objective of the proposals. For various reasons they thought that the new nation was either impractical or undesirable or both.

But what kind of a nation could be built out of four or five scattered colonies which knew either too little about one another, as was the case of the Maritimes and Canada, or too much about one another, as was the case of Canada East (as Quebec was then called) and Canada West (later Ontario)? It is in answering this question that the originality and deviationism of the founders of Canada become clear and the complexity of the problem becomes obvious. While the Fathers of Confederation were intent upon establishing a 'nation-state', they were equally forthright in their rejection of the ideal of the 'nationalist-state'. The nation whose foundations were being laid was not culturally homogeneous. Nor was it the objective of the politicians of the Great Coalition to build a structure that would enforce or produce ultimate homogeneity. In the house of the Fathers of Confederation there were to be many mansions. In explaining why he had forsaken his ideal of a single, unitary legislative union in favour of a federal system, Macdonald, who understood every detail of the scheme, had this to say:

In the first place it [legislative union] would not have met the assent of the people of Lower Canada, because they felt that in their peculiar position – being a minority with a different language, nationality and religion from the majority – in case of a junction with the other provinces, their institutions and their laws might be assailed, and their ancestral associations, on which they prided themselves, attacked and prejudiced; it was found that any proposition which involved the absorption of the individuality of Lower Canada – if I may use the expression – would not be received with favour by her people.[6]

Macdonald, who had successfully trod through the no-man's-land of sectional, religious, and cultural quarrels for twenty years before Confederation, knew that the key to political success and constitutional stability was harmony between French and English Canadians. He defined his formula in 1856 when he told an English-speaking Montrealer: 'Treat them [the French Canadians] as a nation and they will act as a free people generally do – generously. Call them a faction and they become factious.'[7] But how could one build a 'nation' and yet treat the French Canadians as a 'nation'? Macdonald supplied his answer in the Confederation debates. The British constitutional system was one that required no enforced uniformity, but rather provided for the protection of minority rights. 'We will enjoy here', Macdonald claimed, 'the great test of constitutional freedom – we will have the rights of the minority respected.'[8] This point was explained more fully by George Etienne Cartier, the leading French Canadian among the Fathers. Cartier was naturally very sensitive to the charge made by his opponents that the much-talked-about 'new nationality' would engulf the French-Canadian nationality. Had not Lord Durham been one of the first to propose federation of all British North America? And for what purpose? None other than to erase the French-Canadian nation from the face of British North America. Cartier made it plain, however, that the nation whose birth he was attending would be the very antithesis of the Anglo-Saxon nationalism that Durham had supported:

Now when we were united together, if union were attained, we would form a political nationality with which neither national origin, nor the religion of any individual would interfere ... In our federation we should have Catholic and Protestant, English, French, Irish, Scotch, and each in his efforts and success would increase the prosperity and glory of our new Confederacy.[9]

Thus while it is true that in 1867 the political leaders of Canada were engaged in that characteristic nineteenth-century activity, the building of a nation-state, it is likewise true, and highly significant, that they were rejecting that equally characteristic nineteenth-century phenomenon, the nationalist-state. Their concept of Canada was of a community based on political and juridical unity, but also on cultural and religious duality. And the key to that unity in duality was the rejection of the intolerant, conformist, ideological nationalism that was, in these same years, shaking the foundations of Europe and also providing the drive that led to the destruction of the Southern Confederacy by the North in the American Civil War.

The second key to the meaning of Confederation was that the new union was to be a federal one. In this fashion, diversity was to be given specific institutional guarantees. Federalism, as has often been remarked, was not a very well understood system of government in the nineteenth century.[10] And where it was known, in the United States, it did not provide a very encouraging example. Yet federalism was indispensable if there was to be a union of British North America. The Maritime Provinces were quite unwilling to be completely absorbed into the upstart culture of Canada. More important, the French Canadians refused to give up the relative security of the union where Canada East and Canada West enjoyed equal representation for a new union based on representation by population unless they were given the means of protecting their individuality. Arthur Gordon, the Governor of New Brunswick, watched the preliminary discussions on the projected union and reported to the Colonial Secretary, 'The aim of Lower Canada is a local independence as complete as circumstances will permit, and the peculiarities of race, religion and habits which distinguish its people render their desire respectable and natural.'[11] And when Lord Carnarvon, the Colonial Secretary, presented the British North America Act to the House of Lords in February 1867 he noted that 'Lower Canada now *consents* to enter into this Confederation because its peculiar institutions were to be given effective guarantees.'[12] The great compromise of 1867, and at the same time the great victory for the French Canadians, was the federal system of government.[13] Had there been only one 'nation' involved in the negotiations that preceded the establishment of Confederation, the proponents of legislative union would doubtless have fought harder for their viewpoint. Since there was not one nation but two, the result was federalism.

What is perhaps not often enough emphasized in discussions of Confederation is that while the events of 1864 to 1867 produced a union, they also produced a division. From 1841 to 1865 Canada East and

Canada West had been united in a theoretically unitary, but practically federal, state. The experience had been less than satisfying. Moreover, it was not only, or even chiefly, the French Canadians who were anxious to bring this unhappy condition to an end. Indeed, throughout the last years of the union the loudest complaints came from the Liberals in Canada West. Led by George Brown, the Grit party practically made its fortune on two cries: 'French domination' and 'rep by pop'. The federal system adopted in 1867 provided the means whereby this so-called French domination could be ended and representation by population implemented with the approval of the French Canadians. This explains the exuberant tone of the letter George Brown scribbled to his wife at the end of the Quebec Conference in 1864. 'All right!!' he whooped. 'Confederation through at six o'clock this evening – constitution adopted – a creditable document – a complete reform of all the abuses and injustices we have complained of! Is it not wonderful? French Canadianism entirely extinguished.'[14] That last line about 'French Canadianism' speaks volumes about the history of the United Canadas! In the debates that took place in the Parliament of the Canadas on the subject of the Quebec Resolutions, speaker after speaker, in more restrained terms than the editor of the Toronto Globe, noted that the proposed Confederation was 'a separation of the provinces',[15] as the venerable Sir E.P. Taché put it. Once more the complexity of Confederation is obvious: to unity in duality has been added unity in separation.

To the English-speaking Fathers, unity was all-important. Macdonald repeatedly emphasized his preference for a legislative union – which he evidently thought was compatible with cultural duality. Each of the supporters of the scheme emphasized the necessity of a strong central government if the new nation state was to survive in the face of a rapidly changing world. In the newly emerging balance of world power, Britain seemed anxious to retreat from her costly commitments in North America at a time when the United States, the traditional enemy of British North America, was giving proof of its enormous military strength.[16] Both French and English supporters of the Confederation scheme were agreed that a central government capable of initiating effective military and economic policies was necessary if British North America was to survive. Every nation is founded on a will to survive. Canada was no exception and it was that will which united French- and English-speaking British North Americans in 1867. In 1940 the report of a royal commission, the Rowell-Sirois Commission, which had been appointed to carry out a full-scale examination of the Canadian federal system, made the point in this way:

Confederation was conceived as a solution for a number of political and economic difficulties and, therefore, had both political and economic aims. Politically it was designed to establish a new nation to meet the changed conditions of British policy and to brace the scattered provinces against possible American aggression. Economically it was intended to foster a national economy which would relieve dependence upon a few industries and lessen exposure to the effects of the economic policies pursued by the United States and Great Britain.[17]

With these objectives in mind, the men who drafted the British North America Act placed the preponderance of power, including the residual power, in the hands of the central government.[18]

So broad were the powers of the proposed central government, the critics of the scheme charged that to describe the system as federal was to divest the term of all known meaning. 'I am opposed to the scheme of Confederation,' Eric Dorion, the *enfant terrible* of French Canada, announced, 'because the first resolution is nonsense and repugnant to truth; it is not a federal union which is offered, but a legislative union in disguise.'[19] The fear that disturbed these French-Canadian opponents of the plan was quite simple: had the Macdonalds and Cartiers, in their concern for Canadian survival, produced a system of government that would threaten *la survivance de la nation canadienne-française?* Cartier, of course, said no; but his response failed to convince a significant number of his compatriots.[20]

This sharp difference of opinion is another reminder of the duality of the country and also of the duality of the motives that lay behind the union of 1867. Therefore, just as the Rowell-Sirois Report stressed the theme of Canadian survival as the central factor in Confederation, a Quebec royal commission in 1956, the Tremblay Commission, stressed the factor of French-Canadian survival. And just as the Rowell-Sirois Commission emphasized the centralized character of the 1867 scheme, so the Tremblay Commission underlined provincial powers. Here is the way the Quebec commissioners concluded their consideration of the events of 1864–7:

To sum up, the Union of 1867 met the common needs of the provinces. If it assumed a federative character it was doubtless due to their divergencies, but it was especially due to the irreducible presence of the French Canadian bloc which only accepted Confederation because it had been given every conceivable promise that it would be able to govern itself in autonomous fashion and thereby develop, along with all its institutions, according to its special way of life and its own culture.[21]

Those who try to read orthodox nationalist assumptions into Confederation – that is to say, those who argue that Canada is a nationalist-state rather than a nation-state – always fail to realize that survival and *la survivance* are not necessarily interchangeable words. Indeed, rather than being interchangeable, the two realities that the words represent are in a constant state of tension. It was one of the fundamental objectives of the Fathers of Confederation to bring that tension into a state of equilibrium. Confederation was an agreement, pact, or *entente*, whichever of those words best describes the political rather than the legal character of the events of 1864–7. And the terms of that *entente* were that a new nation-state was to be founded on the basis of an acceptance of cultural duality and on a division of powers.[22] The unstated major premise of that *entente* was that both survival and *la survivance* were legitimate objectives and that those objectives could better be achieved within the structure of a single, federal state than in separate states or in a unitary state. The unceasing responsibility of Canadian political leaders since 1867 has been to ensure that the equilibrium between survival and *la survivance*, between the legitimate goals of Canadians and of French Canadians, should not be destroyed. It has never been an easy assignment.

There can be no doubt that a homogeneous nation is more easily governed than one based on cultural duality, though the history of the American federal system, especially before 1865, stands as a constant warning against easy generalization. But in Canada cultural duality adds a second type of potential friction to that inherent in any polity organized on federal lines. Within the Canadian federal system there have been, in general terms, three types of conflict. Each of these conflicts has involved the problem of cultural duality; but two of them have also been entangled in the question of divided jurisdiction.

The first type of conflict has arisen as part of the struggle for political power at Ottawa. There is always a danger, in a society composed of diverse cultural and religious elements, that an ambitious or frustrated politician will attempt to build his fortunes on stimulating antagonism rather than on conciliating differences. On the whole, Canada has been remarkably free of this type of politician. Nearly all of our leaders seem to have realized that party lines must not be allowed to coincide with national lines. Such a party division would be especially dangerous for French Canadians. 'Why, so soon as the French Canadians, who are in a minority in this country, were to organize as a political party, they would compel the majority to organize as a political party and the result would be disastrous to themselves,'[23]

Wilfrid Laurier warned in 1886. Theoretically, as a Conservative tactician argued as recently as 1956,[24] it is possible for a party to win
power by appealing exclusively to English Canada. But even if English
Canadians were united enough to be herded into the same political cor-
ral, it is doubtful if successful government could be carried on.[25]

On at least two occasions a complete French-English division has
nearly been reached. These crises, in 1917 and 1942, both centred on
the question of conscription for overseas service, which the vast majority of French Canadians opposed and most English Canadians
favoured. But in general Canadian federal parties have served the
country well in their role of finding a working consensus in a culturally divided country. Their weakness is that they must be parties of
compromise, and compromise can sometimes become an excuse for the
evasion of responsibility. That is why our party system has most often,
in the twentieth century, been a multi-party system composed of one or
more major 'parties of consensus' and several 'parties of principle or
interest'. The latter type of party has never gained power in Canada,
but if one did it would almost certainly be rapidly transformed into a
party of consensus. The 'price of union' in Canada appears to be parties of compromise and consensus.

A second type of conflict that has produced serious national friction
has grown out of the question of the rights of French Canadians living
outside of Quebec. While both French and English were made official
languages in the federal parliament, the British North America Act
made no special provision for the French language or French schools
outside of Quebec – though the Protestant, English-speaking minority
was well provided for inside Quebec. It is true that some protection
was provided for religious minorities outside of Quebec, and perhaps
the Fathers assumed that their successors would be as liberal as themselves in allowing both religious and national minorities equality of
rights.[26] The hope, if it existed, proved too optimistic.

By its very intention, Confederation was expansionist. It was to provide the answer to American 'manifest destiny' which threatened to
absorb parts of mid-western and far-western British North America. As
George Brown, the voice of Ontario manifest destiny, put it, 'What we
propose now is but to lay the foundations of the structure – to set in
motion the governmental machinery that will one day, we trust, extend
from the Atlantic to the Pacific.'[27] The Confederation scheme could
not be completed without this commitment to expansion; it was a necessary element in the over-all pattern of British North American survival. Yet it was also a threat to the new Confederation – just as Western expansion threatened the American federal system before 1860, so
western settlement would inevitably raise the question of the rights of

French Canada's 'peculiar institutions'. The question was especially difficult since these territories would almost certainly be filled with non-French-speaking settlers. There were those French Canadians who recognized the danger early and appealed to Quebec to send colonists to Manitoba 'in the interests of our future influence in Confederation'.[28] But the appeal went largely unheeded. French-language rights had been recognized in both Manitoba in 1870 and the Northwest Territories in 1875, but these privileges were largely swept away by the end of the century. The privileges were abolished by people who accepted the view of the Ontario member of parliament who told the House of Commons in 1890: 'I say that we have not, that we cannot have and never will have in this country, two nationalities.'[29] It was the belief of such people as these, as D'Alton McCarthy put it at Stayner, Ontario, in 1889, that 'This is a British country, and the sooner we take up our French Canadians and make them British, the less trouble will we leave for posterity.'[30] What these people really wanted was to replace the Canadian nation-state, based on cultural duality, with a Canadian nationalist-state based on a uniform British-Canadian culture.

'McCarthyism,' as it might well be called, insisted that Canada was a British country by right of conquest, and that it could only become a real nation if that right of conquest was used to create cultural homogeneity. Sir John Macdonald rejected these claims completely and in so doing [in 1890] once more defined his view of the meaning of Confederation:

I have no accord with the desire expressed in some quarters that by any mode whatever there should be an attempt made to oppress the one language or to render it inferior to the other; I believe that it would be impossible if it were tried, and it would be foolish and wicked if it were possible. The statement that has been made so often that this is a conquered country is à propos de rien. Whether it was conquered or ceded, we have a constitution now under which all British subjects are in a position of absolute equality, having equal rights of every kind – of language, of religion, of property, and of person. There is no paramount race in this country, there is no conquered race in this country; we are all British subjects, and those who are not English are none the less British on that account.[31]

In 1890 Macdonald had only a little more than a year to live. The theory of equality expressed in his defence of the French language in the Northwest did not live much longer. As the immigrants flocked to the empty plains from all parts of Europe and the United States, the French-speaking minority was rapidly outnumbered. Once more that most difficult of all problems of democracy was raised: the relation of minority rights to majority rule. Mgr Taché, the ecclesiastical and national leader of the French Canadians in Manitoba, foresaw the outcome. 'Number is going to make us weak,' he wrote, 'and since under our constitutional system number is power, we are going to find ourselves at the mercy of those who do not love us.'[32]

First in Manitoba in the 1890s, and then in the new provinces of Saskatchewan and Alberta in 1905, the privileges of the French and Catholic minority were reduced to a minimum. The arguments against minority schools were chiefly of two kinds. One arose from an intense Protestantism or, perhaps better, an intense anti-Catholicism. John Willison, the distinguished editor of the Toronto *News*, explained his hostility to separate schools in 1905 when he wrote to Sir Wilfrid Laurier: 'While I have all this respect and consideration for the natural race sentiment of French Canadians no man could be more strenuously opposed to clerical interference in state affairs. And from Confederation down the plain meaning of the constitution has been deliberately perverted to serve the ends of the Roman Catholic hierarchy.'[33] In those years, to argue against separate schools was to argue against French schools.

The second argument was, in effect, that unless English was made the sole language of all the schools in the West, a Canadian 'nation' could never emerge from the polyglot western population. This view had a natural attraction on the prairies, and the patriotic fervour created by the First World War provided the necessary heat to set the melting-pot boiling. That process, like many experiments in mass produced uniformity, had first been tested in the United States. Its Canadian version rarely distinguished between recent immigrants from Poland and French-speaking Manitobans whose ancestors had arrived in North America in the seventeenth or eighteenth centuries. The process was well illustrated in Manitoba. In 1916, when bilingual schools were finally and completely abolished, a Franco-Manitoban protested in the legislature that 'the French are a distinctive race, and will not be assimilated whether you like it or not'. To this *cri de coeur* a cabinet minister of Icelandic origin replied: 'I want those who agree with that statement to consider what would happen if all the nationalities represented in this province were to adopt that attitude. What kind of a Manitoba would we have a hundred years from now?'[34] The attitude here expressed was that the Franco-Manitobans were a minority like any other minority, and must therefore be cast into the Manitoba melting-pot.

Yet this view was not accepted by all the Western provinces. In 1918, when Saskatchewan made certain modifications in its school laws in order to 'nationalize' its ethnic minorities, a small exception was made for the French-speaking group – though only after a cabinet minister had resigned in protest against an initial plan to homogenize all the minorities. In the debate, one minister of the Saskatchewan government who knew his country's history better than his Manitoba colleague told the legislature: 'Saskatchewan is an integral part of our Dominion. Confederation came as the result of a compromise for the sake of unity. French was the official language of the Dominion and because we have the legislative power to wipe it out I cannot see the justification for violating the principle upon which Confederation unity was founded, just because we have that power.'[35]

It is nevertheless true that increasingly in English Canada the principle of majority rule took precedence over minority rights. Macdonald's tolerant belief that there were at least two ways of being Canadian was replaced by a rigid, even intolerant, adherence to the letter of the British North America Act. John W. Dafoe, a leading exponent of Canadian nationalism, exemplified this new rigidity. Annoyed by some criticisms that a French-Canadian friend levelled at the unilingual Manitoba school system, Dafoe retorted:

You have allowed yourself to become committed to the theory that the Dominion of Canada, as a whole, is a bilingual country in every portion of which the French have precisely the same rights as the English. Canada is not, however, a bilingual country, either by treaty, or in law, or in fact, and you cannot establish that it is by either of the courses open to you: an appeal to the law courts or an appeal to the court of public opinion.[36]

By the strict letter of the law, Dafoe was quite correct. But by insisting on that strict view and backing it up with a scarcely veiled appeal to the tyranny of the democratic majority, he was rejecting the essential spirit of Confederation. 'In all countries the rights of the majority take care of themselves,' Macdonald had remarked in 1865, 'but it is only in countries like England, enjoying constitutional liberty, and safe from the tyranny of a single despot *or of an unbridled democracy*, that the rights of minorities are regarded.'[37]

Dafoe's nationalism, founded on a firm belief in 'unbridled democracy,' was accepted as the standard by most English Canadians. Only a man with the optimism of Henri Bourassa, the founder of the Montreal nationalist daily *Le Devoir*, could maintain his faith in a Canadian nation founded on a genuine dualism. In 1928 he again expressed this primary article in his political creed, which he called 'nationalism', in a letter to one of the many unconverted, J.W. Dafoe:

Most of us are sincerely and profoundly convinced that the federal pact was
based on the recognition of a perfect equality of rights as between English-
speaking and French-speaking Canadians, and also as between Catholics and
Protestants, in all matters relating to education, whether religious or linguistic.
And in this as you know we have the solemn word and testimony of Sir John
Macdonald himself. We not less sincerely believe that Confederation cannot
endure and Canada obtain her full destiny as a nation, unless this broad principle of dualism obtains everywhere.[38]

To quote that statement is to measure the gulf that divided two Canadian nationalists and probably the two most influential Canadian journalists of the twentieth century.

A third type of conflict in Canada is one familiar to every inhabitant
of a federal polity. It is the conflict between federal and provincial
authorities. The history of federal-provincial friction in Canada is as
old as Confederation itself, and it has never been simply a clash
between Ottawa and Quebec. Indeed some of the most vigorous exponents of provincial rights have been EnglishCanadian provincial leaders. Oliver Mowat of Ontario is the grandfather of them all. His
attacks on the federal power in the 1880s were followed by those of Sir
Richard McBride of British Columbia in the early years of the 20th
century, Howard Ferguson and Mitchell Hepburn of Ontario in the
1920s and 1930s, William Aberhart of Alberta and T.D. Pattullo of
British Columbia in the 1930s, and George Drew of Ontario and
Angus L. Macdonald of Nova Scotia in the late 1940s and early 1950s.

Nevertheless the struggle for provincial autonomy has had a particular meaning and appeal for French Canadians. Every premier of Quebec, from Honoré Mercier in the 1880s down to Jean Lesage today
[1960s], has at least paid lip-service to provincial rights, and more
often has carried on a running conflict with Ottawa. Indeed, the most
serious threat to the original concept of Confederation as a nation-
state founded on cultural duality has always been the possibility that
some day French Canadians would come to identify their nation solely
with the provincial state. One of the most serious results of the limitations that were placed on the rights of French Canadians outside Quebec has been the growing feeling that only Quebec was the 'national-
state' of French Canada. This process of 'nationalizing' the provincial
state began in the 1880s shortly after Quebecers were shocked to discover that their delegation at Ottawa had been unable to prevent the
execution of Louis Riel, the Métis leader of two Western rebellions.
But the pace has gathered momentum in the age of industrialization
and urbanization, since both phenomena have raised serious questions
about traditional political jurisdictions. The fact that Quebec was

industrialized largely by 'foreign' capital stimulated the French Canadians' national consciousness. Moreover the development took place
during a period when French Canadians, as a result of their unhappy
memories of 1917 and their fears of a new world war, were exceedingly
suspicious of the federal authority. That, in part, explains the fact that
while many English Canadians have since the Great Depression
demanded increased federal involvement in social welfare, economic
development, and education programs, most French Canadians have
resisted federal largess even when it meant forgoing the kind of wel-
fare-state policies that make life livable in modern society.

Perhaps the key point in this development was the election in 1936
of Premier Maurice Duplessis and his Union Nationale party. For the
first time, a party held office in Quebec that had no federal affiliations.
It was a specifically provincial party and, as its name suggested, it identified the nation with the province – despite the fact that its leaders
paid homage occasionally to the idea of a bicultural or bi-national
Canada. Thus began a period when French Canadians looked more
and more to their provincial government as the primary defender of *la
survivance*. This development took place at the very time when English
Canadians were becoming convinced that Canadian survival depended
on a more active central government. That is the crux of our present
discontents.[39]

During the 1950s English Canadians became rapidly aware of the
vulnerability of their small nation alone in North America with the
giant United States. Survival seemed more than ever to depend on a
federal government capable of implementing new national policies in
the economic, social, and cultural fields that would strengthen Canadian individuality and independence.[40] French Canadians, no less fear-
ful of the all-pervasive influence of the United States, reacted coolly,
even with hostility, to many of the new national panaceas. Typical is
the comment of a French-Canadian nationalist on the *Report of the
Royal Commission on National Development in the Arts, Letters and
Sciences*, better known as the Massey Report. 'When the Massey
Report registers the dangers of the American way of life, it sees accurately,' he wrote. 'When it brings its support to the centralizing movement, it opts for a bad remedy. For one can never assure the defence of
Canada when one contributes to the dismantling of one of its bas-
tions.'[41] What worried French Canadians in the 1950s, as it had worried them a century earlier, was that an all-powerful central government might become the instrument, not of duality, but of a
homogeneous nationalism that would stifle the minority. The fear was
expressed in an extreme form by a group who declared: 'Those who
pretend to work for the formation of a single nation called "Canada"

desire, consciously or unconsciously, the complete assimilation of the weaker nation by the stronger.'[42]

By the beginning of the 1960s many French Canadians had begun to question the validity of the Confederation concept. At the basis of these questions is the belief that the *entente* of 1867 has been broken, that tension between survival and *la survivance* has mounted to a final crisis. 'Canada is a reality whose very existence is only possible by the coexistence of two antagonisms,' a young radical separatist wrote recently.[43] If there is antagonism rather than cooperation, it is because the meaning of Confederation has become blurred. That meaning was that two nations could survive and grow inside a single nation-state, provided each nation refrained from claiming an exclusively nationalist-state. The *entente* of 1867 was based on the belief that the federal government would be the instrument of both survival and *la survivance*. The provinces, of course, also had a role to play. But if they, or even one of them, ever fully assumed responsibility for one of the components of the 'new nation', then the *entente* would be a failure.

Today the experiment is by no means over. But no one can doubt that it is passing through a period of profound readjustment. If the original, imaginative concept of Confederation cannot be reshaped to meet the needs of today's Canada, then, as a wise French Canadian has recently observed, 'the blind forces of national pride will be let loose for good.'[44] At that point the meaning of Confederation will be finally destroyed, for it will mark the triumph of nationalism over the nation-state.

[1965]

NOTES

1 French-Canadian historians have not written much of a scholarly kind about Confederation, but two rather different approaches can be found in Lionel Groulx, *La Confédération canadienne* (Montreal, 1918), and Thomas Chapais, *Cours d'histoire du Canada* (Quebec, 1934), Vol. VIII.

2 Raymond Barbeau, *J'ai choisi l'indépendance* (Montreal, 1961), page 7.

3 Raymond Barbeau, *Québec est-il une colonie?* (Montreal, 1962).

4 Elie Kedourie, *Nationalism*. This book is an indispensable analysis of nationalist ideology.

5 *Confederation Debates*, page 45.

6 *Ibid.*, page 29.

7 Public Archives of Canada, Brown Chamberlin Papers, Macdonald to Chamberlin, February 21, 1856.

8 *Confederation Debates*, page 44.

9 *Ibid.*, page 60.

10 For an account of federal ideas in Canada, see Peter B. Waite, *The Life and Times of Confederation* (Toronto, 1962), and Jean-Charles Bonenfant, 'L'Idée que les Canadiens français de 1864 pouvaient avoir du fédéralisme', *Culture*, Vol. XXV, December 4, 1964, pages 307–22.

11 Public Archives of Canada, New Brunswick, C. O. 189, Gordon to Cardwell, September 22, 1864.

12 Sir Robert Herbert (ed.), *Speeches on Canadian Affairs by Henry Howard Molyneux, Fourth Earl of Carnarvon* (London, 1902), pages 10–11. Italics added.

13 D.G. Creighton, *The Road to Confederation: The Emergence of Canada, 1863–1867* (Toronto, 1964); Thomas Chapais, *Cours d'histoire du Canada* (Quebec, 1934), Vol. VIII, page 162.

14 Public Archives of Canada, Brown Papers, Brown to Anne Brown, October 27, 1864.

15 *Confederation Debates*, page 9.

16 C.P. Stacey, *Canada and the British Army, 1846–71* (Toronto, 1963), and Robin Winks, *Canada and the United States: The Civil War Years* (Baltimore, 1960).

17 *Report of the Royal Commission on Dominion-Provincial Relations, Book I: Canada 1867–1939* (Ottawa, 1940), page 29.

18 Today even French Canadians appear to accept this view of the intention of the Fathers, though traditionally they have been loath to do so. (See Jean-Charles Bonenfant, 'L'Esprit de 1867', *Revue d'histoire de l'Amérique française*, Vol. XVII, No. 1, June 1963, pages 19–38.)

19 *Confederation Debates*, page 858.

20 It is, of course, impossible to know the exact strength of the opposition to Confederation since the matter was not put to a popular test. One French-Canadian writer, after a less than exhaustive analysis, has concluded that a majority of French Canadians probably supported the scheme. (See Jean-Charles Bonenfant, 'Les Canadiens français et la naissance de la Confédération', *Report of the Canadian Historical Association*, 1952, page 45.)

21 *Report of the Royal Commission of Inquiry on Constitutional Problems, Province of Quebec* (Quebec, 1956), Vol. I, page 22.

22 Pierre-Elliott Trudeau, 'Federalism, Nationalism and Reason', in P.A. Crepeau and C.E. Macpherson (eds.), *The Future of Canadian Federalism* (Toronto, 1965), pages 16–35.

23 Canada, *House of Commons Debates*, 1886, Vol. I, page 72.

24 John Meisel, *The Canadian General Election of 1957* (Toronto, 1962).

25 John Meisel, *The Canadian General Election of 1957* (Toronto, 1962). The tactician, Gordon Churchill, added significantly: 'The statement is

frequently made that "you cannot govern the country without Quebec" and to this statement there is no serious disagreement, for in the interests of national unity all parts of Canada should be represented in the government.'

26 Eugene Forsey, 'The British North America Act and Biculturalism,' *Queen' s Quarterly*, Vol. XXXI, No. 2, Summer 1964, pages 141–9.

27 *Confederation Debates*, page 86.

28 Alfred Bernier, *Le Manitoba champs d'immigration* (Ottawa, 1887), page 16.

29 Canada, *House of Commons Debates*, 1890, Vol. l, page 546. The speaker was Colonel W.E. O'Brien of 'Noble Thirteen' fame.

30 Fred Landon, 'D'Alton McCarthy and the Politics of the Later Eighties,' *Report of the Canadian Historical Association*, 1932, pages 43, 50.

31 Canada, *House of Commons Debates*, 1890, Vol. I, page 745.

32 Dom Benoît, *La Vie de monseigneur Taché* (Montreal, 1904), Vol. II, pages 195–6.

33 Public Archives of Canada, Laurier Papers, J.S. Willison to Laurier, March 9, 1905.

34 *Canadian Annual Review*, 1916 (Toronto, 1917), pages 673–4.

35 Hon. S.J. Latta, in *The Language Question before the Legislative Assembly of Saskatchewan* (Prince Albert, 1919), page 13. The Minister who resigned was the Hon. W.R. Motherwell.

36 Public Archives of Canada, Dafoe Papers, Dafoe to Thomas Côté, April 17, 1916.

37 *Confederation Debates*, page 44. Italics added.

38 Dafoe Papers, Henri Bourassa to Dafoe, April 26, 1928.

39 Donald Smiley, 'The Two Themes of Canadian Federalism', *Canadian Journal of Economics and Political Science*, Vol. XXXI, February 1965, pages 80–97.

40 For the standard argument, see the *Report of the Royal Commission on Broadcasting* (Ottawa, 1957), page 9. The same argument underlies both the Massey Commission report (1951), and the O'Leary Commission report (1963).

41 André Laurendeau, 'Y a-t-il une crise du nationalisme ?', *L'Action nationale*, Vol. XL, No. 3, December 1952, page 224.

42 *Canada français et l'union canadienne*, Société Saint-Jean-Baptiste de Montréal (Montréal, 1954), pages 115–16.

43 Paul Chamberlain, 'De domination à la liberté', *Parti pris*, Summer 1964.

44 Claude Ryan, 'The French-Canadian Dilemma', *Foreign Affairs*, Vol. 43, No. 3, April 1965, page 474.

THIRTEEN

Quebec and Confederation: Past and Present

The political problem of the French-speaking minority in Canada is as easily defined as it is difficult to solve: how can a self-conscious minority preserve its distinctiveness in a community governed by the principles of majority rule and representation by population? Clearly in such a society if a public question arises which divides the community along cultural lines French-speaking Canadians inevitably find themselves subjected to what is sometimes called 'the tyranny of the democratic majority'. Such issues have arisen in Canadian life in the past – most seriously in 1885 over the hanging of Louis Riel, during the First World War crises over French-language schools in Ontario and conscription for overseas service, and again over the conscription issue during the Second World War. These crises, which seriously ruptured relations between French and English Canadians, suggest that in Canada something more than simple majority support is necessary if public business is to be transacted smoothly and efficiently. A rough consensus of opinion in both French and English Canada is a primary requirement. The achievement of that consensus has been the objective of most of our political leaders. And the very machinery of government in Canada was, in part, designed to help make that consensus possible. When the Fathers of Confederation sat down at Charlottetown and later at Quebec to formulate the principles of union for British North America, one of the first problems they had to grapple with was that of the place of a minority in a majoritarian state. There were, of course, several types of minorities, including, in Sir John Macdonald's view, the rich.[1] But the most important minority was French Canada. It was not only the spokesmen of French Canada who insisted that the new state be a federal one, but they were certainly the strongest proponents of federal as opposed to legislative union. George Etienne Cartier, the leader of the French-Canadian delegation, told the Quebec Conference:

'We thought that a federation scheme was the best because these provinces are peopled by different nations and by peoples of different religions.'[2]

What federal union provided was that French Canadians, while participating fully in all the common affairs of the new nation, also had one province where they would be in a majority. And the provinces were given control over those matters which, in 1867, seemed most important for the preservation of French Canada's distinctiveness – education, civil law, and matters respecting religious life. Thus, in addition to being a union of the four provinces, Confederation was also a division between Canada East, or Quebec, and Canada West, or Ontario, which had previously been united in a single legislative union. Hector Langevin predicted, too optimistically as events were to prove, that 'in Parliament there will be no questions of race, nationality, religion, or locality, as this Legislature will only be charged with the settlement of the great general questions which will interest alike the whole Confederacy and not one locality only.'[3]

At the same time, French became one of the two official languages of the federal parliament and its records or journals, and of the federal courts. Quebec, alone among the provinces, was made bilingual in its legislature and in its courts. In this sense, as in one or two more minor matters, Quebec was not to be a province like the others. Something that is not always realized is that it was not until 1867 that French became constitutionally one of the two official languages of Canada. French had been used in public business before Confederation, but it was not until the passage of the British North America Act that it obtained legal recognition as an official language.

Despite the federal structure of the new nation and the guarantees given to the French language, by no means all French Canadians were enthusiastic supporters of the new constitution. Many of them feared that their minority position would be more vulnerable than ever in an arrangement that united the Canadas with the maritime colonies and looked forward to the addition of the Prairie West and the Pacific Coast territories in the near future. Moreover, there was a strongly expressed opinion that the new federal scheme placed so much power in the hands of the central government that a legislative union, in all but name, was in fact being established. The future of French Canada would thus rest at the mercy of the central power where English Canadians would always be in a majority. A.-A. Dorion, a leading opponent of the proposed Confederation, expressed these fears when he stated:

I know that majorities are naturally aggressive and how the possession of power engenders despotism, and I can understand how a majority, animated this moment by the best feelings, might in six or nine months be willing to abuse its power and trample on the rights of the minority, while acting in good faith, and on what is considered to be its rights.

Dorion was worried, moreover, by the talk that he heard from the supporters of Confederation about a 'new nationality'. Did this mean a uniform nationality? Did it mean the assimilation of French Canada into an English-speaking melting-pot? It fell to Cartier to deal with these charges. He affirmed that a new nation was being projected but it would be a political nation which allowed for, indeed encouraged, cultural diversity. 'The idea of unity of races was utopian,' he said; 'it was impossible.' As to French Canada's minority position, Cartier had two answers. First he said that the real question before Canadians was whether they would 'obtain British North American Confederation or be absorbed in an American Confederation'. Of these alternatives, Canadian federation was the obvious choice. Then, turning to the question of French Canada's role in the central government, the tough, cocksure Cartier noted that there would always be French Canadians in the cabinet and they would be backed by a phalanx of sixty-five French-Canadian votes in the House of Commons.

While there was no popular vote on the Confederation scheme, the parliamentary division of the members from Canada East in 1865 was very close – twenty-seven in favour of the plan, twenty-two opposed to it. Perhaps François Evanturel, a French-Canadian Conservative, expressed the views of many of his people when he remarked:

I am in favour of the principle of Confederation, and one of those who main-tain that by means of that principle the rights and liberties of each of the con-tracting parties may be preserved; but on the other hand, I am of opinion ... that it may be so applied as to endanger and even destroy, or nearly so, the rights and privileges of a state which is a party to this Confederation. Every-thing, therefore, depends upon the conditions of the contract.[4]

In the first ninety years after 1867 both the supporters and the critics of Confederation were provided with some evidence to support their pre-dictions. There can be no doubt that French Canadians benefited from the new arrangement. They shared in the economic progress that the new country experienced. They took an active part in the formulation of those policies which were designed to acquire full legal nationhood for Canada. Within the province of Quebec, French Canadians were their own mas-ters in political and cultural matters. Economically they did not have full control over their society, but the complicated explanation of that situa-tion had little, if anything, to do with Confederation.

But French Canadians also suffered set-backs and disappointments in the new federal structure. And as setbacks were experienced attempts were made to devise new methods of solving the old problem of minority rights in a majoritarian state. The first serious crisis arose in 1885 when the Macdonald cabinet, including three French Canadians, decided to allow Louis Riel's death sentence to be carried out. Riel, the enigmatic, unbalanced Métis leader of two rebellions in Western Canada, became a symbol of the renewed strife between French and English Canadians within the new federation. To many English Canadians, Riel was the murderer of a young Ontario Orangeman during the Red River Rebellion in 1870. To many French Canadians, the Métis leader was a valiant, if misguided, defender of a French and Catholic minority in Western Canada.

Though strongly opposed to the decision to allow Riel to hang, Macdonald's French-speaking colleagues did not resign from the cabinet, thus hoping to prevent the division of the country into warring cultural factions. Nor were the sixty-five Quebec members of parliament numerous enough, or united enough, to punish the government with defeat. What French Canadians were brought to realize, probably for the first time in 1885, was that when an issue divided Canadians along French-English lines, English-speaking Canadians were the majority and could control decisions at Ottawa. This realization caused French Canadians to look inward and to fall back on their provincial government as the one bastion protecting them against the English-speaking majority. In 1885 French Canada found in Honoré Mercier a new leader and one who was, significantly, a provincial politician who had opposed Confederation. 'We feel', Mercier declared in 1885, 'that the murder of Riel was a declaration of war on the influence of French Canada in Confederation, a violation of right and justice.'⁵ Taking advantage of the emotions aroused by the Riel affair, Mercier called upon French Canadians to cease their 'fratricidal quarrels' and form a solid 'national', that is, Quebec national, front.

It was Mercier who, as premier of Quebec, provided the first important expression of a view of Confederation that has become a standard French-Canadian interpretation. This was the 'compact theory' of Confederation, a theory which insists upon the 'autonomy' of the provinces. Shortly before Mercier's election, a Quebec judge, the Hon. T.J.J. Loranger, had worked out this theory in considerable detail. His essential argument was that 'the Confederation of the British provinces was the result of a compact entered into by the provinces and the Imperial Parliament which, in enacting the British North America Act, simply ratified it. Moreover, the judge argued, the provinces in setting up the Federal government had only delegated certain powers to it. Therefore the provinces were not only autonomous but, as the creators of the federal government, were equal rather than subordinate to it. If the autonomy of the provinces was not recognized, he concluded, the road to a fully centralized legislative union was a short one.[6]

One interesting point about Judge Loranger's exposition of the 'compact theory' was that he made no effort to prove that the compact was an agreement between French and English Canadians. For him the compact was among the provinces regardless of cultural differences. Perhaps the reason for this attitude was that Judge Loranger was really taking his cue from the Premier of Ontario, Oliver Mowat, who throughout the 1880s was engaged in legal combat with the federal government over a series of questions relating to the powers of the provinces. The Liberal premier of Ontario, like the Conservative prime minister of Canada, was one of the Fathers of Confederation. But the two founders differed seriously over the role of the provinces in the new federation. It is worth emphasizing that the doctrine of provincial autonomy found its first effective exponent in an English-speaking premier of Ontario. The French-Canadian Judge Loranger was merely urging Quebec politicians to join Mowat in the struggle against Ottawa.

Mercier, on becoming premier in 1886, quickly accepted the advice; for Ottawa, having bloodied its hands in the Riel affair, could now be easily stigmatized in Quebec. Together with Oliver Mowat, Mercier arranged a conference of provincial premiers in 1887 for the dual purpose of proposing limits to the powers of the federal government, particularly the power to veto provincial legislation, and also to press the federal government for larger financial subsidies to the provinces. Not all of the provinces attended the Interprovincial Conference, a fact which made it easier for Sir John Macdonald to ignore the meeting's resolutions. But the standard of provincial rights had been firmly planted in 1887. Moreover, an unofficial alliance between the country's two largest provinces had been established, an *ad hoc* alliance which in the twentieth century was occasionally renewed by Premiers Taschereau and Ferguson, and Duplessis and Hepburn.

But despite alliances of this kind, Quebec has always had a unique interest in its defence of provincial rights. That interest was Quebec's distinctive French and Roman Catholic culture. Nothing stimulated Quebec's fears of English Canada more than the attacks, beginning in the 1880s, that were made on that culture where it existed in pockets outside of the province of Quebec. Beginning with the abolition of state-supported separate schools in Manitoba in 1890 and stretching through to the tragic years of the Ontario school controversy during the First World War, the rights of the French-speaking minorities were gradually whittled away. Although these beleaguered minorities, supported by Quebec leaders, fought back vigorously, their numbers were small and their opposition numerous. Section 93 of the British North America Act, which gave the federal government power to initiate remedial action when the legitimate school rights of a minority were interfered with by a province, remained a dead letter. The reason was quite simple: the use of the power was politically dangerous for English-speaking politicians, and French-speaking representation at Ottawa was too small and too divided to force remedial action. Ironically, it was Wilfrid Laurier and the Liberals who prevented a Conservative government in 1896 from taking action to restore minority rights in Manitoba.[7]

Whatever the explanation for the ineffectiveness of the federal remedial power, there can be no doubt that the efforts to limit French rights outside Quebec caused French Canadians to look more and more to their own province as the only part of Canada where they were fully at home. As Edmond de Nevers noted in 1896 in his book *L'Avenir du peuple canadien-français*, 'The Northwest is closed to us, thanks to the unjust retrograde law passed by the Legislature of Manitoba prohibiting French schools ...'[8]

Nevertheless, it was during these years of crisis over the rights to the French-language and Catholic schools outside Quebec that the theory of the cultural compact of Confederation began to receive an explicit formulation. As early as 1890 when the attacks on these rights in Manitoba and the Northwest Territories were being mounted, Sir John Macdonald replied with his view that under the Canadian constitution all British subjects enjoyed 'equal rights of every kind, of language, of religion, of property and of person.'[9] Macdonald, of course, was not speaking of a compact. But it was this very statement to which French Canadians like Henri Bourassa appealed in support of the theory of bicultural compact. 'The Canadian nation', Bourassa declared in 1917, 'will attain its ultimate destiny, indeed it will exist, only on the condition of being biethnic and bilingual, and by remaining faithful to the concept of the Fathers of Confederation: the free and voluntary association of two peoples, enjoying equal rights in all matters.' For Bourassa and his followers, Confederation was a federation of two cultures, as well as of provinces, in which French- and English-speaking Canadians had a moral claim to equality of linguistic, religious, and civil rights from coast to coast.[10]

Bourassa and those who spoke of a 'cultural compact' described an ideal rather than a reality and their compact was one which carried moral rather than legal sanctions. The implications of this moral compact are made clear by André Laurendeau, who has written that 'if force of number alone rules the relations *between an ethnic majority and an ethnic minority* then a common life becomes impossible and only separatism remains. The minority must leave the house which has become uninhabitable.'

Thus, while French Canadians have insisted upon provincial autonomy, a position often supported by some English-speaking provinces, they have also developed the theory of the moral compact guaranteeing minority rights.[11] But there have also always been those French Canadians who have rejected Confederation as a fool's paradise. Usually these have been isolated intellectuals such as Jules-Paul Tardivel in the latter decades of the nineteenth century and some members of *L'Action française* group in the 1920s, or idealistic young nationalists like Jeune-Canada in the 1930s. The separatist argument has always been based on the assumption that French Canada is a nation which should acquire all the trappings of complete nationhood including an independent state. In his apocalyptic separatist novel of 1895, *Pour la patrie*, Tardivel wrote,

God planted in the heart of every French-Canadian patriot a flower of hope. It is the aspiration to establish, on the banks of the St. Lawrence, a New France whose mission will be to continue in this American land the work of Christian civilization that old France carried out with such glory during the long centuries.[12]

Tardivel's theme was that Confederation was part of a plan for the ultimate assimilation of French Canadians and the next step would be legislative union. The other alternative, the one that succeeded in the novel, was of course the establishment of a separate French-Canadian, Catholic state. Tardivel thus set the pattern for later separatist groups, most of whom have argued that Confederation will ultimately lead to legislative union and assimilation. In the 1930s separatists frequently warned against the argument that centralization was necessary to deal with the social crisis of the depression. Others contended that the defence and extension of provincial autonomy was a necessary first step toward an independent Quebec.[13]

In the years before 1960 the voices of separatism had very little direct influence on Quebec politics. Nevertheless, the Quebec Legislative Assembly once debated a separatist resolution. In January 1918, a few months after the English-Canadian majority had insisted on conscription for overseas service despite the opposition of most French Canadians, J.N. Francoeur presented the following resolution to the provincial legislature: 'That this House is of opinion that the Province of Quebec would be disposed to accept the breaking of the Confederation Pact of 1867 if, in the other provinces, it is believed that she is an obstacle to the union, progress and development of Canada.' It is probably too strong to describe this motion as a separatist resolution and the debate that followed was characterized more by sorrow than anger. Not a single voice was heard in support of separation, and the motion was never brought to a vote. Sir Lomer Gouin, the premier of the province, could hardly have spoken more firmly of his faith in Confederation. He began by noting that 'federal government appears to me the only possible one in Canada because of our different races and creeds and also because of the variety and multiplicity of local needs in our immense territory'. He said that if he had been one of the Fathers of Confederation he would have attempted to win a better guarantee for French-speaking minorities, but he added: 'Even if it had not been accorded to me I would have voted in favour of the Resolutions in 1864.'[14]

Despite this reaffirmation of Quebec's faith in Confederation, in the years after the Great War the French-speaking province was more jealous than ever of its autonomy. These were the years when Canadians began to expect government to play a larger role in social and economic affairs. And by government many English Canadians meant Ottawa. But French Canadians, still bitter about the conscription issue of 1917, retained a deep suspicion of any attempt by the federal government to increase its responsibilities. For example, Quebec remained out of the Federal Old Age Pension scheme, enacted in 1927, for more than eight years. Then, in 1936, the Quebec voters elected Maurice Duplessis, a premier who was to build his reputation as a staunch defender of provincial autonomy. Duplessis's party was characteristically called the Union Nationale and the national unity to which the title referred was that of Quebec, not of Canada. In 1938 Premier Duplessis refused to co-operate with the Royal Commission on Dominion-Provincial Relations established to examine the powers and responsibilities of all levels of government in Canada. Quebec's view was the traditional one: 'Confederation is a pact voluntarily agreed upon and which can be modified only by the consent of all parties.' Drawing out the implications of the 'compact theory', Duplessis's government, following in the tradition of Mercier, insisted that no alterations could be made in the Canadian federal system without the consent of all provinces. A few years later the Quebec premier explained why Quebec's autonomy was necessary, saying: 'The Legislature of Quebec is a fortress that we must defend without failing. It is that which permits us to construct the schools which suit us, to speak our language, to practise our religion and to make laws applicable to our population.'[15] Here Duplessis was expressing the view of many French-Canadian nationalists that Ottawa was the government of English Canada while Quebec City was the government of French Canada. Underlying this view was the doctrine of two nations: Canadians and Canadiens.

Perhaps the event that most encouraged French Canadians to think of the government at Ottawa as a power dominated by English-speaking Canadians was the conscription plebiscite of 1942. Many French Canadians believed that the pledge made by the King government, and very specifically by Ernest Lapointe, in September 1939, that there would be no conscription for overseas service, was a promise made to French Canadians. In 1942, however, the King government asked not French Canadians but all Canadians to release it from the pledge. One participant in the events of 1942 has since written: 'French-Canadian nationalists were opposed in principle even to the plebiscite. They denied that the government should ask the majority to remove a pledge made to the minority. They denied in advance the validity of the Canadian response.'[16] The outcome of the plebiscite was what F.-A. Angers called 'un vote de race' with more than eighty per cent of French Canadians casting a negative ballot.[17] King's handling of the conscription crises was almost unbelievably adept, so adept that French Canadians are convinced that the crisis took place in 1942 while English Canadians are equally convinced that the date was two years later.[18] The fact is that unlike 1917 when all the poison was administered at once, King, in typical fashion, prescribed two half doses. The result was that the federal Liberal Party continued to thrive in Quebec despite the demise of Premier Godbout's fragile provincial Liberal administration. Nevertheless, the fact remained that when limited conscription for overseas service was adopted in late 1944 the English-Canadian majority imposed its will on the French-speaking minority. To many French Canadians the moral, as M. Laurendeau has written, seemed to be that 'at Quebec one does what one wants, at Ottawa one does what one can.'[19]

In 1944 the Union Nationale was returned to power in Quebec. During the next dozen years the struggle between Quebec and Ottawa was intermittent but unceasing. These were years during which many English Canadians, at least, were becoming convinced that 'Canadianism' had at last triumphed over the country's chronic sectionalism, and only just in time, too, in the face of the growing threat of what many saw as subversive American cultural and economic influences. The report of the Massey Commission epitomized this spirit. But these same events caused profound uneasiness among French-Canadian nationalists who, in turn, feared that 'Canadians' might engulf 'canadienisme.'[20] Premier Duplessis's battle against Ottawa thus won the support of the possessors of these disturbed nationalist consciences.

Even so convinced an anti-separatist and vigorous critic of *dup-lessisme* as André Laurendeau was moved to write in 1955: 'The sep-aratist policy has become a chimera and an absurdity. However, those who have a conscience very alive to the perils into which the policies of Ottawa over the past fifteen years have plunged us, and who are consumed with impatience, prefer absurdity and chimera to death.'[21]

It was during these Duplessis years that the doctrine of 'two nations' received its full-blown exposition and, to some extent, obtained the official imprimatur. The doctrine received formal sanction in the volu-minous *Report of the Royal Commission of Enquiry on Constitutional Problems* in 1956, which was, in effect, Quebec's answer to the report of the Rowell-Sirois Commission and Ottawa's post-war economic, social, and fiscal policies. The report of the Tremblay Commission included lengthy philosophical, sociological, and even theological dis-cussions of the nature of the French-Canadian identity. But its funda-mental postulate was that

... by reason of its history, as well as of the cultural character of its population, Quebec is not a province like the others, whatever may be said to the contrary. It speaks in the name of one of the two ethnic groups which founded Confed-eration, as one of the two partners who officially have the right to live and expand in this country. It is the only one able to represent one of the two part-ners, just as it alone may determine its reasons for refusing federal largess.

But the French-Canadian nation did not live exclusively in Quebec, and the report therefore advocated not only the limitation of federal powers but also the promotion of bilingualism and biculturalism throughout the country. And it put its finger on the central issue of Dominion-provincial relations when it remarked: 'There can be no fed-eralism without the autonomy of the state's constituent parts, and no sovereignty of the various governments without fiscal and financial autonomy.'[22] This was precisely the view that Premier Duplessis, with few philosophical trimmings, had been urging on the federal govern-ment for a decade.

While the autonomist theme was the predominant theme in Quebec during the 1950s, it was not the only one. Indeed, the reactionary social policies and the growing corruption of the Union Nationale régime tended to discredit the provincial-rights cause in progressive cir-cles. French-Canadian nationalism itself became suspect as a tool of reaction; the 'state of siege' mentality, it seemed, was encouraged as much to stifle reform in Quebec as to fight Ottawa.[23]

In 1954 one reformer, Maurice Lamontagne, published *Le Fédéral-isme canadien*, a careful study of the Canadian federal system which, in effect, advocated that Quebec accept fully the implications of the type of centralized federalism that the Rowell-Sirois Commission had recommended and that economic and social planning seemed to necessitate.[24]

While Duplessis lived, neither the Tremblay Commission's theorists of 'positive autonomism' nor the proponents of what Lamontagne called 'une intégration lucide au nouveau fédéralisme canadien' gained control over provincial policy, though, of course, the former received a more sympathetic hearing than the latter. Undoubtedly far more important than the Union Nationale's constant, noisy war with Ottawa was the economic and social transformation that was taking place in Quebec and the gradual growth of a new nationalist impulse – one that was, at least in origin, more aggressive in its advocacy of social reform and in its defence of provincial autonomy than anything Duplessis had countenanced.[25] Since 1960 the turmoil in Quebec has resulted in the revival of all the traditional attitudes toward Confederation, as well as some new ones, stretching all the way from 'co-operative federalism' and autonomism through to the idea of an associate state and separatism. The vague theory of an associate state includes among its proponents spokesmen for the traditionalist Société Saint-Jean-Baptiste, the populistic Créditistes, and the left-wing Parti Socialiste du Québec.[26] The appeal of the doctrine of an associate state obviously lies in its ready solution to the problem of the relation of the minority to the majority without going as far as separatism. In brief, its proponents reject representation by population, whereby French Canadians are increasingly outnumbered, in favour of representation by 'nation.' It is, of course, a Canadian version of John C. Calhoun's 'concurrent majorities', though, strangely, one never sees any reference to the writings of the ante-bellum South's most distinguished theorist in the writings of French Canadians. At least to English Canadians, the idea of an associate state seems hopelessly utopian and perhaps even less acceptable than outright separation. In the first place, the idea would seem to promise only the deadlock which paralysed the union of the Canadas in the 1860s and led to Confederation. Secondly, French Canada's minority status is not as much the result of our present constitutional arrangements as it is of geography. No constitutional changes can alter the fact that French Canadians live in North America.

It is only the future, of course, that can supply fully satisfactory answers to the problems of the present. But the past suggests that it is in the realm of political action rather than in constitutional theorizing that solutions to our present discontents are likely to be found. It is highly significant that in his great struggle to defend the autonomy of his province against what he saw as the encroaching federal power,

Premier Duplessis's chief antagonist was another French Canadian, Louis St. Laurent. And Prime Minister St. Laurent's position was characteristic. In the years since 1867 French Canadians have made their major adjustment to Confederation in the fashion that Cartier had recommended: effective leadership in the federal cabinet where an *ad hoc* system of concurrent majorities seemed at least partly feasible. A long line of vigorous French-Canadian politicians, beginning with Cartier himself and stretching through Laurier and Lapointe to St. Laurent, forcefully upheld the viewpoint of French Canada. It was in political action rather than in legal and moral compacts that these men placed their faith.[27] For them Confederation, while not perhaps the ideal political arrangement, was nevertheless the best one available. All of them recognized that the relations between majorities and minorities in a democratic state can never be settled in an absolute manner. It was Sir Wilfrid Laurier who summed up this tradition best when he wrote just before his death:

There have been found among us limited spirits who have shouted very loudly, 'No compromise; all or nothing.' What an aberration! When a minority affirms that it will concede nothing, that it demands all or will accept nothing less than all, they are three times blind who do not see what the inevitable results will be: nothing. How can they not see that the majority itself will accept the doctrine and apply it without compunction to those who proclaim it! This truth was evident when Confederation was formed, it is equally so today. Salvation consists in administering Confederation in the same spirit as it was conceived, with firmness and always with moderation.[28]

For Laurier, as for Cartier before him and Lapointe afterwards, Confederation was a compromise that provided for cultural coexistence within the bosom of a single political nation. Since the Canadian political community of 1867 had been established in a spirit of compromise it could only be operated effectively in the same spirit. That spirit meant that while the majority must respect the rights of the minority, the minority, for its part, can never forget that majorities also have rights. Only by working through the federal political parties in co-operation with English Canadians can French Canadians hope to have their viewpoint understood. Cartier had defined the underlying assumption of that co-operation when he declared in 1865: 'We were of different races, not for the purpose of warring against each other, but in order to compete and emulate for the general welfare.'

Since 1867 Canadian coexistence has not always been entirely peaceful, competition has sometimes been destructive. Yet, at least until recently, the overwhelming majority of French-speaking and English-speaking Canadians have remained convinced that Confederation, when operated in a spirit of 'firmness and moderation', has been a worthwhile experiment. It may not always be so, but until a more attractive alternative is offered it is perhaps well to remember a recent remark by a French-Canadian writer in summing up the Canadian experience. 'Most nations', he wrote, 'have been formed not by people who desired intensely to live together, but rather by people who could not live apart.'[29]

[1964]

NOTES

1 Macdonald is reported as saying: 'A large qualification should be necessary for membership in the Upper House, in order to represent the principle of property. The rights of the minority must be protected, and the rich are always fewer in number than the poor.' Sir Joseph Pope (ed.), *Confederation, Being a Series of hitherto unpublished Documents Bearing on the British North America Act* (Toronto, 1895).

2 A.G. Doughty, 'Notes on the Quebec Conference, 1864', *Canadian Historical Review*, Vol. 1, No. l, March 1920, page 28.

3 *Parliamentary Debates on the Subject of the Confederation of the British North American Provinces* (Quebec, 1965) (hereafter cited as *Confederation Debates*), page 368.

4 *Ibid.*, page 711. On 'biculturalism' and Confederation, see Eugene Forsey, 'The British North America Act and Biculturalism', *Queen's Quarterly*, Vol. LXXI, No. 2, Summer 1964, pages 141–9.

5 Charles Langelier, *Souvenirs politiques* (Montreal, 1909), Vol. I, page 254.

6 T.J.J. Loranger, *Letters on the Interpretation of the Federal Constitution called the British North America Act* (Quebec, 1884) (first letter), page 61. In 1884, as leader of the Opposition in Quebec, Mercier used Loranger's writings as a source for a speech on provincial autonomy. See J.O. Pelland, *Biographie, discours, conférences, etc., de l'hon. Honoré Mercier* (Montreal, 1890), page 401.

7 Sir Wilfrid Laurier, 'Le Fédéralisme', *Revue trimestrielle canadienne*, November 1918, pages 219–21.. Sir Wilfrid Laurier to the end of his life insisted that Cartier had been mistaken in agreeing to give the federal government this power to interfere in provincial affairs.

8 Edmond de Nevers, *L'Avenir du peuple canadien-français* (Paris, 1896), page 293.

9 Canada, *House of Commons Debates*, 1890, Vol. 1, page 745.

10 Henri Bourassa, *La Conscription* (Montreal, 1917), page 20.

11 Jean-Charles Falardeau, 'Les Canadiens français et leur idéologie,' in Mason Wade (ed.), *Canadian Dualism* (Toronto, 1960), page 25.

12 Jules-Paul Tardivel, *Pour la patrie* (Montreal, 1895), page 7.

13 Dosteler O'Leary, *Séparatisme, doctrine constructif* (Montreal, 1937), page 150; Emile Latrémouille, *Tradition et indépendance* (Montreal, 1939), pages 28–9.

14 *Quebec and Confederation. A Record of the Debate of the Legislative Assembly of Quebec on the Motion proposed by J.-N. Francoeur* (Quebec, 1918), page 124.

15 H.F. Quinn, *The Union Nationale* (Toronto, 1963), cited pages 117–18.

16 André Laurendeau, *La Crise de la conscription, 1942* (Montreal, 1962), page 74. See *L'Action nationale*, Vol. XIX, No. 1, January 1942, pages 48–50. It is worth noting, however, that this argument based on the idea of 'compact' was not used by La Ligue pour la Défense du Canada in its 'Manifeste au peuple du Canada' in 1942, which went out of its way to emphasize the Canadian rather than the French-Canadian character of its appeal.

17 F.-A. Angers, 'Un Vote de race,' *L'Action nationale*, Vol. XIX, No. 4, May 1942, pages 299–313.

18 R.McG. Dawson, *The Conscription Crisis of 1944* (Toronto, 1961), and André Laurendeau, *La Crise de la conscription*.

19 *La Crise de la conscription*, page 152.

20 'Mémoire de la Ligue d'Action Nationale à la Commission royale d'enquête sur les arts, les lettres et les sciences,' *L'Action nationale*, Vol. XXXV, No. 4, April 1950, page 312; see also Michel Brunet, 'Une autre manifestation du nationalisme Canadian, le Rapport Massey,' in *Canadians et Canadiens* (Montreal, 1952).

21 André Laurendeau, 'Nationalisme et séparatisme,' *L'Action nationale*, Vol. XXX, No. 3, March 1955, page 579.

22 *Report*, Vol. III, page 294.

23 See Pierre-Elliott Trudeau, *La Grève de l'amiante* (Montreal, 1956), pages 10–37, and his 'Some Obstacles to Democracy in Quebec' in Mason Wade (ed.), *Canadian Dualism*, pages 241–59.

24 Maurice Lamontagne, *Le Fédéralisme canadien* (Quebec, 1954).

25 Jean-Marc Leger, 'Aspects of French-Canadian Nationalism,' *University of Toronto Quarterly*, Vol. XXVII, No. 3, April 1958, pages 310–29. Hubert Guindon, 'Social Unrest, Social Class and Quebec's Bureaucratic Revolution,' *Queen's Quarterly*, Vol. LXXI, No. 2, Summer 1964, pages 150–62.

26 *Le Fédéralisme, l'acte de l'Amérique du nord britannique et les Canadiens français*, Mémoire de la Société Saint-Jean-Baptiste de Montréal au Comité Parlementaire de la Constitution du Gouvernement du Québec

(Montreal, 1964); *Le Devoir*, August Il, 1964, page 4; Jacques-Yvan Morin, 'The Need for a New Canadian Federation,' *Canadian Forum*, Vol. XLIV, No. 521, June 1964, pages 64–6.

27 Laurier and Lapointe (though not St. Laurent) subscribed to the 'compact theory,' at least in a vague way, but to them the theory was obviously far less important as a device for defending French-Canadian rights than direct political action.

28 Laurier, 'Le Fédéralisme,' page 220.

29 Jean-Charles Bonenfant, 'L'Esprit de 1867,' *Revue d' histoire de l'Amérique française*, Vol. XVII, No. 1, June 1963, page 38.

FOURTEEN

The Canadian Dilemma:
Locke, Rousseau, or Acton?

'There are two miracles in Canadian history,' Professor F.R. Scott of McGill University once maintained. 'The first is the survival of French Canada, and the second is the survival of Canada.'[1] Almost always in the past English Canadians and more particularly French Canadians have believed instinctively that these two miracles were linked indissolubly together. Most French Canadians were convinced that *la survivance de la nation canadienne-française* depended on an alliance with English Canada, and even on the protection of the British Empire. The theme that the 'last cannon-shot which booms on this continent in defence of Great Britain' will be 'fired by the hands of a French Canadian' is an important one in the history of French Canada.[2]

Then, too, one of the most frequently repeated arguments in favour of the acceptance of Confederation in 1865 was that it was the only alternative to annexation. That argument has often been adapted for modern usage. Pointing out the weakness of the French-Canadian separatist case a few years ago, M. André Laurendeau wrote: 'Above all, one of the principal motives which led to the creation of Canada: the proximity of a large country to the south and the necessity of gathering together the British colonies in order to allow them to exist beside the United States, this motive has become more imperious. A segmented Canada would have scarcely more influence than one of the little republics of central America: would it even be able to exist?'[3] From the French-Canadian viewpoint it has always been obvious that although they were a minority in Canada, they would be an even smaller and more precarious group, and therefore less capable of resisting absorption into the United States, if they attempted to exist apart from English Canada.

The irony of today's situation [1960s] is that while a growing number of English Canadians have concluded that the survival of Canada can best be guaranteed by continuing the French-English association, there are now a growing number of French Canadians who are no longer convinced that the miracle of *la survivance* depends on this alliance. This latter is not yet a predominant view, but it is threatening enough to cause James Eayrs to remark recently: 'This crisis of nationhood presents to a Prime Minister of Canada an issue transcending all others in urgency and importance. For many years it was his main concern so to conduct his countrymen's affairs that there would continue to be two sovereign governments in North America, not one. Today his main concern is that there continue to be two sovereign governments not three.'[4]

Canada's present 'crisis of nationhood' is at least partly explained by the old symbol of 'two solitudes'. For reasons attributable largely, though certainly not exclusively, to the majority, French and English Canadians have rarely understood one another's purposes. That is the central failure of the Canadian experiment and one for which we are bound to continue paying heavily until it is rectified. In Canada we have only rarely conformed to Durham's famous description of 'two nations warring in the bosom of a single state'. But, what may be worse, we have been two nations each talking to itself within the bosom of a single state.

Perhaps the most extraordinary thing about Canada is that while French and English Canadians have interacted upon each other to an immeasurable extent, the two people hardly know one another. What is today fashionably called a 'national style' is, in Canada, almost wholly a reflection of the delicately balanced relationship between French- and English-speaking Canadians. Few if any other countries exemplify the obsession with that holy grail of all Canadian politicians, 'national unity'. That is only one example of what has been called the 'bifocal' character of Canada.[5] Nor should it be necessary to insist that the character of French-Canadian nationalism can only be understood when it is placed in the matrix of French-English relations in Canada. But despite the obvious impact of each group on the other, there is only a very limited interchange between the two groups. English Canadians read American and British newspapers, magazines, and novels, and of course watch American movies and television programs. Most of them could not, even if they wanted to, read a French-Canadian novel or understand a French-language television commentator. It is almost certainly true that an undergraduate in an English-Canadian university spends more time reading about the history of Great Britain and the United States than he does reading about the history of French Canada. Whatever else a young French-Canadian undergraduate in history may learn, he spends very little time on the history of English Canada

except where it relates to *la survivance*. Mr. George Ferguson, a shrewd
observer of the Canadian scene, once observed that 'because of differences of race and language, culture and tradition, and, to some extent,
religion, Quebec remains a *terra incognita* to almost all English Canadians.'[6] And English Canada is almost as much of a mystery to French
Canadians.

While language is obviously an important wall between French and
English Canadians, history, perhaps, divides us even more. The central
event in the history of Canada is the British Conquest in 1760. Whatever this event may have meant in the lives of eighteenth-century
French Canadians (and there is a good deal of scholarly dispute on that
subject) it is nevertheless true that since the beginning of the nineteenth
century French-Canadian nationalists have been attempting to overcome it. And the French-Canadian nationalist quite naturally identifies
the Conqueror of 1760 with his rather indirect heir, the contemporary
English Canadian. Actually, though one occasionally hears crude
remarks about the Plains of Abraham, English Canadians are largely
unconscious of their Conqueror's role. But consciously or not the Conquest dominates English-Canadian nationalism, just as it does French-
Canadian nationalism, giving the former a sense of belonging to the
winning side, the latter a yearning for lost glories. The Conquest, then,
is the burden of Canadian history.

It is at least partly the Conquest that explains the different public
philosophies of French and English Canada. Because they are a conquered people and a minority, French Canadians have always been
chiefly concerned with group rights. Their public philosophy might be
called Rousseauian: the expression of a 'general will' to survive. The
English Canadian, as is equally befitting his majority position, is far
more concerned with individual rights and with that characteristic
North American middle-class ideal, equality of opportunity. The English Canadian's public philosophy might be somewhat grandly
described as Lockean. The English Canadian has therefore tended to
look upon privileges asked for or granted to groups as inherently undesirable, indeed undemocratic. This means, then, especially since the
dominant English-Canadian tradition is Protestant, that rights granted
to groups *as* French Canadians or *as* Roman Catholics are at best an
unfortunate deviation from the democratic norm, at worst a devilish
plot to undermine Canadian, that is English-Canadian Protestant, civilization. The English Canadian instinctively makes the natural but
nevertheless arrogant majoritarian assumption that the only fair and
just way to run a society is according to the well-known Australian
principle of 'one bloody man, one bloody vote.' The French Canadian
just as instinctively makes the no less natural, and not always less arro-

gant, minoritarian assumption that a truly fair and just society would be based on something closer to the principle of representation by groups. And most French Canadians insist that there are only two groups in Canada. It is this basic difference in public philosophy that divides Canadians. To an extent, I think to a quite successful extent, our political and constitutional machinery was designed to overcome or at least blur this difference. The federal system has meant, or at least was intended to mean, that those things most fundamental to the survival of the minority culture are placed safely beyond the reach of the majority. By defending provincial autonomy French Canadians could, in the past, defend at least a large part of the French-Canadian nation. At the same time our federal parties have usually worked in such a way as to ensure that if vigorous leaders were sent to Ottawa by Quebec something very near to a French-Canadian veto could be exercised within the federal cabinet, at least in matters that touched on French-Canadian affairs. It is true that the veto has not always been effective, though history unfortunately records more clearly those cases where it failed – Riel, conscription, and so on. History says less about the cases where the veto succeeded. When the complete story of Canadian foreign policy in the inter-war years is revealed, the influence of a man like Ernest Lapointe will almost certainly appear enormous. But the main point is, and it has often been made, that the Baldwin-Lafontaine, Macdonald-Cartier, Laurier-Sifton, King-Lapointe, St. Laurent-Howe tradition has given French Canadians a role in federal politics somewhat greater than a strict adherence to the principle of representation by population would have provided. Within the federal cabinet, the leading French Canadian is not a minister like the others.

But while our federal constitution allows Quebec a large measure of autonomy and our federal parties are especially susceptible to French-Canadian influence, one part of the French-Canadian community is left unprotected in practice if not in theory. These are the French Canadians living beyond the frontiers of the mother province. And it is here that English Canada's Lockean approach takes its toll. While Quebec is a constitutionally bilingual province, the other provinces, except for a brief two decades in Manitoba, have been unilingual. English-speaking Protestant majorities in every province, as far as the constitution permitted, have reduced the privileges of Roman Catholic and French-speaking minorities to a minimum. Whether the reason has been religious or national is difficult to decide with certainty, though it was probably religious in Manitoba in 1890 and national in Ontario in 1912. While the constitution in some cases (Ontario for example) has protected religious separate schools in a limited way, it gives no protection to French-language rights. The Fathers of Confederation had not seen fit to provide such guarantees; so where French-language schools existed by custom they have been eliminated by measures that are, according to the courts, within the letter of the constitution. Whether these measures are also within the spirit of the constitution is a matter that neither courts nor historians can decide with certainty. The effect of these actions has been to make French Canadians outside Quebec a minority like any other, subject, in matters of education, to the same laws as others.

Nowhere has this point been better established than in the case of Manitoba. Under the Laurier-Greenway settlement of 1897, which was designed to restore some of the privileges that the Roman Catholic and French-speaking minorities had been deprived of by the Manitoba School Act of 1890, bilingual schools meant English and any other language demanded by a minority group. And in 1916, when these bilingual schools were abolished, the public-school system's *Kulturkampf* was directed not only against German, Ukrainian, and Icelandic immigrants, but also against Franco-Manitobans. The survival of the French-speaking minorities outside Quebec, and they have survived in varying degrees, is a minor miracle attributable only to the will of these people to live according to the dictates of their culture. It is only recently, and very belatedly, that a growing number of English Canadians have recognized that the survival of the French-speaking minority groups is one important guarantee of Quebec's continued interest in Confederation.

Not unnaturally, French Canadians have developed a profound sense of grievance about the manner in which their compatriots were treated in the other provinces. This sense of grievance has been deepened enormously, of course, by the presence in Quebec of an English-speaking minority enjoying complete equality of rights in the educational system and bilingualism in public affairs, and to a large extent dominating the economy of the province. Despite repeated rebuffs in their attempts to extend French-language rights outside Quebec, most French-Canadian nationalists before 1945 refused to abandon the hope that one day the minorities in the other provinces would receive more equitable treatment. In 1913 Henri Bourassa stated the basic argument for this view when he said: 'The Canadian Confederation ... is the result of a contract between the two races, French and English, treating on an equal footing and recognizing equal rights and reciprocal obligations. The Canadian Confederation will last only to the extent that the equality of rights will be recognized as the basis of public law in Canada, from Halifax to Vancouver.'[7] As long as the French-Canadian nationalist believed that a bicultural Canada was possible, then he refused to identify the nation with the province.

Since 1945, and especially during the last decade, there has been a growing tendency for French-Canadian nationalists to write off the minorities, maintaining that the unending ransom being paid for these hostages to Confederation is a poor investment. As René Lévesque commented, referring to the Royal Commission on Bilingualism and Biculturalism: 'It is infinitely more important to make Quebec progressive, free, and strong than to devote the best of our energies to propagating the doubtful advantages of biculturalism.'[8] The assumption underlying this view is, of course, that the province is identified with the nation. This explains the significance of the recent but now common usage, *l'Etat du Québec*.

But this 'nationalization' of the province is not merely the result of disillusionment about the fate of the minorities. It is also a response to a series of developments in English Canada. In the years immediately following the Second World War, English Canadians became increasingly self-conscious, even nationalistic. For one thing, they had played an important role in defeating the Axis powers. And largely because of the political skill of Mackenzie King and the political realism of Louis St. Laurent, the country that emerged from the war's two conscription crises had only a few scars on its unity.

Then too after 1945 Canadians suddenly realized that the traditional balance of power in their North American world had been badly upset. Where Britain had once stood as a material and psychological counterbalance against Canada's closest neighbour, the war had exhausted Britain and catapulted the United States into a position of world preeminence. This is what Professor F.H. Underhill has called 'the revolution of 1940' when 'we passed from the British century of our history to the American century ... And', he added, 'our American century is going to be a much tougher experience for us than our British century was.'[9] Faced with this new situation, many Canadians concluded that public policies, national policies, would have to be devised to bolster up Canada's lonely independence. For English Canadians this meant action by Ottawa in economic, social, and cultural affairs on an unprecedented scale. And if these fears of the American giant were not enough to impel our politicians in the direction of the interventionist state, then the wartime industrialization and urbanization provided the necessary additional impetus.

Most English Canadians, the majority of whom voted for a federal party led by a French Canadian, were unpleasantly surprised to find that Quebec was hesitant about accepting the new nationalist role that the federal government was assuming. After all, we were all Canadians (though evidently some were more Canadian than others). Ottawa belonged to all of us. Why should the federal government not, therefore, move into these new fields even if it did encroach on such traditionally provincial responsibilities as education and social welfare? The difficulty with this point of view was that many French Canadians feared that the new 'Canadianism', promoted by Ottawa, ignored or perhaps even threatened *'Canadienisme'*. As the Ligue d'Action Nationale remarked in its submission to the Royal Commission on the Arts, Letters and Sciences in 1950: 'Current language frequently makes use of the expressions "Canadian nation", "Canadian culture". This manner of speaking is not in itself reprehensible provided that no one draws from there a complete theory of Canadian national unity.'[10]

But few English Canadians paid any attention to this view, for in their eyes provincial autonomy and French-Canadian nationalism had been largely discredited. After all, Premier Duplessis was not only a nationalist and an autonomist but also remarkably illiberal and corrupt. Most English Canadians concluded, therefore, that French-Canadian nationalism was merely a tool used by a reactionary provincial politician to undermine the progressive policies of Ottawa. Thus, happily, the new Canadian nationalism seemed to coincide with progressivism and modernism. French-Canadian nationalism was just as obviously backward and obsolete. M. Duplessis and his Union Nationale abundantly proved everything that most English Canadians had long, secretly or openly, believed about French-Canadian nationalism. And they were often encouraged in this view by the foes of *duplessisme* in Quebec.

Thus there developed the opinion in English Canada that if Quebec was ever to come to terms with the chromeplated, modern world of North America it would first have to shed its parochial nationalism. As late as three years after the death of Premier Duplessis, and two years after M. Lesage's reforming Liberals had entered office, the Toronto *Globe and Mail* expressed [in 1962] exactly this view in explaining its opposition to the appointment of a royal commission on bilingualism and biculturalism: 'A wiser course, in our view,' the editor noted, 'would be to let Quebec complete the task it has set itself. The Province is now in good hands, and the necessary basic reforms have been initiated. If we have patience, the discovery already made by its leaders, that English is the language of commerce and is as essential to Quebec as to the rest of us, will spread throughout the populace. We will find wider areas of agreement. French-speaking Canadians will retain their culture, as the Welsh and Scotch have done. We will be able in time to find the unity we seek.'[11]

That comment is enormously revealing. First, one may note, it was the type of attitude that was driving many young French Canadians into the nationalist and separatist catacombs. M. André Laurendeau, the editor-in-chief of *Le Devoir*, wrote in commenting on the *Globe*'s condescending observations: 'Were the *Globe and Mail* editorial a true reflection of English Canada today, I, with many others, would become a separatist. I would go to this extremity without joy; and would, in self-defence, curse those who had forced me to it. But a fundamental instinct and desire to live despite it all would nevertheless keep me going.'[12] M. Laurendeau is now, as the co-chairman of the Royal Commission the *Globe* unsuccessfully opposed, engaged full-time in attempting to discover how far the Toronto paper's views were the views of English Canada. It should be added that in the last year or so the attitude of the *Globe and Mail* towards Quebec has been enormously liberalized.

M. Laurendeau was probably right in thinking that in 1962 the *Globe*'s opinions were not those of all English Canada. Two years earlier the case might have been different. Most English Canadians welcomed the defeat of the crumbling, corrupt Union Nationale government in June 1960. The victory of the Liberals led by the familiar former federal minister, Jean Lesage, seemed to promise the end of corruption, authoritarianism, and even that parochial spirit that French Canadians insisted on calling 'nationalism.' For most English Canadians autonomism and *duplessisme* were inseparable. It was for this reason that they had almost completely ignored the report of the Tremblay Commission in 1956. This commission, established by Premier Duplessis to examine the constitution, provided the most complete statement of autonomism ever devised. Had English Canadians read it they might have been better prepared for the events of the last two or three years. But since it was a product of the Union Nationale régime it was largely ignored.

With the Union Nationale gone, it was widely assumed that autonomism would soon disappear too. The new Quebec premier was given an exceedingly good press in English Canada during his first two years in office. He was often paid that highest English-Canadian compliment of having his name suggested as the successor to Lester Pearson. This suggestion may, of course, have been as much a reflection on Mr. Pearson as it was on M. Lesage. Anyway, M. Lesage was seen as the new Laurier who would bind up the nation's wounds as they were beginning to appear at the end of the Diefenbaker era. And among M. Lesage's ministers few were more popular during those early years than M. René Lévesque, who seemed, at least to liberal intellectuals always in search of an idol, to be the epitome of the intellectual *engagé*.

Of course there were still troubles between Ottawa and Quebec. But it was well known that all Quebec politicians, even Liberal ones, had to pay lip-service to provincial autonomy. And, moreover, there was the fact that Liberal provincial governments were almost duty-bound to fight with Conservative federal administrations – and vice versa. On towards the second year of the Lesage régime a growing number of people were happy to see the Quebec government adding its weight to the anti-Diefenbaker forces. This would surely aid in the return to office of the federal Liberals who, as everyone knew, have always been the trusted guardians of that highest Canadian virtue, 'national unity'. Indeed, there were many who still believed – or were convinced by Mr. Diefenbaker – that the late Mackenzie King, following a recipe secretly passed on to him by Sir Wilfrid Laurier, had actually invented 'national unity'. Once the country was returned to that almost divinely ordained condition of 'rouge à Ottawa et rouge à Québec', all would be for the best again.

Yet even before that blissful condition was achieved in the spring of 1963, there was a growing amount of evidence to suggest that the Lesage Liberals were not entirely orthodox. First there was the decision to place the privately owned power companies under Hydro-Québec. While public ownership of electricity is hardly an unorthodox policy in Canada, the Quebec move was preceded by an election in which the Liberals campaigned on the nationalist slogan 'maîtres chez nous'. The nationalization was carried off in such a businesslike fashion, especially when compared with the much more arbitrary actions a year earlier of that Lochinvar of the West, Premier W.A.C. Bennett, that whatever fears had been raised were quickly laid. If English Canadians had known much about the educational history of Quebec they would have had another warning of the untraditional character of the Lesage Liberals when the decision to establish a ministry of education was announced. Here, in cold fact, was the civil authority imposing its will in an area traditionally held sacrosanct by the Church. But to most English Canadians a minister of education was the most natural thing in the world. Indeed, it was just another sign that French Canadians were at last recognizing the value of English-Canadian practices. Many English Canadians, of course, also approved of actions designed at last to put the Church in its place. It is worth adding that while for Quebec the Lesage reforms represent sizeable changes, most of them are fairly orthodox in the English-Canadian provinces. That is one reason why English Canadians did not get overly excited about the early events of 'la révolution tranquille'.

As the quiet revolution grew noisier and more expensive, English Canadians began to grow disturbed and to some extent hostile. The Quebec noise stretched all the way from the much-publicized separatist groups to the increasing number of statements by Premier Lesage and his ministers that the constitution, at least as it was being operated, was too restrictive of the ambitions of the 'Etat du Québec'. M. René Lévesque, known to be the *éminence grise* behind the power national-ization, was increasingly viewed with suspicion as he dropped off-the-cuff remarks that showed a shocking lack of respect for national unity. Indeed, by 1962 Quebec was more of an enigma to most English Cana-dians than it had ever been under M. Duplessis. In those good old days Quebec had seemed to have only one face and one voice. Moreover, since M. Duplessis had been a sound conservative, his autonomism had not cost the federal government much money. In both these respects the new régime in Quebec was quite different.

In the first place the autonomism of the Lesage government was guided by a program of positive nationalism. This included large expenditures for economic development, educational expansion, and social welfare programs. These were to be provincial policies designed and paid for by the provincial government. But to pay for these poli-cies M. Lesage had to begin a campaign to push the federal government at least part way out of the fields of direct taxation that under the British North America Act are shared by the federal and provincial governments. This new conflict in federal-provincial relations might best be explained by noting that under M. Duplessis the provincial state was largely non-interventionist and passive; under M. Lesage the role of the state is positive and thus comes into direct competition with another interventionist state, Ottawa. By April 1963, when M. Lesage issued his famous 'ultimatum' or 'request' (depending on your transla-tor) that Quebec should have 25 per cent of income taxes, 25 per cent of corporation taxes, and 100 per cent of succession taxes, English Canadians had come to realize that living with the new Quebec would cost money.

But the second upsetting fact about the new Quebec was that it no longer had one face and one voice. Indeed there were times when it appeared that even the government had several voices, of which the soothing tones of Jean Lesage and the rasping wit of René Lévesque were but two. And in addition to this multi-voiced government, after the 1962 general election, there appeared an even more confusing phe-nomenon in the person of M. Réal Caouette and some two dozen Social Credit M.P.s. If to some English Canadians René Lévesque was becom-ing a beardless Castro, M. Caouette was more reminiscent of an earlier generation of authoritarian radicals. And, if this was not enough, there was soon also an unharmonious chorus composed of nearly every French-Canadian newspaper, periodical, academic, radio and television commentator, student organization, and what not, advancing criticisms of Quebec's place in Confederation. And more often than not these crit-icisms were more precise than were the proffered alternatives – except of course in the case of separatism. While it annoyed French Canadians to hear it said, it is really no wonder that, faced with this babel of raucous voices, English Canadians began to demand somewhat impatiently, 'What does Quebec want?'

And here we arrive at the nub of the problem. English Canadians had grown used to hearing one voice from Quebec – whether it was Laurier or Duplessis. M. Duplessis had often made clear what he wanted; English Canadians had more often than not rejected his demands. Now, since 1960, there is no longer one voice. (Of course, there never really was only one voice, but M. Duplessis succeeded in making it seem so.) What distresses English Canadians is their inability to get a single, clear statement of what Quebec would like to have done to make Confederation more habitable. And this makes them suspect that either there is no real grievance or the list of demands knows no end. Many English Canadians, however, believe that enough of what they call 'concessions' have already been made to Quebec – perhaps too many. First there was the establishment of the Royal Commission on Bilingualism and Biculturalism; next the obvious steps to increase bilingualism in the federal civil service; then the gradual decentralization in order to allow more tax resources to the provinces and more freedom to the provinces in policy choices. Then came the crowning touch – the flag! Much of the debate has centred on the flag because it is the kind of issue that ordinary minds, like that of the leader of the Progressive Conservative Party, can understand. But the heat of that debate is at least partly attributable to a vague feeling of unease about Quebec's 'demands.' In fact the somewhat hostile response to the so-called 'concessions' to Quebec is explained by the instinctive English-Canadian suspicion of special treatment. Once more Locke and Rousseau have come into conflict.

English Canadians are right in believing that French Canadians are asking to be treated as though they were not the same as other Canadians, and as though Quebec 'n'est pas une province comme les autres'. What French Canadians are asking for is equality. There are, of course, many different prescriptions being offered for the achievement of that equality. English Canada's response to the demand for equality depends on how far the prescription requires them to give up their traditional Lockean assumptions. The more nationalist the prescription, that is to say, the closer the French Canadian comes to saying that our present system based on a modified version of 'rep by pop' must be replaced by a system of representation by nations, the less sympathetic English Canadians are likely to be.

Recently, a young journalist who over the past three years has done much to try to inform English Canadians of events in Quebec published 'An Open Letter to the French-Canadian Nationalists', which probably sums up a good deal of the thinking among English Canadians who have been somewhat sympathetic to the aspirations of Quebec. These people have been upset by the increasing intensity of the nationalism of Quebec, and the apparent unwillingness of Quebecers to pay any attention to the people of good will in English Canada. 'You are winning your revolution,' Peter Gzowski wrote. 'In many senses you have already won it. And yet – as though the battle had become more important than the victory – you grow ever more strident. Those of us who have listened to your demands from the outset, and have agreed with your principles, wonder if it isn't time you listened to what *we* have to say, and whether you might want to entertain some principles of ours, such as the one that nationalism isn't the most important issue in the world of 1964.'[13] That letter is a clear sign of the times in English Canada; it strongly suggests that the more radical demands of the French-Canadian nationalists will find little sympathy outside of Quebec.

The most extreme, clear-cut version of the one-nation-one-vote doctrine is separatism. The supporters of this doctrine reject the view that two nations can live peacefully in the bosom of a single state. The separatists' counterpart in English Canada would be assimilationists, who are nearly, if not completely, non-existent. At present, most English Canadians would refuse to consider seriously the possibility of a separate Quebec, and therefore it is nearly impossible to judge what the response might be if the majority of Quebecers opted for independence. Most English Canadians view the separatists as a rag-tag and bobtail collection of irresponsible students and people in or near the criminal fringes of society. At present, nevertheless, there are probably more people in English Canada who would deplore than applaud the recent bellicose remarks of one English-Canadian historian. Speaking at the Progressive Conservative Conference on Canadian Goals, Professor W.L. Morton declared: 'I deny that any province has the right to secede. I think that any such attempt should be resisted by every means, including force if necessary ...'[14] While these remarks may remind some of the pre-Civil-War years in the United States, they could equally remind others of the pre-American-Revolution years in Great Britain!

Many thoughtful French-Canadian nationalists believe separation would create as many problems as it would solve. But many of them nevertheless believe that our polity should be reorganized to give clear recognition to the 'two nations' theory. In various forms these people have suggested that a system of 'associate states' should be established, held together by a weak central government in which each nation

would be equally represented. English Canada's response to this suggestion has been almost completely negative. The Winnipeg *Free Press*
described the proposal as a 'prescription for national suicide', while the
Montreal *Star* branded the idea in its various forms as 'half-way houses
to separatism.'[15] M. Maurice Lamontagne, a member of the Pearson
cabinet from 1963 to 1965 and a man with a broad knowledge of
Canadian federalism, told his compatriots quite bluntly that English
Canada 'would never negotiate with Quebec a formula of associate
states in which the federal government would be reduced to nothing.'
He added that in economic terms the idea was completely lacking in
realism. In fact, as one French-Canadian wit recently quipped, the theory of 'associate states' might better be called 'co-operative separatism'.

English Canadians are probably quite unprepared to search for solutions to our present problems outside of our present constitutional and
political system. At the same time there is a considerable willingness to
make modifications within the system. Perhaps this is merely the satisfied conservative's instinctive preference for the familiar; perhaps also
it is a realistic reluctance to disturb that precarious balance that has
been built up over the years. Still, there is some willingness to modify
the balance. Many English Canadians, though probably not a majority, have become convinced that French Canadians have a legitimate
claim to better treatment for minority groups outside Quebec. These
people, and Professor Morton is among them, favour the extension of
bilingualism and biculturalism across the country. This would mean
that wherever practical (that is, in terms of numbers of French Canadians), French would become an equal working language in the civil
service, a teaching language in minority schools, and even an official
language in the courts and legislatures of the provinces. Naturally,
most of these improvements would have greater application in New
Brunswick, where the French-speaking population is very large, than in
British Columbia, where it is tiny.

The major obstacle to these changes is the constitution itself, for
education is a provincial matter and will certainly remain one as long
as Quebec has any influence in Canadian politics. The provincial
politicians whose electorates are largely English-speaking are much less
aware of French-Canadian pressures than federal politicians. The truth
is, of course, that the French Canadian, though a provincial autonomist, has always received more just treatment from the central government than from the provincial governments. One example of this tru-
ism is the Canadian Broadcasting Corporation's autonomous, publicly
supported French-language network. The establishment of the French-
language radio station CJBC in Toronto recently is a service provided

by the federal government that would not have been provided (even if it were constitutionally possible) by the provincial government.

It will be difficult to overcome the reluctance of provincial politicians to grant 'special' rights to French Canadians. One suggestion has been a federal department of education for French- and English-language minorities. On paper the idea is attractive; in practice it is doubtful that either Quebec or the English-speaking provinces would accept it. One group that would certainly accept it is the French-language minorities. It remains to be seen what the Royal Commission on Bilingualism and Biculturalism will have to say on this and other matters. In the meantime, it is worth noting that Ontario and Saskatchewan have to a considerable degree made an effort to place French-language and Roman Catholic minorities in a more equitable position. The situation in New Brunswick, while not perfect, is fairly satisfactory, and there is some hope that Premier Roblin in Manitoba will be able to move his province gradually in a direction more satisfactory to the Franco-Manitobans.

Biculturalism and bilingualism are one thing; decentralization is quite another. At present, decentralization is probably the first item on the agenda of the Quebec government. English Canadians, on the whole, have been brought up to believe that strong central government is a necessity in a country as spread out as Canada. Moreover, there is the completely defensible view that only a strong central government can make the transfer and equalization payments necessary to keep the have-not provinces viable. Therefore decentralization is approached with caution and hostility by many English Canadians. It should be added that rich provinces like British Columbia or Ontario are less concerned about decentralization than poor provinces like Newfoundland or Saskatchewan.

Nevertheless, in their usual stumbling way, Canadians are groping towards an *ad hoc* working arrangement. This pragmatic formula, if it can be given so precise a description, has been dignified by the title of 'co-operative federalism'. The concept was first written into the platform of the New Democratic Party at its founding convention in 1961; it has since been taken over by the Liberal Party. In essence, the formula admits that institutions are less important than practices, and calls for careful and frequent consultations between the various levels of government on an increasingly wide range of policy matters. It places no stock in rewriting the constitution, realizing that the Canadian society is dynamic, not static, and that the present constitution is flexible enough to meet this situation. As one apostle of 'co-operative federalism' recently [1964] told a Montreal audience, 'Rewrite the constitution? What an unbelievable waste of time. It is rewritten daily in the facts.'[17]

It may be that this approach will prove too little and too late. Certainly it has been criticized by at least two members of the Lesage government, René Lévesque and Pierre Laporte, as too vague. But it has, in addition to its obvious commitment to careful study of facts and figures rather than heady appeals to rhetoric, one important merit that is not always noticed. That merit is a political one. Realizing that attempts to gauge public opinion in the present unsettled state of Quebec are hopeless, our present federal government has quite rightly chosen to act as though Quebec had only one voice. That voice is the government of Quebec speaking through the Premier, Jean Lesage. And Premier Lesage's latest pronouncement on constitutional matters sounds very like a commitment to the idea of 'cooperative federalism' as it has been expounded by such federal Liberals as Maurice Lamontagne and Jean-Luc Pépin.[18]

On September 28, 1964, Premier Lesage told the Montreal Canadian Club that he did not believe the time was opportune for a full-scale constitutional revision. He went on to state, however, that French Canada had two minimum demands. (No Quebec politician ever states French Canada's maximum, or even intermediate, demands.)

The first of these is a status for the French-speaking Canadian equal in all respects to that of the English-speaking Canadian. This means in the immediate future: French as a working language in the federal administration and French as a teaching language for French minorities outside Quebec. The second claim is that of a genuine decentralization of powers, resources, and decision-making in our federal system. Quebec, I have often said, believes in harmony through consultation and discussion among equals, not through a uniformity imposed by an all-powerful central government. At the moment we believe our political framework to be flexible enough, especially if it were to be adapted to the present circumstances, to allow for a centring in the Quebec government of all the means necessary to the development of a French-Canadian nation mainly concentrated within our borders. This political framework, grounded as it is on historical, geographical, and economic realities, is resilient enough to secure the permanency of a country that stretches from coast to coast.[19]

Premier Lesage may be wrong, though no one as yet has questioned his political sagacity. He may be swept aside in the next rebound of the powerful nationalist tide that is still sweeping Quebec. But in the meantime he is the person who speaks for Quebec. He is the person with whom English Canadians must, and will, co-operate. Of course the success of this pragmatic Pearson-Lesage approach depends on the triumph of reason in both French and English Canada. M. Lesage will have difficulty selling his moderation to some French Canadians, but no more than Mr. Pearson will have with some English Canadians.

For those English Canadians who have attempted to understand the French-Canadian viewpoint, and for those French Canadians who recognize the dangers in the separatist and quasi-separatist siren songs, the future of Canada lies in the construction of a society in which national differences are accepted and where that abstraction 'the nation' is not made the norm of all political, economic, and cultural activity. This is what Claude Ryan, the director of the Montreal nationalist daily *Le Devoir*, has called the 'Canadian hypothesis'. He defined this hypothesis recently, writing [in 1964] that

Canada offers us the chance of constructing a new type of political society, a society whose political boundaries will be advantageous for the development of different cultures without being rigidly or exclusively conditioned by one culture alone. We are convinced that this type of society will reveal itself as more favourable to the cultivation of fundamental liberties, in the long run, than societies calculated too closely on the single reality of a particular culture. In affirming this conviction we are conscious of enunciating an ideal which is far from having been attained in the Canadian reality. But the difficulties and setbacks of the past have not yet been decisive enough to justify pure and simple abandonment of the ideal which presided at the birth of Confederation.[20]

M. Ryan, in fact, proposes that French and English Canadians exchange Rousseau and Locke for Lord Acton and build a multinational society. It will require a good deal of practical ingenuity to devise the institutions capable of containing the 'Canadian hypothesis'. But our federal system has proven flexible in the past and our politicians are not entirely lacking in the practical skills of political adjustment. And today some of the most thoughtful people in both English and French Canada have recognized the potential value of a Canadian version of the Actonian state. In 1962 Pierre-Elliott Trudeau wrote, in a brilliant analysis of French-Canadian nationalism:

The die is cast in Canada: there are two ethnic and linguistic groups; each is too strong and too deeply rooted in the past, too firmly bound to a mother culture, to be able to swamp the other. But if the two will collaborate inside of a truly pluralist state, Canada could become a privileged place where the federalist form of government, which is the government of tomorrow's world, will be perfected.[21]

More recently, John Holmes, the president of the Canadian Institute of International Affairs, wrote:

One purpose Canada can serve in a world threatened by tribal anarchy is to prove that state and nation are not necessarily coterminous, that people of different cultures and languages can co-exist within a single sovereignty. It is not the same lesson as that of the United States – that divers people can be melted into a successful nation with one official language. Noble as that example has been, it is less applicable than the Canadian experience to new countries which must embrace distinct tribes and clans as founding members within the framework of one effective state.[22]

If there is a solution to the ever-present, but at present critical, problem of the relations between French- and English-speaking Canadians, it must lie in this Actonian direction. Of course, there never will be a perfect or final solution, for the problem is one of human relations. But then there are good reasons, of recent memory, which warn loudly against those who offer a Final Solution.

[1964]

NOTES

1 F.R. Scott, 'Canada et Canada français,' *L'Esprit*, August-September 1952, page 178.
2 E.P. Taché speaking in the Canadian Assembly in April 1846.
3 André Laurendeau, 'Nationalisme et séparatisme,' *L'Action nationale*, Vol. XLIV, No. 7, March 1955, page 575.
4 James Eayrs, 'Sharing a Continent: The Hard Issues,' in John Sloan Dickey (ed.), *The United States and Canada* (New York, 1964), page 93.
5 Malcolm Ross, *Our Sense of Identity* (Toronto, 1954), page ix.
6 G.V. Ferguson, 'The English-Canadian Outlook,' in Mason Wade (ed.), *Canadian Dualism*, page 9.
7 Henri Bourassa, *La Langue française et l'avenir de notre race* (Quebec, 1913), page 15.
8 'René Lévesque Speaks of Quebec, National State of the French Canadians,' originally published in *Le Devoir*. Printed in translation in F. R. Scott and Michael Oliver, *Quebec States Her Case*, pages 144–5.
9 F.H. Underhill, 'Canada and the North Atlantic Triangle,' in *In Search of Canadian Liberalism* (Toronto, 1960), page 257.
10 'Mémoire de la Ligue d'Action Nationale à la Commission royale d'enquête sur les arts, les lettres et les sciences,' page 312.
11 Toronto *Globe and Mail*, December 21, 1962.
12 *Le Devoir*, December 22, 1962. Translated in Scott and Oliver, *Quebec States Her Case*, page 104.

13 Peter Gzowski, 'An Open Letter to the French-Canadian Nationalists,' *Maclean's* Magazine, October 17, 1964, page 28.

14 Toronto *Globe and Mail*, September 8,1964.

15 Winnipeg *Free Press*, June 19, 1964; Montreal *Star*, October 1,1964.

16 *Le Devoir*, September 10,1964.

17 Jean-Luc Pépin, reported in *Le Devoir*, October 31,1964.

18 Maurice Lamontagne, speech to the Club Richelieu de Québec, September 9, 1964; Jean-Luc Pépin, speech to the Institut Canadien des Affaires Publiques, September 12, 1964.

19 Speech to the Canadian Club, Montreal, September 28, 1964.

20 *Le Devoir*, September 19,1964.

21 Pierre-Elliott Trudeau, 'La Nouvelle Trahison des clercs,' page 15.

22 John W. Holmes, 'The Diplomacy of a Middle Power,' *The Atlantic*, November 1964, page 106.

FIFTEEN

"I never thought I could be as proud ...":
The Trudeau-Lévesque Debate

It is not the idea of nation that is retrograde; it is the idea that the nation must necessarily be sovereign.

Pierre Elliott Trudeau, "New Treason of the Intellectuals,"
Federalism and the French Canadians (Toronto, 1968)

What does this French Quebec want? Sometime during the next few years, the question will be answered. And there are growing possibilities that the answer could very well be – independence.

René Lévesque, "For an Independent Quebec," *Foreign Affairs*
(October, 1976)

... only two positions seem logical to me: that of Mr. Trudeau, who won the referendum of 1980, and that which preaches the independence of Quebec. The rest look like a kind of constitutional embroidery.

Marcel Rioux, *Une Saison à la Renardière* (Montreal, 1988)

Many Canadians and doubtless foreigners, too, found the Canadian constitutional debate of the 1970s something of a puzzle. Quite apart from the confusion created by arcane constitutional details best left to lawyers and other addicts, there was the dominant role played by two Francophone Quebecers: Pierre Elliott Trudeau and René Lévesque. If this was a Canadian drama, surely central casting had been mischievous in failing to assign one starring role to an English-Canadian thespian. And the theatre analogy could be carried further: the particularly obtuse Premier of Newfoundland, Brian Peckford, once described the debate as "The René and Pierre Show." That suggested it was just a soap opera in which two middle-aged matinée idols made increasingly melodramatic gestures in a personal competition for the hearts of their sentimental viewers. Sunset Boulevard North. Or, if another simplifying analogy were needed, there was always sport. Now Levesque and Trudeau could become aspiring champions lurching round after round from corners marked "Quebec" and "Canada" urged on by their seconds to deliver the final knockout block. Muhammad Alis in the federal-provincial ring. In the age of television, personality simplifies, ideas confuse. Or so we are told.

But reducing the debates of the 1970s to mere personality clashes, however dramatic, banishes confusion at the risk of introducing obfuscation. Trudeau and Lévesque were powerful personalities and ambitious men. One had been a television star, the other an accomplished athlete. Each, doubtless, wanted to finish first in his chosen sport: politics. But each was also a politician with fixed conclusions on an issue that went to the very essence of the history and existence of the community in which they were both deeply rooted. Neither Trudeau nor Lévesque created the issue that divided them: it existed before they came on the scene and lives after them. It can be simply stated: "All we need to know is this: is it in the interests of French-speaking Canadians to be a majority in a pluralist Quebec state, or a minority in a pluralist Canadian state? That is what the whole debate is about."[1]

Those are Trudeau's words, but Lévesque could easily have uttered them. They agreed on the question; they disputed the answer. Yet both were champions of the community Trudeau called francophones canadiens, though Lévesque would have used the term "French Quebecers." The debate turned on that nuance. It measured the gap between the federalist and the nationalist and made it appropriate, though not necessary, that both gladiators should be Francophone Quebecers. But the nuance also created confusion for those who would have preferred a simpler dichotomy: French against English, Quebec against Canada. That Trudeau and Lévesque were both Francophone Quebecers made that simplification impossible. The confusion can be dispelled only by examining the ideas they expounded.

As Canada's centennial celebrations drew to a close in 1967, two Quebec politicians published books setting out proposed courses for the future of Canada, French Canada, and Quebec. *Le Fédéralisme et la Société canadienne-française* appeared just as Expo '67 was closing its doors on Ile Ste-Hélène in Montreal. Its author, Pierre Elliott Trudeau, was the federal Minister of Justice, a post that included responsibility for tending Canada's constitution. A politician of only two years' experience, he was just beginning to develop a public profile. Long known among Quebec intellectuals – and by a few in English Canada – as a brilliant lawyer, political writer, and one of the founders of the little magazine *Cité libre*, he seemed always out of step with the dominant views of his province's leaders, and, by 1967, increasingly so. In English Canada he was hardly known at all except as something of a non-conformist bachelor who coined the aphorism that the state had no place in the bedrooms of the nation.

Trudeau's book, a series of essays and documented polemics, had been written over a period stretching from 1957 to 1964. The essays were devoted to analysing Canadian federalism and the place of French Canadians in that system. The focus was on Quebec. The earliest articles were critical of the centralizing tendencies of Ottawa and of those French Canadians – usually on the left – who supported that tendency. The later essays were sharp, even shrill, assaults on those French Quebecers who, by the early 1960s, had taken up various versions of the slogan, *Québec d'abord*. A book of this sort, with chapter headings like "De libro, tributo ... et quibusdam aliis" and "Federalism, Nationalism and Reason," was hardly, at least in normal times, expected to hit the bestseller list. But in fact the book, and the English version that appeared early in 1968, was soon on that list (though not all buyers were readers), and Trudeau was launched on a trajectory that would make him Prime Minister of Canada for over a decade and a half.

The author of the second book, this one entitled *Option Québec*, whose sales in French and English were also brisk, was much better known both inside and outside Quebec. René Lévesque, former journalist and television *vedette*, had joined Jean Lesage's *équipe du tonnerre* in 1960 and played a leading part in launching the Quiet Revolution. As Minister of Natural Resources in the Lesage government, he had led a successful campaign in 1962 to bring the last eleven privately owned power companies into the publicly owned Hydro-Québec. Later, as Minister of Family and Social Affairs, he had continued the building of the Quebec *état-providence*. But he also acquired the reputation of being a loose cannon on the deck of the Quebec ship of state. And as that ship heaved through the sometimes heavy waves aroused by fundamental reforms in education, the economy, labour laws, the civil service, and social policy, Lévesque became increasingly, if unsystematically, critical of the federal system. He also became more openly nationalist in his outlook and discovered that nationalist rhetoric was effective in mobilizing popular support for government measures. In 1963 he defined "nation" as "a group of men of the same cultural family with a place on the map," and went on to say that "nationalism" had to be used to overcome the "economic sickness" of Quebec. "The question," he said, "is to use it as much as possible, because no one is ever sure of controlling it, no one can actually control this force."[2] Hydro nationalization, in Lévesque's hands, was not merely an economic measure; rather, it was a step toward French Quebecers becoming masters in their own house.³

While Lévesque's frequent jabs at Ottawa and at the "Rhodesians of Westmount" (the English-Canadian establishment in Quebec) made him something of a hero among French Canadians, especially with the student populations among whom nationalism had witnessed a new birth,⁴ they also jarred English-Canadian complacency. In 1963 he bluntly told an English-Canadian television audience that "I am a Quebecer first, a French Canadian second ... and I really have ... well, no sense at all of being a Canadian."⁵ His use of terms revealed a lot – being a "French Canadian" apparently meant being a French-speaking Quebecer, not a French-speaking Canadian. But those implications, and others, were only gradually becoming clear.

Lévesque's remarks – he rarely used prepared texts – were those of a man who, in contrast to the more academic approach of Pierre Trudeau, thought as he acted, or better, talked as he thought. As a radio and television journalist by trade, Lévesque was more at home with the spoken word than the written word. (At one of their early meetings Trudeau, waiting for Lévesque to finish a promised article for *Cité libre*, had snapped, "Say, Lévesque, you talk damn well, but I'm beginning to wonder if you can write at all." "Write ... write ...," Lévesque replied, "first I've got to have the time ..." And Trudeau shot back, "And something to say."⁶) Of course, Lévesque would prove to have lots to say, but he reacted more than he analysed. He was always a man of action, where Trudeau, at least until 1965, was an intellectual, one whose critics claimed was nothing but a dilettante in a Mercedes. Lévesque's book, *Option Québec*, was characteristic: it was not really a book at all, but rather a compilation of newspaper articles, government documents, snippets of speeches written and spoken by a variety of people. Lévesque's *imprimatur* was on it, since he had led the group of former Liberals and bureaucrats out of Lesage's Liberal Party in the fall of 1967. He made the founding of the Mouvement souveraineté-association possible. He would be the leader of the Parti Québécois when it was established in 1968.

During the 1950s Trudeau and Lévesque had become casual acquaintances. Lévesque's work and interests had concentrated on international affairs – his program *Point de Mire* had brought the world's events into hundreds of thousands of Quebec living rooms. Trudeau, whose wealth made permanent employment unnecessary and whose liberal views kept him out of regular academic life, concentrated his attention on Quebec, though foreign travel and international affairs also appealed to him. But Quebec politics and the trade union movement absorbed much of his time.

The events of the 1960s drew Lévesque and Trudeau into closer touch. Trudeau was part of a small group of intellectuals who met fairly regularly with Lévesque, now a minister, who used them as a sounding board for ideas he hoped to advance in cabinet. Obviously, the two men were fascinated by each other, but each had reservations. In his marvellous memoir, *Les Années d'impatience 1950–1960*, Gérard Pelletier provides a revealing glimpse of the two men. Trudeau, he writes, admired

René's vitality, his lively intelligence, his aptly chosen words, his unexpected turns of thought, his imagination, the quirkiness of his learning, his extensive knowledge of history and astonishing memory for the smallest items of news – all this left Trudeau breathless ... I suspected him at the time of thinking privately that a journalist's background, combined with a star temperament, could only produce a tainted or at least dubious political philosophy.

As for Lévesque, he

could not help having a deep respect for the other's intelligence ... Trudeau's political erudition clearly impressed him ... For Lévesque, Trudeau embodied the scholar type, whose profound, authoritative knowledge he envied, but also the ivory tower intellectual, insensitive to certain realities, whose facetious brand of humour irritated him exceedingly.[7]

These attitudes, doubtless hardened and occasionally touched with anger, remained constant after Trudeau entered federal politics in 1965 intending to defend the federal system (Lévesque, interestingly, had urged Jean Marchand not to go alone to Ottawa but to take his two "*copains*" with him)[8] – and after Lévesque moved to establish a political party whose goal was to destroy that system. At that point in 1968, Trudeau and Lévesque agreed on at least two fundamental propositions. The first was that Quebec's future had to be settled democratically. Each man believed profoundly in the sovereignty of the people. Second, they agreed that the time of choice, individual and collective, was fast arriving. What that meant was that each had concluded that the fuzzy, rhetorical debates about Quebec's place in Canada, which had consumed so much energy for the previous decade, were futile. The proposed panaceas – *une province pas comme les autres*, a particular status, a special status (today [1980s] we call it "distinct society") – all missed the point. French Canadians would either be equal partners in a federal system that gave full guarantees to their rights throughout Canada or they would achieve equality through the establishment of a sovereign state. Special status, Trudeau and Lévesque agreed, was neither fish nor fowl.

By 1968 Trudeau's option had been worked out systematically and tested in numerous intellectual jousts. The essence of his position was contained in a paragraph that formed part of a bitingly sarcastic attack on the early proponents of separatism. In "La Nouvelle Trahison des clercs," published in 1962, he declared:

The die is cast in Canada: there are two main ethnic and linguistic groups; each is too strongly and too deeply rooted in the past, too firmly bound to a mother culture, to be able to engulf the other. But if the two will collaborate at the hub of a truly pluralistic state, Canada will become the envied seat of a form of federalism that belongs to tomorrow's world. Better than the American melting pot, Canada could offer an example to all those new Asian and African states ... who must discover how to govern their polyethnic populations with proper regard for justice and liberty. What better reason for cold-shouldering the lure of annexation to the United States?[9]

If Trudeau's option was intellectually elegant and idealistic, Lévesque's option carried a powerful emotional resonance. His book began, "*Nous sommes des Québécois*," and went on to explain:

What that means first and foremost – if need be, all that it means – is that we are attached to this one corner of the earth where we can be completely ourselves; this Quebec where we have the unmistakable feeling that here we can really be at home ...

At the core of this personality is the fact that we speak French. Everything else depends on this essential element and follows from it or leads infallibly back to it.[10]

Where Lévesque had once described himself as a *Quebecer* and a *French Canadian*, the second designation had now disappeared: he was a *Québécois*. Early in 1969 he told a reporter that "I've never had any feeling of being Canadian, but I've always had an incredibly strong sense of being North American. The place where I'm most at home outside Quebec is the United States."[11] Trudeau and Lévesque differed not only about Canada; they felt quite differently about the United States.

The origins of Lévesque's nationalism and his gradual transition into an *indépendantiste* are difficult to trace in detail. Nor do his published memoirs help much. But like many young French Canadians, he was introduced to nationalist sentiments at school, and living side-by-side with the English in New Carlisle may have made him a ready subject. At seventeen he wrote in the student newspaper at the Collège des Jésuites in Quebec City that "French Canada will be what

French Canadians deserve,"[12] sentiments remarkably like those held by Pierre Trudeau. He learned some Canadian history, and like all Quebec nationalists came to see the Conquest of 1759 as both the source of Quebec's inferiority and the historical event that needed undoing. In later years he recalled his admiration for abbé Groulx's novel, *L'Appel de la race*, the story of the breakup of a mixed marriage that symbolized Confederation.[13] But action, not theory, always attracted Lévesque, and he drew his general conclusions from personal experience. As a journalist who had devoted most of his attention to international events, his mind was turned to Canadian affairs by a strike of French-language Radio-Canada producers in 1959. He joined that strike as a sympathizer and soon came to share the frustration of the producers at the failure of the federal government to step in and settle the dispute in the publicly owned network. Lévesque concluded that nothing of the kind would have been allowed to happen in the English network. "Of such signal advantages," he told the Montreal *Gazette*, "is the privilege of being French made up in this country. And even at the risk of being termed 'horrid nationalists,' we feel that at least once before the conflict is over, we have to make plain our deep appreciation of such an enviable place in the great bilingual, bicultural and fraternal Canadian sun."[14] Here was an expression of that minority sensitivity that would lead to the idea of independence.

Lévesque's years in the Lesage government made him increasingly impatient with what he believed to be the intransigence of the English-speaking business elite in Quebec and the rigidity of the Canadian federal system. In these years, when French-Canadian representation at Ottawa under John Diefenbaker's Conservatives and in the early Pearson years was ineffective, Lévesque became convinced that Quebecers were ready to run their own affairs. "Now that our new generations are bringing us more and more proficiency every year," he observed in 1967, "there is no reason which can, which should prevent Quebec from realizing that thing that's been kicking around in our collective back room for the last two hundred years, which is to get our chance to make our own way as a society."[15]

The term Lévesque preferred to use to describe the option he chose by 1967 and that he would defend so ably and determinedly until his departure from office in 1985, was not "nationalist" or "separatist." Even *indépendantiste*, though he used it, was less preferred than *souverainiste*. And that was important. Though Lévesque never felt "Canadian," he never proposed complete separation from English Canada. Instead, he favoured a continuing economic association within a structure where each "nation" would be equal, despite differences of size. He once called it "sovereignty-cum-association," and that position revealed his moderation, even conservatism. For all his rhetoric about "colonialism" and "Westmount Rhodesians," Lévesque knew that Quebec and Quebecers neither were oppressed in the manner known in the colonial world nor did Francophones hate Anglophones in any systematic way. As he wrote in 1976, "undoubtedly French Quebec was (and remains to this day) the least ill-treated of all colonies in the world."[16] Hardly the language of a firebrand nationalist. Moreover, it should be added that René Lévesque, for all of his suspicions of the Anglophone minority in Quebec, consistently defended that minority's right to the use of its language, though not as an equal right with French. This was not always a popular view in his party.

The Lévesque vision of Canada, if he can be said to have had one, was based on a view of what was convenient, necessary, and practical. For him, that had to be a relationship between equal nations. In that vision Quebec was central, Quebec was first. In preparation for the 1980 referendum, the Parti Québécois issued a program whose title summed up the objective: *D'égal à égal.*

For Trudeau, too, Quebec was central. Though perhaps the most clear-headed defender of federalism in our history, Pierre Trudeau was French Canadian from Quebec. Before he entered politics, his writings were almost exclusively about Quebec. His goal was to help rid his province of the reactionary, paternalistic, nationalist regime of Maurice Duplessis, and the road to that goal, as he saw it, was to educate Quebecers in the values and uses of democracy. To those who cried *"Québec d'abord!,"* he replied *"Démocratie d'abord!"* His brilliant essay entitled "Some Obstacles to Democracy in Quebec" and the popular articles published in *Vrai* and collected later in *Les Cheminements de la politique* (1970) were passionate pleas for democratization and attacks on the nationalism he thought stood in its way. For him, the checks and balances of federalism provided desirable guarantees for pluralism and freedom.

In his youth Pierre Trudeau may have been attracted to French-Canadian nationalism. He campaigned in 1942 on behalf of a nationalist candidate named Jean Drapeau, who was an opponent of conscription for overseas service. And in 1944, at age twenty-four, after a long canoe trip in the Canadian North, he wrote a lyrical essay entitled "L'ascéticisme en canot" ("Asceticism in a Canoe"), which concluded: "... I know a man who had never learned 'nationalism' in school, but who contracted this virtue when he felt the immensity of his country in his bones, and saw how great his country's creators had been."[17]

This "nationalism" was not connected with ethnicity, but rather with a sense of place and pride in ancestral achievement. That perhaps

explains why he altered the word to "patriotism" when it was translated into English a quarter of a century later.[18]

If René Lévesque's political baptism during the 1959 Radio-Canada
producers' strike led him to a nationalist conclusion, Pierre Trudeau's
first association with the Quebec working class resulted in a quite different analysis. In the spring of 1949 Trudeau travelled to Thetford
Mines with his friend, the labour journalist Gérard Pelletier. There he
met Jean Marchand, the secretary-general of the Confédération des tra-
vailleurs catholiques du Canada, who was leading an illegal strike in
the asbestos industry. Trudeau addressed the workers, joined the pick-
ets, and concluded that the union movement represented the best hope
for the future of democracy in Quebec. In that strike he witnessed an
alliance between an American-owned corporation and the nationalist
government of Quebec, an alliance sanctioned by many of the leaders
of the Roman Catholic Church, and that that was devoted to crushing
a French-Canadian workers' organization. This reactionary provincial
government promoted a narrow ideology founded on "clericalism,
agriculturalism and paternalism toward the workers,"[19] an ideology
utterly out of tune with the dominant industrial order of Quebec. That
ideology and the institutions that promoted it, Trudeau concluded, had
to be undermined.

In the years after the Asbestos strike, when Trudeau worked as a
legal adviser to various union movements, his conviction that nationalism was a primary obstacle to French-Canadian progress hardened
into an unshakable conviction he would never change. In his lengthy
polemical introduction to a collection of essays entitled *La Grève de
l'amiante*, he set out to dismantle traditional social and nationalist
thought and to call upon his contemporaries to replace *a priori* nationalist idealism with a hard-headed empirical approach to Quebec's
social realities. He concluded: "An entire generation is hesitating at the
brink of commitment. May this book provide elements to enlighten its
choice."[20] Thus he was dubbed an "antinationalist" and, unlike some
of his comrades in the fight against Duplessis who later found the
"reform" nationalism of the 1960s appealing, Trudeau maintained
that stance, and, if anything, intensified and clarified it in the battle
against the so-called "new nationalism." In 1964 he and six other
intellectuals – all younger than Trudeau – set out their answer to the
"national question" that was once more consuming so much energy. In
their "Manifeste pour une politique fonctionnelle," published in *Cité
libre* and *Canadian Forum*, they proclaimed:

In the present political context, what matters is to put the emphasis back on
the individual, regardless of what his ethnicity, geography or religion happens

to be. The social and political order must be founded primarily on the universal attributes of man, not on what makes him different. A set of political and social priorities based on the individual is totally incompatible with an order of priorities based on race, religion or nationality.[21]

Thus, by the time he chose to plunge into federal politics in 1965, he had become a fierce critic of nationalism – though he never denied the existence or value of nations. He had also become a proponent of Actonian ethnic pluralism as the soundest basis for a liberal democracy. By working to strengthen federal representation from Quebec in Ottawa, the balance could be restored to a situation in which Quebec, under Lesage's Liberals, appeared to be pulling itself, step by step, out of Confederation. Moreover, since he and his friends believed that nationalism in Quebec was the product of the failure of Canadian federalism to provide enough space for French Canadians to exercise their rights, that space would have to be made by reforming federalism, not by seceding from Canada. "The most effective way to cure nationalist alienation would probably be to put in a better kind of government," he explained to his somewhat unhappy readers of *Cité libre*. As Dorval Brunelle has put it so exactly, the goal was twofold: "against both French Canadian nationalism and passive federalism."[22]

Separation, independence, sovereignty – all these, in Trudeau's view, meant the identification of state and nation, an inward-turning by French Canadians and, at least in the worst-case scenarios implied in some of the early separatist writings, a return to the reactionary society of pre-1960. This was counter-revolution, a return to what he disdainfully called "the wigwam complex."[23] Where Lévesque accepted nationalism as a positive sentiment that could energize reform, Trudeau believed that nationalism based on ethnic homogeneity was negative, bound in the end to stifle reform. Actonian pluralism, a state in which ethnic distinctions balanced each other and were accepted as positive virtues, guarantees of liberty, was Trudeau's ideal; that stood at the heart of his political ideas and was the basis of his vision of Canada. And it was the point on which he and René Lévesque differed irreconcilably.

Well before the *trois colombes* – the labour leader Jean Marchand, the journalist Gérard Pelletier, and Trudeau – set off for Ottawa, Trudeau had set out explicitly the conditions necessary if his gamble was to succeed. There were two conditions for successful federalism:

First, French Canadians must really want it; that is to say, they must abandon their role of oppressed nation and decide to participate boldly and intelligently in the Canadian experience ... The second condition is that the dice not be loaded against French Canadians in the "Confederation game." This means that if French Canadians abandon their concept of a national state, English Canadians must do the same. We must not find Toronto, or Fredericton, or above all, Ottawa exalting the *English* Canadian nation ...[24]

Thirty months after his decision to join the Liberals – they were not sure they wanted him at first – and work in Ottawa, Pierre Trudeau was Prime Minister of Canada. At about that same time his old associate, René Lévesque, no longer a cabinet minister, began to build a new political party devoted to his ideas and his leadership. His ascent to power was almost as spectacular as that of Trudeau: on November 15, 1976, his party was elected on its third attempt. ("We're not a minor people," he told his joyous supporters that night, "we're maybe something like a great people.") [25] The road to sovereignty-association had opened up. The stage was set for what seemed to be the final act in the great debate about Quebec's future and Canada's future. It would last six years, and would include the defeat and resurrection of Pierre Trudeau and then the referendum. On May 20, 1980, Quebec voters, by a sixty/forty split, rejected Lévesque's request for permission to begin negotiations on the sovereignty-association question. Trudeau now moved to patriate the Canadian constitution, complete with a new Charter of Rights and Freedoms and an amending formula. Lévesque, on behalf of his province, rejected that constitution, demonstrating that the referendum had not ended the debate.

When Pierre Trudeau left office in 1984, he knew that while Lévesque had lost, he himself had not won – at least not unconditionally. Speaking at Laval University in the spring of 1984 he once again defended his conception of Canadian federalism. In closing, he admitted that there was still much work to be done to harmonize the several "little homelands" with "the bigger homeland." He continued:

Our Canadian attachment will probably always be more distant, less deeply rooted in the soil than our attachments as Quebecers, Newfoundlanders or Albertans. But, exactly for this reason, we must make sure our institutions can embody our collective will to live and instill it in the minds of all Canadians, and in the minds of foreigners wishing to do business and build a better world with us. [26]

In 1962, Hubert Aquin, who would soon be recognized as one of Quebec's finest novelists, explained to his fellow Quebec nationalists that while hostility to English Canadians was at the root of the quest for independence, the English were not the essential problem. "It's the French Canadians we have to fight," he explained. [27] That was a shrewd judgement. Indeed, it is the key to understanding the history of Quebec and of Canada between 1960 and 1980.

Pierre Trudeau and René Lévesque: two Quebecers devoted to the survival and full flowering of a modern French-speaking society. In Lévesque's view that could be achieved only if his "minor people" became a "great people": sovereignty for Quebec. Trudeau believed that the future of his "little homeland" would best be guaranteed through participation in the "bigger homeland," a federal system built on equality between French- and English-speaking Canadians throughout Canada. For the *francophone canadien*, Trudeau, Canada was central; for the *Québécois*, Lévesque, Canada was marginal – at best. Nevertheless, both leaders, Trudeau and Lévesque, were, in Gérard Bergeron's happy phrase, "our two-sided mirror" – both reflections of the same community.[28] On the evening of November 15, 1976, following the Parti Québécois's stunning victory in that day's election, René Lévesque, in a state of barely controlled emotion, told his supporters: "I never thought I could be as proud to be a Quebecer as I am tonight."

On the evening of May 20, 1980, following the victory of the federalist option in the Quebec referendum, Pierre Elliott Trudeau, his reason only just controlling his passion, confessed: "I never thought I could be as proud to be a Quebecer and a Canadian as I am tonight ..."[29]

The parallel was intentional; the summary perfect.

[1990]

NOTES

1 *Le Devoir*, 17 juillet 1980 [translation].

2 René Lévesque, "Quebec's Economic Future," in *The Montreal Star, Seminar on Quebec* (Montreal, 1963), p. 78.

3 Albert Breton, "The Economics of Nationalism," *Journal of Political Economy*, 72 (August, 1964), pp. 376–86.

4 Jacques Lazure, *La Jeunesse de Québec en révolution* (Montréal, 1970), pp. 23–62.

5 Quoted in Gérard Bergeron, *Notre miroir à deux faces* (Montréal, 1985), p. 42.

6 Quoted in Gérard Pelletier, *Les Années d'impatience 1950–1960* (Montréal, 1983), p. 49 [translation].

7 *Ibid.*, pp. 50–51 [translation].

8 Gérard Pelletier, *Le Temps de choix 1960–68* (Montréal, 1986), p. 214.

9 Pierre Elliott Trudeau, *Federalism and the French Canadians* (Toronto, 1968), p. 179. For detailed accounts of Trudeau's ideas, see Reg Whitaker, "Reason, Passion and Interest: Pierre Trudeau's Eternal Liberal Triangle," *Canadian Journal of Political and Social Theory*, 4 (Winter, 1980), pp. 5–32; Ramsay Cook, The Maple Leaf Forever (Toronto, 1977), pp. 22–44.

10 René Lévesque, *Option Québec* (Montréal, 1968), p. 14.

11 Jacques Guay, "Comment René Lévesque est devenu indépendantiste," *Le Magazine Maclean* (février 1969), p. 27 [translation].

12 Jean Provencher, *René Lévesque: portrait d'un Québécois* (Montréal, 1973), p. 33 [translation].

13 René Lévesque, *Memoirs* (Toronto, 1986), p. 74. Lévesque doesn't help much by writing that "the nation-state has had its day" and that "one cannot be any thing but federalist ... at least in world terms" (p. 117).

14 Quoted in Jean-Louis Rioux, "Radio-Canada, 1959," in *En Grève* (Montréal, 1963), p. 265. It is interesting that the editor of the nationalist daily, *Le Devoir*, Gérard Filion, rejected Lévesque's claim, writing sarcastically, "when honour is lost, nothing is left but shame." *Ibid.* (translation).

15 *La Presse*, 2 novembre 1967 [translation].

16 René Lévesque, "For an Independent Quebec," *Foreign Affairs*, 54 (1976), pp. 737, 742.

17 Pierre Elliott Trudeau, "L'Ascéticisme en canot," *JEC*, 6 (juin 1944), p. 5 [translation]. The official English version (not this translation) appears in Borden Spears, ed., *Wilderness Canada* (Toronto, 1970), p. 5.

18 Spears, ed., *Wilderness Canada*, p. 5.

19 Pierre Elliott Trudeau, ed., *La Grève de l'amiante* (Montréal, 1956), p. 41 [translation].

20 *Ibid.*, p. 404 [translation].

21 "Manifeste pour une politique fonctionelle," *Cité libre* (mai 1964) [translation].

22 Quoted in Pelletier, *Le Temps*, p. 222; Dorval Brunelle, *Les Trois Colombes: essai* (Montréal, 1985), p. 18 [translation].

23 Trudeau, *Federalism*, p. 211.

24 *Ibid.*, pp. 31–32.

25 Bergeron, *Notre miroir*, p. 124 [translation].

26 Pierre Elliott Trudeau, "La Consolidation du Canada passe par le renforcement organique de la fédération," *Le Devoir*, 2 avril 1984, p. 8 [translation].

27 Hubert Aquin, "L'Existence politique," *Liberté*, 21 (mars 1962), p. 69 [translation]. See also Elie Kedourie, *Nationalism* (London, 1960), p. 101: "These movements are ostensibly directed against the foreigner, the outsider, but they are also the manifestation of a species of civil strife between the generations; nationalist movements are children's crusades ..." Brunelle, in *Les Trois Colombes*, also touches on this theme of generational conflict. No one has applied it, in detail, to Quebec and it could not be done mechanically, since Trudeau and Lévesque were of the same generation.

28 Bergeron, *Notre miroir* [translation].

29 *Le Devoir*, 16 novembre 1976; *Le Devoir*, 22 mai 1980 [translation].

Index